Companionism

Why companies need democracy as much as countries

Madoc Batcup

Copyright © Madoc Batcup 2006

British Library Cataloguing In Publication Data
A Record of this Publication is available
from the British Library

ISBN 978-1-84685-680-8

First Published 2007 by
Exposure Publishing,
an imprint of
Diggory Press Ltd
Three Rivers, Minions, Liskeard, Cornwall, PL14 5LE, UK
and of Diggory Press, Inc.,
Goodyear, Arizona, USA
WWW.DIGGORYPRESS.COM

The Road Not Taken

TWO roads diverged in a yellow wood,
And sorry I could not travel both
And be one traveler, long I stood
And looked down one as far as I could
To where it bent in the undergrowth;

Then took the other, as just as fair,
And having perhaps the better claim,
Because it was grassy and wanted wear;
Though as for that the passing there
Had worn them really about the same,

And both that morning equally lay
In leaves no step had trodden black.
Oh, I kept the first for another day!
Yet knowing how way leads on to way,
I doubted if I should ever come back.

I shall be telling this with a sigh
Somewhere ages and ages hence
Two roads diverged in a wood, and I—
I took the one less traveled by,
And that has made all the difference.

Robert Frost (1874–1963)

To my family

Contents

Introduction

"It was the best of times, it was the worst of times, it was the age of wisdom, it was the age of foolishness, it was the epoch of belief, it was the epoch of incredulity, it was the season of Light, it was the season of Darkness…" These were the words with which Charles Dickens opened his novel 'A Tale of Two Cities'. At the beginning of the twenty first century, when the developed world has never been wealthier, when great countries like China and India are lifting themselves out of poverty and tremendous scientific progress continues to be made on many fronts, there is nevertheless a sense of deepening malaise, of a season of Darkness to accompany this season of Light. There are heightened concerns about threats of world-wide terror; there are fears for personal safety and for personal liberties. The impact of globalisation, and the way in which the benefits of the increase in worldwide productivity are being distributed, is causing us to question our way of life. There is great uneasiness that our incessantly expanding economic activity is causing irreversible damage to our environment. After a great increase in the number of countries with democratically elected governments over the last 20 years or so there is a fear that we are becoming jaded by democracy. Turnout in many western democracies has seldom been so low, and the greater slickness of the political parties has bred cynicism rather than interest.

At the same time there are also considerable concerns about the way in which companies govern and regulate themselves and how corporate greed and malfeasance can be contained and controlled, with the salaries and compensation of company directors and senior executives growing far faster than those of the people who work for them.

These many and different concerns and fears are not unrelated. They are in fact intimately connected with one of the most important phenomena of our time - the corporation. The modern company dominates much of our society; our working conditions, what we eat, where we go on holiday, what we want, what we expect, what we buy and how often.

It affects our thought processes – we look at the world to some extent through corporate eyes. It affects how we treat others, and how we think of ourselves. The priorities of corporates shape our society and our lives. What are these amazing entities? Where did they come from? Are they friend or foe? Can we now imagine our modern world without them?

The development of the corporation bears witness to the ethical cross currents of western society, with influences from both the Christian and the Classical world. The Christian message is one of benevolence, but also of discipline and obedience, where absolute truth is revealed: its goal is knowledge, its approach prescriptive, and it seeks to answer the question 'Why?'

The Classical world inspired the concept of the freedom to seek out and understand truth, (which may well be relative): its goal is understanding, its approach descriptive and it seeks to answer the question 'How?'

The one looks to maximising good, the other enables the maximising of goods. The corporate world which is a mechanism to achieve the latter more efficiently has nevertheless acquired the prescriptive structure of the former. We appear to have contrived to have the worst of both worlds - an authoritarian system where benevolence is only admitted on sufferance.

Although the way in which companies operate in Japan or China is very different from the way in which they operate in most western democracies, they owe their origin to outside influence. The legally independent corporation with an identity of its own has not made its appearance naturally in different societies over the centuries – it is a creature of 'Western' civilisation which has taken root in other soil. For the most part corporate capitalism has spawned few variants. Rather it has stood as a contrast to communism for many, and has derived much of its support for its economic efficiency, for 'delivering the goods'.

The very meaning of capitalism and the extent to which it is susceptible to being modified has received rather less publicity than declarations of simple support on the one hand or opposition and calls for its abolition on the other. The corporate capitalism that is such a dominant factor in our economic activity today is a rather different creature from the capitalism described by Adam Smith[1], who thought that the use of corporations should be limited to a very small number of activities. In his day corporations were often synonymous with monopoly, and he wrote some telling criticisms of the East India Company in 'The Wealth of Nations'. It is doubtful that he would have been much more impressed by the dominant positions of some large corporations today.

It is perhaps ironic that, partly as a result of the Cold War, corporate capitalism has also enjoyed the advantage of often being linked with democracy, to heighten its distinction of not being communism. And yet for all this, the vehicle through which capitalism is most powerfully expressed today – the corporate structure - is wholly undemocratic. It is one of the curiosities of our society that at the beginning of the 21st Century while we aspire to democracy in the social/political sphere we seem to unquestioningly accept absolutism in the corporate sphere. While political structures and institutions have moved on from the values and mores of the early 19th century, the decision making process of the joint stock company has not changed nearly as much. In the political process property is no longer a qualification to vote in the United Kingdom (or in other democratic countries); it remains the only qualification to vote in the corporate structure of many countries. It is psychologically intriguing that we have arrived at this point of schizophrenia – we demand the right to vote at intervals for our governments, as citizens, but wearing (or perhaps doffing) our employee hats we, by default, do not question our inability to exercise our rights within the corporate structure. Political sovereign but corporate serf.

---

[1] (1723-1790)

It is these tendencies of inequality both within societies and between societies that has been one of the factors in an increasing undercurrent of concern. This concern has not necessarily been well focused and has been coupled with a feeling of helplessness. This is not surprising since the vector of these changes has often been multinational corporations seeking to expand their markets, and, by their nature they are both non-democratic and amoral organisations. Indeed their importance and their enormous resources enable them to lobby government in a much more concerted, effective and focussed way than any of the various pressure groups, either individually or collectively. The importance of corporations as vehicles through which governments seek to deliver policy and their vital role in the economic well being of a country as well as the intimacy of government and business born through working together put them in a uniquely favourable position to defend their interests against modern day angst with its inchoate demands.

In this respect it could be said that the democratic process of decision making is being increasingly sidelined; that decisions are to a greater and greater degree being taken in a forum to which the general public have no realistic access, and from which they realise they are excluded. The feelings of powerlessness and frustration are therefore not without foundation.

So while large corporations like over-mighty subjects roam the world, figments of legal fiction, but powerful vehicles for those who have fought their way to the top, the individual citizen as employee has only those rights bestowed on him or her from outside the corporate structure, which is not itself concerned with the status of employees, merely property ownership.

As corporations become larger and large corporations become more powerful there is an increased sense of helplessness. The departments of many large corporations dealing with employee matters describe their function as 'human resources' and this is perhaps a telling distinction from the previously used words of 'staff' or 'personnel'. Resources are there to be used and exploited. They can of course be husbanded, but in any event their role is a passive one.

So for the many individuals who work for large corporations there is no formalised way in which they can influence the institution for which they work. They are deprived of the rights which as citizens they take for granted. It may perhaps be one of the causative factors why democratic rights are less exercised than once they were. For the many who work for large organisations it is clear that their opinions don't count, and yet the decisions of their employers often have at least as much importance in their daily lives as those of government. Is it any surprise that when the time comes to vote in elections many people shrug their shoulders and assume that their vote will make little or no difference?

In addition the treatment of these 'human resources' by companies is guided not only by the obligations of the companies while they work for them but also by their obligations, or rather their lack of them, once they have left the company. In Victorian times and for many years after, huge damage was inflicted on the environment because the cost of cleaning up the disposal of waste from a company's manufacturing process was borne not by the company, but society at large. There was therefore little incentive for the company to look for a more responsible method of dealing with its waste, since it would almost always end up as an additional cost and therefore be an unnecessary burden on the shareholders. In the same way once a company pays the often minimal amount of redundancy, the obligation for looking after ex-employees falls upon society at large – almost a form of human pollution of society. In both cases the company does not pay the full economic cost to the society in which it operates of its commercial activities.

When in difficult times thousands and even tens of thousands can be made redundant by 'downsizing' or 'right sizing' it is the democratic social structure that bears the brunt of the problem, not the autocratic corporate control structure. But then the latter's sole allegiance is to maximise the return of profit to their shareholders – in short institutionalised greed. If they take any other course of action management lay themselves open to criticism. As management their obligation is to invested money and as such, within whatever regulations the law may require from time to time, they have the obligation to squeeze as much profit as possible out of the resources at their disposal, whether animate or inanimate, regardless of the human cost.

It might be thought that such attitudes are more redolent of the 1980s (or even the 1880s), than the beginning of the 21st century, but they are intrinsic to a company's mission, an inherent part of the structure we have created for them. If von Clausewitz could describe war as 'not merely a political act but… a carrying out of the same by other means', it could perhaps be equally said that in the global economy corporate capitalism is the carrying out of war by other means. Victory at all costs is what the corporation demands, and the fixity of purpose is comparable. This was highlighted in a recent management book reviewed in the Financial Times[2]. The six killer strategies described in the book include unleashing 'massive and overwhelming force', threatening your competitors' profit sanctuaries' 'take it and make it your own' and 'entice your competitor into retreat'. The military language is unmistakeable, and should not be surprising. Nor should references to the corporate jungle: having breathed legal life into the corporate being, it is unsurprising that we should witness the Darwinian struggle in which corporates naturally engage.

The growth of the size and power of corporations is a real and substantial threat to democracy. The following chapters attempt to trace the way in which this has happened, highlighting fundamental contradictions and inconsistencies in our value systems. They seek to explain why much of the

---

[2] FT 7th October 2004, book review by Stefan Stern of "Hardball, Are you playing to play or playing to win?" by George Stalk and Rob Lachenauer, published by the Harvard Business School Press

problem lies in the legal nature of the corporate model itself, examining why we are guilty of double standards; applying one set of rules to the corporate world and another to the political world and they contain a suggested solution to this dilemma, one that is simple yet radical. It is only by understanding the essential contradictions and differences in our society, and the need to reconcile them, that we can make a start towards a coherent integration of corporate and political aspirations and actions.

If we as a society wish to rectify the degree to which corporations influence us, then it is necessary to go to the root causes of what makes companies act in a particular way. In a world where we aspire to engineer substantial changes to the DNA of living organisms, the fact that we have not yet even managed to create a legal entity without pathological tendencies is not an encouraging precedent.

Companies are in some ways like firearms – while morally neutral they put vastly more power in the hands of individuals than they would normally have. Their very force engenders behaviour and delusions of power that would otherwise be absent. Currently both firearms and companies are mono-functional. The former's function is to kill people and that of the latter to make money. The larger the weapon, from rifle to nuclear device, the greater the potential consequences. So too for companies: the larger they are, the greater their ability to cause enormous damage. The companies are not to be blamed – they are merely inert instruments in the hands of humans who have a particular agenda. However it is possible to re-engineer companies, to provide them with more than one function, and to improve the mechanism of their safety catch. If we fail to do this we may all, as Shakespeare wrote, be hoist by our own petard.

The problems of democracy and the rise of corporate capitalism are also part of larger historic themes. Human societies have always been buffeted by the tensions of three sets of opposing desires: the transfer of power between the many and the few; the influence of secular and religious priorities; and the retention of power in a personal or an institutional capacity. The corporation today stands at the fulcrum of these three sets of countervailing forces. It has been an immensely effective means of transferring power back from the many to the few; it has been a vector for secular rather than religious priorities, and it has become increasingly efficient in channelling the exercise of power into an institutional form (through the corporate structure) and away from individuals.

In the past institutional power has either been based on religion, or very strongly connected to it, exemplified by the pharaohs of Egypt, the Emperors of Japan, the deified Roman emperors, or even the concept of the divine right of kings. The aim of the religious institution was to become the single central source of power in its area of influence. This was true even when there was no established titular head of a religion, as in the case of much of Islam, both historically and geographically. The rise of corporatism is unique; it is really the first time that secular institutions with no ultimate single source of authority have been so powerful, and where there has been a multiplicity of such powers. However we should not assume that such a situation is stable. We should anticipate that in the absence of effective anti-trust laws certain companies will become more and more powerful, and that quasi monopoly corporate power in a number of different business areas is a possible, even a likely, outcome.

It is intended that this book will help to explain how corporations have changed the way in which people relate to one another. It will look at the evolution of democracy and of the corporate structure, and analyse how these have been affected by the value systems of the societies in which they grew and how, in turn, they have moulded and to some degree displaced these same value systems. It will look at the roots of our current corporate society and suggest an alternative form of corporate decision making, and how it is possible to start to reconcile corporate and democratic structures in a way that will ameliorate the conflict between the principles we claim to value on the one hand and the way in which our every day actions are straight–jacketed by an entirely different set of principles geared to corporate priorities on the other.

What is clear is that a corporate based society is unstable. It requires and even craves continuous growth; the current corporate model is ill-suited to stability. It assumes potential for limitless growth, either through expanding markets and greater use of resources, or at the expense of market competitors. As we approach the limits of the damage that we can inflict on the environment and of the resources that the world can provide it is clear that we need to temper the gargantuan appetite of the corporate world. The developed world has long acted as Earth's profligate 'upper class'. Like the rake's progress, it is not that we have not enjoyed the experience of using up our inheritance and borrowing from that of others to feed our spendthrift habits; it is rather that without reform ruin beckons. And we have become almost as profligate with our politics as we have been with our environment. While seeking to dispense democracy abroad, to countries with no such tradition, we increasingly dispense with it at home, with low voter turnouts and increased apathy, inured as we are to impotence. If present trends continue it seems increasingly likely that international companies will come to dominate their democratic host societies. A symbiotic relationship between corporate society and civic society is increasingly becoming a parasitic one. Without adequate controls mega companies may in the future achieve global monopoly, and this could result in growth becoming less important than continued economic domination. But at the same time a world dominated by a handful of immensely powerful corporations would be a profoundly undemocratic one. As we continue on this path of globalisation we need to understand clearly that democracy is increasingly the victim of corporate power, not its beneficiary.

Chapter I

The moral matrix

Stranded

Underlying the way in which we govern society and the way in which companies are governed are the values of the societies in which the companies are constituted. There are two strong sets of values which permeate the thinking and beliefs of most western societies. Although most would refer to their Christian roots, the impact of the values of classical culture, of Greece and Rome have also been of vital importance in influencing the present value system of Western society. Many of the moral values of Christian society and the values of the classical heritage are similar; but the origin of these values is different and so is their implication. While the values of the Classical World are by no means a universal canon of principles, the philosophy, the value judgements, thoughts and precepts as well as concepts of law and justice of Greek and Rome have been immensely influential in forming the values of our own society. Athenian democracy and the Republican virtues of the early Roman state have exerted a powerful influence on the kind of governance which we value today. This latter was certainly of great importance to Rousseau in his views of how a society should be properly governed, and permeates 'The Social Contract'[3].

---

[3] Jean-Jacques Rousseau (1712-1778) published 'The Social Contract' in 1762. It famously starts with the sentence "Man is born free and everywhere he is in chains". The book was a very important influence of the French Revolution. It constructs the justification for a democratic society based on the 'General Will'. Chapters 4-7 of the fourth book in the Social Contract are given over to a discussion of different aspects of the constitution of Republican Rome, and the whole book is peppered with references to the Classical world. Rousseau was born in protestant Geneva in

It is impossible to do justice here to either the philosophical richness of the Classical period, or the moral complexity of the Christian faith. However it is possible to discern certain key elements in both traditions which inform the way in which we think and underpins our view of the world.[4] It is fair to say that the great philosophical and mathematical achievements of Greek society derived from the notion that knowledge and, perhaps it can be said, truth could be obtained by rational speculation and investigation. Christianity, however, believes that truth and knowledge come from God and are to be sought in the Bible. The one tradition tends to favour questioning, the other acceptance. The Classical tradition is imbued with an approbation of open discussion, the Christian tradition with one of obedience. The contrast between mediaeval European society where the values of the Catholic Church had no real competitor, and its post Renaissance, post Reformation counterpart, highlight to a degree this dissonance between the two value systems.

The Renaissance marked a turning point for Western society in many different ways. The growing interest in and acceptance of the thinking of the Classical World resulted in a syncretism of Christian and Classical viewpoints which permeated society in a way that undermined not only the authority of the Church but also the integrity of the Christian value system. Over the following decades and centuries Europe acquired a bi-polar Christian and Classical value system. The humanism of Erasmus and the authority of the Roman Catholic Church were uneasy companions.

1712, which was under the influence of Republican Switzerland, and he died in 1778 in a Paris deeply affected by his work. During the French Revolution Robespierre praised it and had Rousseau's ashes moved to the Panthéon. However when Rousseau published the book even in comparatively liberal Geneva it was thought to be deeply offensive, and it was burnt. Rousseau fled to London.

[4] What the Germans would call a 'Weltanschauung', or world view or philosophy of life.

The Catholic Church recognised, by excommunicating Galileo for his assertion that the Earth revolved round the Sun and was not the centre of the universe, that its authority was under threat.[5] The Church was the guardian and interpreter of

---

[5] Galileo was first summoned to Rome in 1616 by Pope Paul V (1605-1621) for suggesting (in 1610 in Sidereus Nuncius – the starry messenger) that the earth moved around the sun. He was faced with the following two accusations:

The first proposition, that the sun is the centre and does not revolve about the earth, is foolish, absurd, false in theology, and heretical, because expressly contrary to Holy Scripture.
The second proposition, that the earth is not the centre but revolves about the sun, is absurd, false in philosophy, and, from a theological point of view at least, opposed to the true faith

Galileo agreed not to publish his research and left Rome in 1616. However by 1632 he was allowed to publish a work which included both his and the traditional point of view. This upset the then Pope, Urban VIII (1623-1644). He summoned Galileo to Rome, and forced a recantation from the 70 year old man:

"I, Galileo Galilei, son of the late Vincenzio Galilei of Florence, aged 70 years, tried personally by this court, and kneeling before You, the most Eminent and Reverend Lord Cardinals, Inquisitors-General throughout the Christian Republic against heretical depravity, having before my eyes the Most Holy Gospels, and laying on them my own hands; I swear that I have always believed, I believe now, and with God's help I will in future believe all which the Holy Catholic and Apostolic Church doth hold, preach, and teach...

I abjure with sincere heart and unfeigned faith, I curse and detest the said errors and heresies, and generally all and every error and sect contrary to the Holy Catholic Church. And I swear that for the future I will neither say nor assert in speaking or writing such things as may bring upon me similar suspicion; and if I know any heretic, or one suspected of heresy, I will denounce him to this Holy Office, or to the Inquisitor and Ordinary of the place in which I may be...

the truth, which came from God and it was not for a mere scientist to gainsay its interpretation of that truth. The reverberations of this clash between religious and scientific knowledge continue to this day[6], and the then attitude of the Catholic Church was perhaps not so very different from those who believe in creationism today. This challenge to the Church's authority was undertaken more directly by the rise of Protestantism, but for a different reason – the Protestants, like the Catholic Church, believed that truth was God's truth, but they felt no need for a sacerdotal interlocutor to understand the Bible's revelation of that truth.

Inevitably such changes took time to take root, but the European Enlightenment of the eighteenth century, based as it was on Classical teachings, had its origins in the cultural revolution that was the Renaissance. It is perhaps no surprise that an area of activity, such as banking, which had been so misprized by the mediaeval Church should have found its first modern European origins in Italy during the time of the early Renaissance, and in those other areas of Europe whose trading links meant that new ideas travelled to them quickly, such as the major German trading towns and the Netherlands. The taking of interest which during the Middle Ages had been so frowned upon by the Church that it became the specialism of

---

In Rome, at the Convent della Minerva, this 22nd day of June, 1633."

[6] Galileo's propositions were only taken from the Roman Catholic Index of proscribed books in the 19th century. Pope John Paul II in 1979 asked the Pontifical Academy of Sciences to investigate the Galileo affair. They reported back in 1992. In his comments on the report, the Pope said "There exist two realms of knowledge, one which has its source in Revelation and one which reason can discover by its own power. To the latter belong especially the experimental sciences and philosophy. The distinction between the two realms of knowledge ought not to be understood as opposition. The two realms are not altogether foreign to each other, they have points of contact. The methodologies proper to each make it possible to bring out different aspects of reality."

the Jews gradually became an acceptable profession, and the wealth that it generated, if not on a par with landed wealth, was at least not wholly tinged with disgrace and shame.

These twin strands of Western cultural inheritance continued to intertwine through the centuries. From the very earliest times in Europe there had always been a tension between the temporal power of the powerful nobles and the spiritual power of the Church. However before the Renaissance the rules by which such relationships were governed were essentially those of the Church. It was their enforceability not their applicability that was in question.

Even though it was the prerogative of Henry II to choose Thomas Becket as the Archbishop of Canterbury it was by the Church's norms of behaviour that he was judged by the wider populace when Becket was killed in 1170. The canonisation of Becket by Pope Alexander III in 1173 resulted in Henry doing penance in the following year. It is difficult to imagine post Renaissance monarchs feeling compelled to take such action in a similar way, even in such countries which have traditionally been religiously conservative such as Spain.

In a country with as robust a religious tradition as the United States, however, even today Christian values act as a strong benchmark for acceptable behaviour. In a modern context, perhaps the contrition shown by President Clinton over the Monica Lewinsky affair, and the involvement of his church was not so very different from the penance required of a mediaeval monarch. But it is fair to comment that matters of sex and reproduction are some of the few issues that have not yet succumbed to being judged wholly by the litmus test of commerciality and profitability. This was also demonstrated in March 2005 when Henry Stonecipher was relieved of his post of Chief Executive of Boeing for having an affair with another employee of the company (his predecessor had also left for similar reasons). As the chairman of Boeing, Mr. Platt, remarked "when we looked into it, if certain details were disclosed, it would cause embarrassment to the company."[7]   Such comments highlight the way in which companies are now deemed to have personalities. People can be embarrassed; companies cannot. They can only have their reputation damaged, resulting in possible loss of sales. The absurdity of claiming that companies have feelings is part of the cult of the corporate personality.   Companies are deliberately amoral, which, as we will see, results in some of them becoming immoral and lying, cheating and stealing when they think it suits their profit line. Their behaviour and its results today are dealt with later, but the roots lie deep in history, and in the clash of our values.

While the battle for allegiance of these two value systems has ebbed and flowed there can be no doubt that the Classical heritage has become increasingly dominant over the centuries, despite the continuing claim of many countries to be Christian. It is of course true that in a number of countries which have experienced revolution, such as the United States and France there has been a deliberate secularisation of the State, either to avoid religious conflict or to diminish the role of the Church. Notwithstanding this formal division between Church and State the importance of Christian belief as opposed to other values continues to inform debate in these societies, perhaps particularly in the United States where issues such as abortion serve to encapsulate this clash of views. The tension between the Christian view of the world and the Classical view is still with us today, very visible, and far from being resolved.

The Classical spirit of rational enquiry was instrumental in changing attitudes within the Church and notwithstanding the earlier movements such as the Hussites and the Lollards there can be little doubt that the Reformation was shaped by the wider dissemination of knowledge of the Ancient World. The fall of Byzantium in 1453 is often cited as a key catalyst in

---

[7] See New York Times 8th March 2005, article by Leslie Wayne. It is perhaps notable that this article can be found readily on the website theocracywatch.org, which concerns itself with the influence of religion on politics.

this respect. The Protestant practice of knowing the Almighty through a careful reading of Scripture rather than through obedience to the Church hierarchy was fundamentally different. A literate mind trained to rationally analyse the Bible could find such a skill useful in other areas of life. The process through which knowledge could legitimately be obtained – through questioning rather than through just learning – became increasingly more important in shaping believers' views of the world.

This way of looking at the world gradually affected viewpoints, particularly where the scriptures did not accord with the world in which people lived.

Although, as Max Weber pointed out, it was Protestants who took to capitalism more readily than their Catholic counterparts[8], this process was by no means an easy one. Heilbroner[9] gives the example of a Boston Merchant in 1639, one Robert Keayne, who made a profit of more than sixpence on the shilling. The church court considered excommunicating him but relented and fined him £200. On the subsequent Sunday the minister of Boston included in his sermon castigation of some false principles of trade, such as:

I. That a man might sell as dear as he can, and buy as cheap as he can.
II. If a man lose by casualty of sea, etc., in some of his commodities, he may raise the price of the rest.
III. That he may sell as he bought, though he paid too dear..."

---

[8] Max Weber. 'The Protestant Ethic and the "Spirit" of Capitalism', Penguin 2002. See for example the opening paragraph "With relatively few exceptions the occupational statistics of a denominationally mixed region [of Protestants and Catholics in Germany].....business leaders and owners of capital, as well as the skilled higher strata of the Labour force...tend to be predominantly Protestant", although his book ranges more widely.
[9] Robert Heilbroner. 'The Worldly Philosophers', Penguin 1991, p.23

It scarcely needs pointing out that a system run on such Christian lines would be somewhat different from the one we know today.

However these concepts, alien as they are to our modern Western mindset perhaps chime more readily with the outlook of Islamic Sharia law which still steadfastly prohibits the taking of interest, and with that of Islamic countries, particularly in the Middle East. The existence of theocratic Islamic states in the Middle East illustrates the fusion of Church and State in contrast to the West. It is certainly arguable that the value system of mediaeval Europe, intolerant as it was of dissent, certain in its conviction of unchanging values and ambivalent in its attitude towards work not dedicated to sustenance, the glory of God or military valour, would be more comprehensible to Islamic countries than the amalgam of values that constitutes Western society today. The primacy of religious authority, whether in the Roman Catholic Europe of the time or even in Calvinist Geneva is surely far more aligned with the Islamic view of the world, than the focus on profit and growth that is one of the most visible facets of Western society today.

Indeed as touched upon above today's capitalism would perhaps be as equally alien to the religious societies of mediaeval Europe as it is to Islam. Max Weber in 'The Protestant Ethic and the Spirit of Capitalism' alludes to one of the initial problems of capitalism – a non-capitalist mind set. Greater payment to workers for jobs such as gathering in the harvest often resulted in less work not more. i.e. the workers did not seek to maximise their income, but to minimise the work required to maintain the standard of living they were used to. As Weber pointed out, when this approach failed the opposite approach was tried of paying the workers less money to try to force them to work harder to maintain their standard of living.[10]

---

[10] Max Weber. Ibid, p.15-16

In his seminal work on the way in which capitalism found in Protestantism and particularly Calvinism a combination of attitudes and practices which facilitated its growth, Weber goes into great detail in analysing the precise religious beliefs which led to the creation of this fertile ground. There is no doubt that the attitudes of diligence, of conscientiousness and of fair dealing that he identifies, and illuminates for example by quoting the writings of Benjamin Franklin, were of great importance in enabling capitalism to grow, even though paradoxically the gaining of personal wealth was the very antithesis of the core of their beliefs – it was the behavioural pattern marking them out as one of the chosen that was of most importance, particularly to the Calvinists and Puritans.

However diligence, conscientiousness and hard work are not a monopoly springing from the Protestant sects' sense of a 'calling' ('Beruf'). What may have been lacking in other societies however was the ability to put these virtues into practice in a way that brought real benefit to the individual. On the contrary it was just as likely to result in resentment and opprobrium.

In many societies, both in the West and the East the business class was looked down on, whether it was the merchants of mediaeval Europe or the shonin in Japan. However hard one toiled one had a fixed place in society, and to try and alter this was potentially undermining the stability of society. Even Luther, as Weber points out[11], like Thomas Aquinas before him, thought that men's occupations and position were divinely ordered by God, and that they should continue in the position assigned to them.[12]

---

[11] Max Weber. Ibid, p.108

[12] Indeed this attitude was still prevalent in Victorian times, typified by the hymn 'All things bright and beautiful', written by Cecil Alexander in 1848. It has as its second verse "The rich man at his castle, the poor man at his gate, God made them high or lowly and ordered their estate" This verse is now often deleted as a recognition that social mobility is now to be applauded, rather than frowned upon.

The monastic orders were extremely successful in the Middle Ages – a similar combination of asceticism and industry enabled them to gain enormous wealth and power, a fact which did not escape Henry VIII of England. No doubt he felt that it was unacceptable to have potential papal power bases across his kingdom, once he had made his fateful split with the Pope, but he was probably less than averse to the wealth that the monasteries yielded up on their dissolution in 1536-40. The difference here is that while industry within the monastery was rewarded, and promotion within its hierarchy entirely possible (as indeed for the Church as a whole, as exemplified by Cardinal Wolsey), it was separate from society, a world apart, though touching at the edges.

The monastic model has relevance for our times and to the corporate model. The problem it raised of an equitable distribution of the surplus resulting from the endeavours of the monks and their employees was solved by the communistic nature of the community. The surplus belonged to the monastery and the order and was to be used for the greater glory of God as understood by the senior priests of the order. Poverty and wealth creation were combined in one eternal cycle of self denial and surplus. The fact that the surplus could often be diverted to ease the less spiritual concerns of the senior prelates confirms only the lack of rigorous enforcement of the ethical standards, not their absence. Indeed the monastic orders suffered from the same problems as the protestant communities. They both committed themselves to a way of life that created surpluses which generated wealth for which they had no proper personal use and which undermined the very values which created it.

The virtues of hard work and application were equally present in other parts of the world. Adam Smith[13] noted that in China even "the artificers" are "continually running about the streets

---

[13] Adam Smith. "An Inquiry into the Nature and Causes of the Wealth of Nations" ('Wealth of Nations'), Book I, viii (Oxford World Classics Edition, p.71)

with the tools of their respective trades, offering their service, and as it were begging employment".

The potential for improving one's lot, however, was a much rarer phenomenon. The patchwork of small states across Europe and the emergence of Europe from feudalism created a cultural background that allowed challenges to the established order. The very lack of centralisation in Europe allowed different ideas to flourish in different power centres. The emergence of republican Switzerland in 1291, the many independent states in Italy and Germany, the triumph of the commercially advanced Netherlands against Spain, (and its declaration of independence in 1581), and the English Civil War in the 17th century were all important indicators of the multi-faceted nature of the European polity. There existed an understanding, born from political realities, of different ideas and philosophies. The powerful commercial heritage of the Netherlands was not only an important factor in engendering its quest for freedom, but also in enabling it to happen[14]. Its attachment to Protestantism not only provided it with an additional reason to free itself from Spain (unlike Catholic Flanders to the south) but also the basis for a much more open society[15].

This instability and tension across Europe allowed a certain social flexibility as well, particularly in Protestant countries. The freedom to discuss new ideas together with sufficient social fluidity to benefit from changed ways of doing things encourages innovation. In Europe the established order knew that there was an alternative. New ideas were able to penetrate, and there was an incentive to innovate. It was not a coincidence, for example, that David Hume[16], the great Scottish philosopher and friend of Adam Smith, came from a

---

[14] According to Davies, "Europe, a history", p.356, the Spanish Netherlands brought Spain seven times more in taxes than the bullion of the Indies.

[15] See for example The Wealth And Poverty of Nations by David Landes pp. 137-139.

[16] Lived between 1711-1176

Calvinist background and was fond of reading Cicero. The fact that he was never appointed to a university post in Scotland, partly due to his suspected atheism, and published his works anonymously illustrate that the path of open minded speculation which might clash with religion was strewn with danger, even in Protestant societies.

By contrast China sought stability, and even by the close of the eighteenth century looked down with disdain at the products of this rather chaotic continent of Europe from what it considered to be an unassailable position.

"Now England is paying homage.
My ancestors' merit and virtue must have reached their distant shores.
Though their tribute is commonplace, my heart approves sincerely.
Curios and boasted ingenuity of their devices I prize not.
Though what they bring is meagre, yet,
In my kindness to men from afar I make generous return,
Wanting to preserve my good health and power."

Poem by the Qienlong emperor on the occasion of the Macartney embassy[17] (1793).

Enlightenment

In Europe the competition of ideas caused a creative friction and a dynamism that led to a changed way of looking at the world. It was also an environment that encouraged, or at least permitted, change itself based on the new ideas. Initially this was in the field of agriculture, as new techniques increased crop yields, and the British aristocracy in particular took a great deal of interest in improving their estates. Indeed such was the profitability of the new techniques that the enclosure of common land (which had been taking place gradually over

---

[17] Quoted in David Landes' "The Wealth and Poverty of Nations", Abacus, p.335.

the preceding centuries with the waning of the mediaeval system) rapidly speeded up, with scant compensation paid to the commoners for the land lost.

This agricultural revolution which started during the eighteenth century was both the precursor and the enabler of the industrial revolution. Agricultural efficiency resulted not only in rising living standards and increased prosperity, but also a rising population for whom there was not enough work in the countryside. Population growth proved a welcome resource to the emerging small scale factories and foundries; a comparative abundance of labour undoubtedly assisted their growth and their profit margins as well as increasing their potential market.

The eighteenth century was called the Age of Enlightenment as a result of the significant changes that were taking place in the spheres of science, philosophy and religion. As previous knowledge was increasingly questioned and new advances were made, the old religious certainties became less secure. The eighteenth century saw a rather more perfunctory approach to religion. This attitude no doubt percolated down from the upper classes, who increasingly felt that religion was not much removed from superstition. In many ways the attitudes of the eighteenth century towards religion paralleled our own. There are doubtless many explanations as to why the agnosticism of the eighteenth century gave way to the robust Christianity of Victorian Britain, from spiritual emptiness to the appalling suffering caused by the industrial revolution.

Through a glass, darkly; but then face to face

In Victorian times the moral matrix of Europe and particularly of the United Kingdom shifted once more towards Christian rather then secular values. The profitability of the new technologies and the wealth they created, particularly for the upper classes, meant that little attempt was made to change the way of life that made this possible. The poor found in religion a support for lives which were often in the phrase of Hobbes 'nasty, brutish and short'. The wealthy found in religion not only the comforting thought that inequality was not of their doing, but a matter of divine providence, and also a salve for any guilty thoughts they might have, sure in the knowledge that the poor could look to the next world for their reward. There were many stalwart Christians on both sides of the Atlantic who regarded slavery with equanimity, and were happy to send small children down mines and up chimneys.

It is in Victorian times that we start to see the emergence of almost institutionalised hypocrisy and a kind of moral schizophrenia. Perhaps it was in Victorian times that the old aphorism that a Christian prayed on his knees on a Sunday and preyed on his neighbours for the rest of the week was coined. It is difficult to equate the compassion of Christianity with the exploitative commercial model that was engendered in that era.

The influence of religion has waned greatly in the United Kingdom since Victorian times (but to a far lesser extent in the United States), and it has failed to recapture much ground as the guide for every day life in the way it was for mediaeval Europe. Although many centuries of Christian heritage permeate our culture and shape our moral outlook, nevertheless religious practice and principle has increasingly accommodated itself to economic priorities. It is rather in the non-economic sphere that religion is seen today. The vigour with which the abortion debate is carried out may reflect not only the depth of sincerely held views on both sides but also the fact that it is one of very few areas where the religious viewpoint is not trumped by the economic imperative of profit. The principle of the good Samaritan and turning the other cheek may be observed in private lives and taught to millions of children, but they are not values which business finds congenial except from the viewpoint of good PR. Good neighbourliness is only to be encouraged when it hones a company's competitive edge; for a company an act can never be good in itself, it must, in some way, potentially enhance the bottom line

Western society at the beginning of the twenty first century may now be suffering from the inconsistencies of its moral matrix rather than benefiting from them. The very success of the technologies which emerged from our willingness to question received wisdom has resulted in the means becoming the ends. Much of the pre-occupation of modern society is with increasing economic growth and consumption, with the (usually) unspoken assumption that more goods are what people want and need. There is simply no concept of enough. As Professor Layard has pointed out, as societies become richer they do not necessarily become happier.[18]

The acceptance of materialism in Western societies has had enormous impact across the globe. The technological advances which were both catalyst and effect of the rise of materialism have provided the Western world with a dominant influence in world affairs. China and India are starting to emulate the West in their aspirations for growth.

The success of the Chinese economy today should be a matter of rejoicing – many millions of people are being lifted out of absolute poverty as a consequence. The position of China today is very different from 500 years ago, or even 50 years ago. China now looks to Deng Xiaoping's aphorism that it does not matter if a cat is black or white as long as it catches mice. The ability to benefit from one's endeavours, which was formerly enjoyed largely by overseas Chinese merchants, less constrained by the proprieties of their own culture, has become widespread in China, and social mobility has engendered geographical mobility. However this acquisition of wealth is not tinged with Protestant sobriety, but rather by a desire to 'get on' and the social milieu has changed to enable this to happen - as the test bed of Hong Kong has so clearly demonstrated. It is not the industriousness of the Chinese that has changed, but their ability to benefit from such efforts.

---

[18] See "Happiness: Lessons from a New Science." Allen Lane 2005. See also Layard's Lionel Robbins Memorial Lectures 3-5 March 2003, delivered at the LSE,
http://cep.lse.ac.uk/events/lectures/layard/RL030303.pdf.

The acquisition of wealth has rapidly permeated public consciousness as the desirable norm to emulate, whether for purposes of state power or for private indulgence. As discussed elsewhere, however, the desired social destination that this additional wealth will bring may be very different from the social priorities of the West.

Just at the time when the translation of the work ethic into personal advancement is becoming more acceptable in a larger number of countries, the results of its unconstrained growth are becoming more and more apparent. We in the West, whose inability to understand the concept of 'enough' has led to increasing problems of obesity and a cavalier disregard of many of the real limitations of raw material and energy resources, will need to revisit the beliefs that underpin our society.[19]

A conjuring trick: how to make society disappear

These moral conundrums have been enlarged by the growth of companies. By focusing so single-mindedly on profit they have accelerated the unravelling of the delicate interweaving of our different value systems. Companies have magnified the pursuit of profit in the interests of efficiency. Indeed they have been designed specifically for this purpose. As the old moral guidelines (whether Christian or classical) have been elbowed aside by simple commercial priorities, the way in which money is earned is less important than how much is earned. The rise of large quoted gambling companies, reality television and the huge amounts placed on lotteries in the

---

[19] Indeed, Professor James Lovelock, who created the concept of the world as 'Gaia', a single integrated organism, has suggested in his latest book 'Revenge of Gaia' (Allen Lane 2006), that it may already be too late. He has come to the conclusion that given the enormous climatalogical impact of man's economic activity nuclear power may be the only way of minimizing the tremendous changes in climate for which we have largely been responsible and which will render large parts of the earth uninhabitable.

hope of a windfall are just some of the indicators of the way in which our societies have become, if not morally bankrupt at least deeply uncertain about codes of conduct and highly materialistic.

In the last quarter of a century the West has become increasingly affluent, but in a number of countries, such as the US and the UK, the distribution of that wealth has become more and more unequal; the goal of corporate efficiency has crowded out considerations of humanity.

In the terrible floods of New Orleans in 2005 after hurricane Katrina, the huge numbers of armed security forces (at one point some 60,000 when there were only 10,000 people left in the city), and the battles with looters indicated a society which had broken down. Even before the flood the city had 10 times the national murder rate, and of the two thirds of the population that was black half lived below the poverty line. This is perhaps emblematic of a preoccupation with profit to the detriment of decency that has caused decay in Western societies, and the decay is often greatest in those societies where profitability and the corporate agenda are most prominent.

Civilisation is not just, or even mainly, about technological superiority; it is about the values inherent in a society. How decisions are made and what beliefs are shared are important attributes of civilisation and determinants of its resilience. Companies have reached a dominant position in society, and their message of profitability above all else has increasingly drowned out other considerations.

Part of our classical heritage that we now take somewhat for granted are the concepts of freedom and democracy that imbued the civilisations of Athens and republican Rome in contrast to their neighbours.

Democracy is a curious animal in that it conflates both an ideal and a delivery mechanism for decision making. It is a highly unusual and fragile form of government, often only

35

arising in the most fortuitous of circumstances and constantly vulnerable to powerful special interests. Its painful birth pangs in the UK and elsewhere bears testament to the complexity of its construction, like those of humankind. As we shall see in the next chapter modern democracy, at least in Britain, owes its philosophical (although not historical) origins to our classical inheritance. However in our progress towards a secular society we have restricted the democratic principle to the political sphere; we have not sought to apply the logic of its underlying principle on a wider scale. In particular, as mentioned in the introduction, the application of democratic principles to the corporate structure is rudimentary to the point of being illusory. We have yet to make the philosophical leap from the sphere of politics to the sphere of commerce.

The moral matrix of the West with its partly conflicting messages which created modern society has been largely subsumed by its own creation. It has been relegated to the sidelines, to be applied in areas of no great or compelling economic interest. This mix of moral values still informs our civic society, but has been excluded as much as possible from the corporate structure. While tolerant societies provide different à la carte meals from the value menu on offer, corporates have a much more limited offering of fixed fare. We need to find a way of integrating the values we profess as individuals, and try to hand down to our children, with the way in which we carry out our commercial activities. This is no easy task. Like all societies we are at least partly prisoners of historical accident, and if we do not try to understand the forces that shaped Western society today then critical questions in respect of what we aspire to, what kind of society we really do want to create tomorrow will go begging. If we fail to deal with these issues, then the spectacle of the Louisiana looters is likely to have its successors.

Chapter II

Democracy's Dance

"If once [the people] become inattentive to the public affairs, you and I, and Congress and Assemblies, Judges and Governors, shall all become wolves. It seems to be the law of our general nature, in spite of individual exceptions."[20]

The first faltering steps

In examining the relationship between democracy and the corporate world we need to look at the origins of democracy and how it has become the system of government that we have today. We take democracy for granted in the United Kingdom. So much so that in the General Election of 2005 for the first time ever more people did not bother to vote at all than voted for the government. As Jefferson remarked, this is a very dangerous state of affairs. Yet it is a system of government of which we are understandably proud, and the benchmark by which we judge the governments of others. It is therefore worthwhile to ask some fundamental questions about the nature of our democracy, how it has evolved, and whether it has fulfilled what some might call the Whig interpretation of history – i.e. a gradual evolution to a better and better way of doing things. Why is democracy thought to be such an appropriate system today when through most of history since the Greeks it was regarded as next to demagoguery and of little practical use in the governance of a state?

Although they share similar social origins the way in which corporate governance and democratic governance have evolved has been quite different. Corporate governance is almost wholly undemocratic. Should this be a matter for

---

[20] Thomas Jefferson to Edward Carrington, 1787. ME 6:58

concern? It is essential to understand the way in which this has come about in order to assess the degree to which democracy and current corporate governance are compatible.

Although the strands of evolution of democracy are many, it is essentially about the transfer of power. The industrial revolution, for example, resulted in the evolution of a much wealthier merchant or business class of people who became economically more powerful, and found themselves insufficiently represented in deciding the affairs of state, and in particular those matters which affected their livelihood. In Britain the rise of the independent farmer, the independent merchant and subsequently the independent businessman was one of the most important factors in forcing the expansion of the electorate. As mentioned elsewhere the landed classes ceased to represent a sufficiently large slice of the economy to justify their continued overwhelming dominance of the institutions of power. In Classical times democracy came as much out of desperation as a position of growing strength.

It required a remarkably benign combination of factors to enable modern democracy to develop. For most of recorded history democracy has largely meant the degree to which members of the elite have shared powers more widely. Even in Athens there was a large slave population, and in their way the free Athenians were an elite, not only in respect of their own slaves, but in respect of the tolerated Greek foreigners in their midst (the metics) and in respect of the citizens of the other Greek cities which owed allegiance, and paid tribute, to Athens. British democracy for centuries only involved a tiny part of the population, and even then many of the MPs were in the pockets of the great landed families. Modern democracy is really a very unusual phenomenon whose staying power has yet to be fully tested.

Although British democracy has its historical roots elsewhere, much of the discussion about democracy refers to the classical societies of Athens and Republican Rome, from Jean-Jacques Rousseau's 'Social Contract' to John Stuart Mill's 'On

Liberty', and much else besides. The concept of democracy in these societies is therefore an appropriate chronological starting point in following, albeit only in outline given the huge scale of the subject, the evolution of democracy in western Europe and beyond.

A curious couple

Greek democracy is almost invariably associated with Athens, but its great rival Sparta also operated a democracy of sorts. Although there was a (dual) monarchy, there was also a council of twenty eight nobles who were elected by the Spartans, and who could approve or veto the acts of the council. In addition there was a group of five men, known as the ephors, who held a great deal of power. They were elected by all the Spartans, and did not need to be noble themselves. Despite or perhaps because of its apparent complexity the Spartan system appears to have been very stable, and with its mixture of monarchy, aristocracy and democracy bears a passing resemblance to some aspects of the British political system. The Spartans were famous for being, well, Spartan and reminiscent of the stiff upper lip attitude so associated with the British. However the domination and enslavement by the Spartans of the Messenians (often referred to as helots), particularly after their revolt, and the single-mindedly military nature of their society has not generally endeared them to subsequent societies as appropriate role models, at least in the political sphere.

The cultural dominance of Athens means that our view of Sparta is inevitably coloured by an Athenian gloss, and given that Sparta ultimately triumphed over Athens in the Peloponnesian Wars this is perhaps not the most objective of influences. What emerges from the Spartan experience, however, is an early attempt at the balancing of different political powers, and the acknowledgement of the importance of limiting the mandate of most powerful officials to one year. It is also an object lesson in the ways in which a society has to adapt in order to deny power to others. Because the Spartans feared the potential uprising of their helot slaves, who vastly outnumbered them, they turned themselves into a very militaristic society, where the interests of the individual were very much subject to those of the state. The liberty of the Spartan people as a whole was bought at a considerable cost to their individual liberty.

The Athenian experience was very different. They were not dependent on the labours of a more numerous conquered people for their survival. Athens was in a rich agricultural area, enjoyed the wealth of silver mines and was a great maritime trading city. A naval rather than a land power. Its solutions to sharing power were rather more varied. Athens started off with a 'basileus', or king, whose power was superseded by the nobles who formed a council called the 'areopagus', together with nine elected officials called 'archons', the chief of whom gave his name to the year of his office and acted as a de facto head of state, another acting largely in a religious capacity, and a third the polemarch, who was the chief military leader, together with six judges. To this complicated mix was added the 'ecclesia', which was the assembly of all free male Athenians of voting age, and the 'boule' a council of 500 men[21], which prepared the agenda for the ecclesia and advised the areopagus.

An amazing series of steps

The way in which these constitutional changes occurred bears some examination. In the seventh century BC there was an increasing divergence of wealth in Athenian society. Among the poorer folk were many wheat farmers, who suffered very badly as a result of cheaper imports from other Eastern Mediterranean countries. By contrast the wealthy tended to own estates growing olives and wine (which required rather

---

[21] Originally consisting of 400 men from the four original tribes, the boule was reformed as a council of 500 men, 50 from each of the 10 new tribes instituted by the reforms of Cleisthenes.

more capital to establish), for which there was a thriving export market. The situation resulted in many of the poorer Athenians incurring very substantial debts, and even selling themselves into an effective slavery (not dissimilar perhaps to the situation of some of the farmers of the United States today[22]). The situation was explosive; so much so that in 594 BC the areopagus and the people of Athens not only made Solon chief Archon, they subsequently asked him to reform the constitution.

Solon instituted substantial constitutional changes to the previous laws of Draco (whence Draconian), but also granted a debt amnesty, with all debts being forgiven, brought people back out of the slavery into which they had sold themselves and generally tried to balance the interests of the contending classes, giving different rights to the different classes according to their wealth, but trying to achieve a balance of power, often acting against the wishes of the nobles.

However the situation was not stable, and a would be dictator came on the scene by the name of Pisistratus.[23]

---

[22] See Eric Schlosser 'Fast Food Nation', Penguin 2002, p. 141, where he points out that the typical chicken grower in the US is mired in debt and earns about $12,000 per year because of the nature of his contract with the large chicken meat processors, such as Tyson.

[23] Aristotle in his description of the Athenian constitution (c 350 BC), from part 5 onwards describes the reforms of Solon. In part 11 he explains that since there were a number of dissatisfied people (the poor wanted more land distribution and the wealthy wanted a return to the status quo ante) Solon could not satisfy them all so he took himself off to Egypt for ten years (to let the Athenians sort the new constitution out for themselves). After five years they were no longer able to elect the Archons, and there was general disorder. The feuding factions split up into the people of the Plain, the people of the Shore and the people of the Highlands, the latter under Pisistratus.

Pisistratus had the brilliant idea of wounding himself and his mules and then going into the Athenian market place the 'agora' and accusing his enemies of the act. He was allowed a club wielding bodyguard for protection as a result, which he then used to seize the Acropolis. He was able to exercise power for some five years before being ousted and sent into exile. Some eleven years later he came back after making a deal with one of his former enemies, which included marrying his daughter. This time he rode into Athens on a chariot with a rather impressive looking female called Phye dressed as the goddess Athena. This apparently overawed the populus, and he again ruled Athens, this time for a further six years, before he lost power once more. However Pisistratus was somewhat persistent and after a further period of exile when he managed to become extremely wealthy he decided on the more straight forward method of attacking Athens with the aid of mercenaries. He won the battle of Pallene in 546 BC, and subsequently disarmed the rest of the Athenians. He then ruled Athens until his death in 527 BC.

The curious thing about Pisistratus is that he was that most unusual of men, a benign dictator.[24] He also encouraged the arts and architecture and great religious festivals. In many ways therefore, although the Athenian constitution may have been created by Solon, it was actually the persistence of a benign dictator that enabled it to bed down successfully. History is seldom so kind, and after his death took her revenge – one of the Athenian noble families called in the

---

[24] Although he was what the Greeks called a 'tyrannos' or tyrant, both Herodotus and Thucidydes confirm that he left the constitution of Solon basically untouched, and Aristotle in part 16 of his history of the constitution wrote of him:

"His administration was temperate, as has been said before, and more like constitutional government than a tyranny. Not only was he in every respect humane and mild and ready to forgive those who offended, but, in addition, he advanced money to the poorer people to help them in their labours, so that they might make their living by agriculture"

Spartans to oust Hippias, the son and successor of Pisistratus, after a rule of 17 years. The Spartans duly obliged and conquered Athens in 510 BC, and Hippias fled to the court of Darius in Persia.

Cleisthenes, an Athenian nobleman who had been a brother in law to Pisistratus, and another nobleman, Isagoras, then struggled for power. Isagoras seemed to have the upper hand until Cleisthenes suggested substantial reforms to the constitution making it more democratic, and the people rallied to his cause. Isagoras then asked for help from his friend King Cleomenes of Sparta, who duly attacked Athens and sent Cleisthenes into exile. In unprecedented fashion the people of Athens then rose up and trapped the Spartan army and Isagoras on the Acropolis for two days. On the third day, a truce was declared; Isagoras and the Spartans were allowed to leave, but 300 of their supporters were killed.

Cleisthenes was recalled and became chief archon in 507 BC. Cleisthenes is credited with being the father of Athenian democracy; he re-organised the tribes of Athens to make them less factional, and he re-instituted the Boule, as a council of 500, 50 representatives from each of the ten new tribes, which would be able to deliberate matters between the meetings of the assemblies of the whole adult male population. The Athenian democratic model had reached a defining moment.

The vital battle of Marathon against the Persians (including Hippias) was some 20 years away (490 BC), and the pivotal naval battle of Salamis 30 years away. The golden age of Athens during the latter part of the fifth century BC onwards was yet to come. This golden age lasted for much less than a century, a substantial part of it in war against the Spartans. The towering figure of this period, Pericles, although a supporter of the people and direct democracy came from an aristocratic family. However the democratic framework in place during this tremendous cultural flowering was brought to an end by 404 B.C. when Athens finally lost the second Peloponnesian War to Sparta.

A half hearted encore

Throughout the development of the Athenian constitution there was continual tension between the wealthy and the nobility on the one hand and the people on the other. Even in the most democratic period the aristocracy played a very prominent role. Athenian self government was resurrected in various guises after the peak of Athenian civilisation and democracy had passed. When Aristotle (or possibly one of his students) was writing his history of the Athenian constitution, democracy was still in place in Athens, but within 12 years the Macedonians invaded Greece, defeated the combined Greek army at Chaeronea, and brought Athenian independence to a close.[25]

The point of this brief examination of the history of democracy in Athens is to underline how much it changed over time, how much it owed to strong leaders, how fragile it was, how special the circumstances were which enabled it to come about, and how ultimately that it lasted for such a brief, if brilliant, period. We should not be surprised at the fact that although the Athenians produced many ideas for a balance of power between the elite of society on the one hand and the people as a whole on the other, even using expedients such as electing many officials by lot (i.e. on an arbitrary basis of chance, to avoid favouring the aristocracy) rather than voting for them, the end result was a brief cultural flourishing followed by defeat by more militaristic and organised societies; firstly the Spartans and later the Macedonians. Finally, of course, they were to succumb to a very determined and initially semi-democratic power – that of Rome.

---

[25] The Greeks did not regard the Macedonians as Greek; Demosthenes in one of his speeches against Philip of Macedon (the Philippics) referred to Philip as 'not only no Greek, nor related to the Greeks, but not even a barbarian from any place that can be named with honour, but a pestilent knave from Macedonia, whence it was never yet possible to buy a decent slave'.

The tensions that existed within the Roman Republic were not dissimilar to those of Athens. As is well known, Rome started off as a monarchy until the overthrow of Tarquinius Superbus (King Tarquin II, the Proud) in 510 BC. Although there had been a Senate at the time of Tarquin's predecessors, he instituted a more despotic kind of monarchy and ruled without consulting the Senate. However, it was the alleged rape of Lucretia by his son Sextus, triggering a revolt by her outraged relatives, that was to lead to his expulsion.[26]

After the expulsion of King Tarquin, and the founding of the Roman Republic in 509 BC, the place of the king was taken by two consuls, who exercised the 'imperium' i.e. the power

---

[26] It was somewhat surprising that Tarquin had not anticipated this turn of events. After all, according to legend he had purchased the Sibylline books from the Cumaean Sibyl. She had originally approached him with an offer of nine books for a stupendous sum of money, which he had resolutely refused to pay, and she had then burnt three of the books, offering him the remaining six for the same amount of money. When he again refused to pay the price she burnt a further three books, and offered him the last three for the original price. At this stage King Tarquin re-considered his position, and bought the remaining three books, which clearly had required a rather rapid rarity value. These books were thereafter consulted by the Romans for many hundreds of years at times of great crisis, preserved in a vault under the Temple of Jupiter on the Capitoline Hill. Perhaps because Tarquin was away attacking the city of Ardea he did not have time to consult them. They had the distinction of being written in Greek, and doubtless open to substantial variations of interpretation.

The Roman monarchy was resented because by this stage it was of Etruscan origin. It was not surprising that Tarquin should therefore go to a neighbouring Etruscan king, Lars Porsenna, for assistance in regaining his throne. The story of Horatius defending the bridge over the Tiber into Rome against the attack of Lars Porsenna is well known, and a famous instance of the Roman willingness to fight against the odds.

of the state in place of the king. They were elected for only one year, and had a veto over the decision of the other. The first two consuls of the City of Rome were Lucius Tarquinius Collatinus, the husband of the raped Lucretia and Lucius Iunius Brutus, his friend and one of the main leaders of the revolt against the monarchy.[27]

After Rome ceased to be a monarchy, it became an oligarchy – i.e. run by the patricians or wealthy and noble families of Rome. However after 15 years, the plebeians, or common people, were sufficiently upset by this state of affairs that they organised a 'secession' in 494 BC. They took themselves off to the Sacred Mount outside Rome in what appears to have been a mass withdrawal of labour in order to exert far more influence. Rather like the situation in Athens this action was triggered by economic causes – the grabbing of public land by the patricians, and the increasing debt of the plebeians resulting in many of them selling themselves into slavery.

The plebeians decided to elect two Tribunes each year who would be their representatives, and gave them the power of the veto over any legislation enacted by the Senate. It was a move that would have greatly impressed the trade unions of the 21st century. They also gradually made into a permanent institution the meetings that they held from time to time, called the concilium plebes, passing decisions called plebiscita (hence the word plebiscite), which were binding on the plebeians.

This was the first of a number of times that the plebeians were to use this technique of 'secession' to achieve their objectives. A further withdrawal in 451 BC resulted in a new set of rules

---

[27] Although he acknowledged it was disputed, the Greek writer Plutarch (circa 45-125 AD) claimed that Marcus Brutus, one of Caesar's murderers was the descendent of Lucius Iunius Brutus. The story of Republican Rome therefore took place between one Brutus driving out a king, and another killing the man he thought had become a tyrant.

being created, the so-called Twelve Tables, by a body of 10 men. From the fragments that survive it would appear that the Twelve Tables were not so much a constitution, rather a rudimentary legal (civil and criminal) code, making e.g. a careful distinction between the permissibility of killing a thief during the night, but not during the day. Dusk must have been a rather uncertain time for thief and householder alike. It appears that the early Romans did not care much for satire – Table VIII provided that "If any person had sung or composed against another person a song such as was causing slander or insult to another....he should be clubbed to death" – presumably you had to be very careful and stick to prose.

However the way in which the Twelve Tables were arrived at is indicative of the power of the plebeians in Roman society at an early stage. Interestingly Table XI prohibited the marriage of patricians and plebeians. This was one of two additional laws added in 450 BC after the plebeians were unhappy with the previous draft of ten laws. The final law provides that "whatever the people last ordained should be held as binding by law". It is difficult to know whether the one law was a trade-off against the other; it is difficult to imagine that the plebeians would not have welcomed the opportunity to marry into the patrician class. The tension between the upper and lower classes of Rome is evident. However the ability of the Romans to resolve these differences in a non violent way and create a working relationship between these two parts of society was distinctive, and led to their proud motto of SPQR – Senatus Populusque Romanus – "the Senate and the People of Rome", thus encapsulating the importance of this partnership. (Indeed the initials SPQR are even used in Rome today, although they have acquired a rather different Italian interpretation – Sono pazzi questi Romani – "they're mad these Romans").

The attempt by the patricians to exclude plebeian bloodlines was a forlorn one, and five years after the Twelve Tables were promulgated, in 445 BC, plebeians and patricians were allowed to inter-marry. There were a number of important constitutional changes in the years ahead, but by and large as the patricians lost power to the plebeians the emerging system came to be seen as more acceptable to both sides, and consequently the social solidarity of Rome was strengthened. Even in the most adverse of circumstances, such as the sack of Rome by the Gauls in 390 BC, the Romans were quick to recover and renew their attacks on the Etruscans and their other neighbours, rather than suffering social collapse. Although there was substantial unrest after the Gaulish invasion of Rome and dire poverty among the plebeians, the Romans were still able to maintain social solidarity and to reach a solution between themselves peacefully with the passage of the Licinian laws, thought to have been passed in 367 BC. These increased the eligibility of plebeians to be elected to high office, provided for some debt forgiveness and made plebeians as well as patricians eligible to receive distributions of public land, with the condition that the amount of land that any one person could receive would be capped.

The gradual removal of many of the disabilities and unfair and arbitrary treatment of the plebeians, and the establishment of a coherent body of laws ushered in a period of tremendous expansion for Rome. At this stage the city was still only a moderately important city state, with the Etruscans and the Samnites pressing in on their borders. Within a hundred years Rome had conquered the whole of southern and central Italy and was starting (in 264 BC) the first of its overseas wars against Carthage. By the end of its third and final war against Carthage (the third Punic war), in 146 BC Rome was master of the Western Mediterranean and much of Greece.

The military success of Rome put enormous strains on the Roman polity. The Romans created a patchwork of rights among their subject peoples, from full Roman civic rights and incorporation for some tribes near to Rome, to the absence of those rights and the requirement of the payment of tribute in many of the provinces. A new class of aristocracy had arisen in Rome, called the optimates (the best), who effectively controlled the Senate. The influence of the institutions of the people (now called the populares) was waning. There had been an enormous growth in the disparity of wealth as a result of the various Roman wars, with vast quantities of plunder, enormous quantities of new land, and regular tribute filling Roman coffers to the benefit of the rich. In addition there had been a massive influx of slaves into Italy as a consequence of the conquests. Rome had started out as an agrarian society, and it was becoming impossible for free Roman farmers to compete with slave labour on the large estates of the wealthy.

The tempo slows

The cause of the ordinary people was taken up by the Gracchus brothers, first by Tiberius and then by Gaius Gracchus. They both ultimately lost their lives in trying to further the situation of the poorer people. [28] During this period the senate was becoming increasingly corrupt. A remarkable self-made soldier, Marius, who had won his spurs fighting in north Africa, was so successful in defending Italy from tribal invasions from the north that he was elected consul six times. However, he was not as adroit a politician for the people as he had been a soldier. He also became embittered against his former lieutenant Sulla, who was firmly on the side of the senate. The end result was a civil war between these two protagonists, with Roman legions being used in Rome for the first time by Sulla, and then when

---

[28] Gaius Gracchus, when he was tribune in 123 BC, instituted a law providing for cheap food for the citizens of Rome, only to find that rather than relieving poverty it actually resulted in Rome being flooded by people who wished to benefit from the cheap food. However the law of unintended consequences was not the exclusive result of his work – he was also clever enough to divide the senatorial class from the other element of the aristocracy – the equites, who were the wealthy, if less blue blooded, part of the Roman upper class. He also wanted to give the right to vote to all the Italian subjects of Rome. In this he was not successful, but it resulted in considerable unrest in Italy in the following years. The Italians revolted against Rome in 90 BC. They lost the war, but they gained the right to become Roman citizens.

he was away fighting Mithridates in Asia Minor, by Marius in a far more bloody way. Marius died before Sulla returned from Asia Minor, but his partisans were ruthlessly swept aside by Sulla who not only went on an orgy of revenge killing against the supporters of the 'popular' party across the whole of Italy, butchering 6,000 Samnite prisoners in cold blood along the way, but also appointed himself as dictator.

This latter was a post of absolute power to which generals in Rome had been historically appointed when the city was in extreme danger, the appointment to last no longer than the emergency required. Sulla then proceeded to emasculate both the office of tribune and the comitia tributa (the committee of tribes) which was one of the assemblies of the people. He emancipated and enfranchised 10,000 slaves to manipulate election results, and he entrenched the power of the senate. Rather remarkably after three years he retired as dictator, having tried to ensure that the senate was in his control. He died within a year, in 78 BC.

However the constitutional changes of Sulla would not greatly outlast his death. It was followed by increasing unrest and the rise of Pompey, who after military victories in Spain, was appointed consul together with Crassus who had recently put down the slave rebellion of Spartacus in 70 BC. Together they reversed nearly all the constitutional changes instituted by Sulla.

Pompey briefly retired until asked to rid the Mediterranean of pirates, and then finished off the war with King Mithridates in Asia Minor. In order to allay suspicions of his intentions, he disbanded his army on returning to Italy. The senate then refused to provide his returning veterans with the grants of land he had requested. Together with Caesar, who was made consul in 59 BC, and Crassus, he formed part of the first triumvirate, which dominated the governance of Rome. However, ultimately he and Caesar were to fall out. Caesar spent the next years conquering the rest of transalpine Gaul and making a few forays into Britain. Caesar had been promised the consulship on his return, but the senate demanded that he disband his army first. Caesar had learnt from Pompey's experience and refused. By crossing the Rubicon river, which was the border between his province of cisalpine Gaul and Italy proper, Caesar committed himself to civil conflict. Rome was plunged headlong into a series of events which would lead to Caesar's assassination, the extinction of the republic and the start of Empire.

What emerges from the formation and subsequent fall of the Roman republic is the degree to which it constituted not a democracy in the modern sense, but mainly an oligarchy; the rich and the powerful making the key decisions, and the ordinary people making fleeting appearances from time to time – often as a result of the greedy demands of the ruling classes becoming unbearable. The surprising fact perhaps is not that the influence of the poorer classes was so weak, but that it existed at all.

The Romans did not perfect the device of representative democracy, except to the extent of electing tribunes, and the requirement of being physically present in Rome severely limited the participation of the people in the process in reality. As the Roman state expanded the old checks and balances of power became increasingly difficult to enforce. The military might required to keep the captured territories in check could be used against the civil authorities. The executive part of Roman government became, in practice, increasingly militarised. The greater the military conquests the more Rome moved from its republican roots. The larger the number of slaves the more vulnerable the position of the average citizen. The introduction of the state food handouts hastened the emergence of a class with civic rights, but with an economic dependence on the state. This was hardly an encouragement of a responsible citizenry.

As the military requirements of the state grew, one of the most attractive career paths for the poorer classes was the army. It provided regular pay and food, and seems to have allowed, at least to a certain degree, promotion based on merit. It is hardly surprising that with these incentives, the loyalty of the army should have become increasingly given to the commanding general rather than to the state. The creation of a standing army provided a temptation to move from civilian to military power, particularly in uncertain constitutional times.

The collapse of the Roman Republic into Empire was not the tragic fall of a noble institution. The senate had often proved itself to be exercising power on behalf of the wealthy classes to the detriment of the rest of society. The Roman virtues of perseverance, honour, fortitude and loyalty were found in a number of its famous men, but not necessarily always in the actions of its institutions. Ruthlessness was also a defining characteristic – in the single year of 146 BC the Romans totally devastated two of the great cities of the ancient world, Carthage and Corinth, with the slaughter and enslavement of their populations on a massive scale.

After the banishment of the kings Rome had been governed as an aristocracy tempered by the influence of the ordinary people. The influence of the plebeians of the early years created a mechanism which allowed a degree of social mobility, providing the most successful of them access into the upper echelons of society and a way of limiting the worst excesses of the ruling classes; it was the power of veto rather than of policy making. The expansion of the Roman state is a tale of the fitful economic decline of the citizenry compared with the wealthy; they were not dangerous because they had become wealthy enough to challenge the existing order; they were dangerous because they were sometimes in a position of having nothing left to lose, and the social solidarity of the Roman state was vulnerable to disintegration.

After the collapse of the Roman Republic and its replacement by Empire the notion of democracy as a practical form of government is consigned to the history books. In the strong centralised state that was to follow, and in the chaos of its collapse, little thought was given to the concept of the rights of individual citizens to have a say in government. The early Christian church which initially exhibited democratic tendencies within its congregations soon succumbed to the attractions of discipline, order and orthodoxy.

The experience of Greece and Rome also shows that excessive concentration of property held in a few hands is not conducive to democracy, but rather repressive of it, at least until the point when the poor feel that they have nothing left to lose. The rise of democracy has, on the whole, been contemporaneous with a changing of the distribution of wealth. It is entirely logical that this should be so. If wealth and power is held in the hands of the few, what is the incentive to distribute it to the many, except as a result of yielding to force?

After a long intermission

As Norman Davies has pointed out in his book 'History of Europe'[29] democracy is very much the exception, not the rule. Indeed the origins of the Anglo-Saxon democratic institutions lie not in the mists of Greek antiquity, however much philosophical sustenance they have drawn from that source, but from the more tribal accommodations of the Germanic and Norse peoples from which they sprang, who had assemblies in very early historical times, including, for example, the Tynwald on the Isle of Man, founded in 979 AD, the oldest continuously sitting Parliament in the world. It is to the warrior societies of the Vikings and the Danes, which have tended to receive a rather bad press, rather than to any lingering memories of Greece or the early days of the Roman Republic that we owe the genesis of British parliamentary institutions.

These institutions represented societies which did not have large amounts of accumulated wealth in a few hands. The distribution of wealth between their members was of a completely different order compared with that which we experience today. The same can be said for the early days of

---

[29] Norman Davies 'A history of Europe, p.130.

the Roman Republic. The disparities of wealth and power were by no means as large as they were to become in the period leading up to Empire and beyond. Simple nomadic societies have few surpluses to provide for substantial asset accumulation. In simple agrarian societies, particularly those which are pastoral, and where it is difficult to grow arable crops, the general poverty of society militates against great disparities of wealth. Early agricultural societies in favourable arable locations, such as Egypt, the Middle East, parts of India and China were able to accumulate greater surpluses and this gave rise to much greater disparities of wealth. Where resources such as water were scarce, there was inevitably a greater tendency to centralisation as a result of the economic advantages gained from co-operation, or at least co-ordination. This in turn enabled an even more effective avenue for the accumulation of wealth and control.

There is more scope (and less need) in societies where such agricultural co-operation is not required to adopt a less autocratic decision making mechanism. It is easy to imagine that in the more unstructured societies of northern Europe in the early Middle Ages it was necessary to persuade warriors to come on raiding parties rather than merely ordering them. The living conditions and the lack of urbanisation made for a much flatter social structure. In such circumstances there was at least the potential for a broader based oligarchy, if only initially on military lines.

Also in these societies power had not been institutionalised through the use of religion. In Egypt and in imperial Rome the status of the ruler was made divine to bolster their authority. Even in the Byzantine Empire, the Emperor had a pivotal status in the life of the church.

Changing partners

However in western Europe as the power of the Pope grew the separation between Church and State became far more clear cut. The Papacy had little secular power but the failure of the early Holy Roman Emperors to exert significant religious authority for any period of time meant that the earthly authority of kings though immediate was not considered supreme.

This idea of monarchs being subject to a higher authority was an important factor in that it promulgated the idea that kings could do wrong, and would be answerable for their deeds.[30] The separation of an institutionalised monarchy and an institutionalised church was to provide a rudimentary balance of powers.

This relationship between Church and State was no less difficult in England than elsewhere in Europe, as the martyrdom of Thomas Becket, the Archbishop of Canterbury, in 1170, during the reign of Henry II (1133-1189) clearly showed.

The democratic rights of Athens and Rome seem to have been born at least in part out of desperation, with the ordinary citizen in dire economic circumstances. The slowly evolving democracy of the English parliament owed more to the increasing economic power of those in society below the level of the aristocracy.

Follow the Leader

During periods of weak kingship (such as during the reign of King John (1199-1216)) the most important subjects were in a more powerful position to get their grievances dealt with. The signing of the Magna Carta in 1215 was a significant first

---

[30] Frederick Barbarossa, Holy Roman Emperor (1155-1190) fell out with the papacy on numerous occasions, supported an anti-pope, was excommunicated, took an army from Germany to Italy six times, and fell on his knees in front of Pope Alexander III on 24th July 1177 at St. Mark's cathedral in Venice to obtain absolution after a disastrous defeat at the battle of Legano in the previous year. He died in 1190 in Anatolia on the Third Crusade.

step in wresting power from the monarch and establishing certain fundamental rights.[31]

The Angevin Empire of John's father, Henry II, covered not only England, but large parts of France. Governing and defending such an Empire was a costly and difficult undertaking, particularly in a feudal system where the tax system was rather rudimentary, and where the king was supposed to "live off his own". Henry was not helped by the fact that his sons (and his wife Eleanor of Aquitaine) had an unfortunate tendency to rebel against him, and the interests of England were subordinated to those of his overseas possessions.[32] These financial tensions became even more

---

[31] It is perhaps interesting to note that the first confirmation of rights is for the English Church to be free. Like his father John had been excommunicated by the Pope, and the refusal of the Church to marry or christen anyone during his excommunication had caused considerable consternation since the unchristened were believed to go to hell and infant mortality was high. The interests of the nobility come next, particularly with regard to inheritance, followed by confirmations of the liberties of the City of London. This is followed by provisions for fixed courts and for punishments to match the severity of the crime. At points 38-40 some of the more crucial issues of general justice are tackled:

"(38) In future no official shall place a man on trial upon his own unsupported statement, without producing credible witnesses to the truth of it.

(39) No free man shall be seized or imprisoned, or stripped of his rights or possessions, or outlawed or exiled, or deprived of his standing in any other way, nor will we proceed with force against him, or send others to do so, except by the lawful judgement of his equals or by the law of the land.

(40) To no one will we sell, to no one deny or delay right or justice."

(See translation of Magna Carta in British Library http://www.bl.uk/treasures/magnacarta/translation.html)

[32] Henry II was the first of the Plantagenet kings of England, but the name of his empire, the Angevin Empire, derived from the fact that the family came from Anjou in France. He married Eleanor of Aquitaine, and his son married the Duchess of Brittany. Henry was

difficult during the reign of Henry's eldest son, Richard I, 'the Lionheart', who spent most of his time, (and his subjects' money)[33] crusading in the Holy Land.[34]

By the time King John came to the throne royal finances were already extremely fragile. Further troubles in France resulted in the need for even more taxes, causing considerable resentment, and culminated in the Magna Carta. This need to raise taxes for dynastic reasons and the friction it caused was part of the background for the calling of parliaments, both to raise money and discuss grievances.

There was a substantial change in the role of parliament during the long and troubled reign of Henry III (1216-1272). During his absence in Gascony in 1254 Henry appointed his younger brother Richard, Earl of Cornwall as regent. In the Easter of that year Richard summoned a parliament, and made the innovation of including two representatives from each of the shires – perhaps to further widen the available pool of funds for the substantial military expenditure in France.

This action was to set an important precedent which others

Count of Anjou, including Maine and Touraine, and Duke of Normandy as well, and ruled the Aquitaine. He spent much of his life expanding protecting and defending his French possessions. So too in death. He, like his wife Eleanor and his son Richard I, lies buried not in England, but in Fontevrault in Anjou. It is ironic therefore that Richard I's statue should occupy such a prominent position in front of the Houses of Parliament. His contribution must be reckoned one of putting royal finances in such a parlous state that the Crown became greatly dependent on the financial resources of its subjects to carry out its policies.

[33] Richard I only spent some six months of his reign in England and imposed a 'Saladin tithe' or tax to finance his exploits on the Third Crusade.

[34] The Crown's financial position was not helped either by the fact that Richard was captured by Duke Leopold of Austria on the way back from the Crusades, and was held to ransom for the sum of 150,000 marks.

were to build on. The initial step was taken in 1258 when the barons, weary of the foreign exploits of Henry III, and the entanglements of his relatives abroad[35], created the Provisions of Oxford, with plans for regular parliaments (three times a year), and a permanent council, which the King swore to support (although he subsequently obtained papal absolution for breaking his oath in 1261).[36]

Friction between the barons and the monarchy continued, and civil war broke out. At the Battle of Lewes in 1264 King Henry III and his son Prince Edward[37] were captured, and taken hostage. Simon de Montfort then proceeded to summon a parliament attended by 120 churchmen 23 barons, two knights for every shire and two burgesses for every borough. The summoning of burgesses from the boroughs was a further innovation, and an indication of the increasing inclusiveness of parliament. De Montfort had no time to build on this novelty; Prince Edward escaped and at the Battle of Evesham in 1265 defeated and killed him.

However Simon de Montfort's innovations had widespread appeal and did not die with him. In 1272 Prince Edward became Edward I, and during his reign he was to show that he had seen the advantages of a more broadly based parliament as compared with a council of nobles, at the very least for

---

[35] For example Richard of Cornwall, not only went on Crusade, but also was a candidate for becoming the Holy Roman Emperor, and was given the title of King of the Romans. He was also offered (but refused) the Crown of Sicily by Pope Innocent IV, although King Henry III accepted it for his second son Edmund.

[36] It is one of the ironies of the Provisions that one of their central conditions was that the realm of England be ruled only by native born men. Ironic not only because England through the Tudors, Stuarts, the Hanoverians and the Saxe-Coburgs has had scarcely any native dynasties, but also because some of its most illustrious sovereigns have been women. It was even more ironic that the baronial rebellion was led by Simon de Montfort, who was born in Montfort l'Amaury, near Chartres in France.

[37] Often referred to as 'The Lord Edward'

raising the huge amount of money he needed to pursue his military campaigns and meet the enormous cost of his massive castle building programme in Wales. The form of parliaments varied, and sometimes no representatives of the shires and towns were summoned, but in 1295 Edward I, in more need of money than usual, summoned what has been described as the 'model parliament', which also included members of the lesser clergy. At this stage parliaments had many functions, including acting as a court (it retains its designation as 'the high court of parliament' to this day) and dealing with pleas and many administrative matters, as well as passing laws and allocating taxes. It is perhaps notable that the model parliament was not requested to pass any laws although it was asked to grant taxes.

This dependency of the monarchy on a wider group of people than just the nobles and great prelates, (and without adequate royal resources for such ambitious projects) doubtless led to an awakening of a feeling of importance in the middling class of people. The social dislocation and demographic catastrophe caused by the arrival of the Black Death in 1348 and again in 1361, as well as subsequent outbreaks[38] was to provide an awareness of economic importance to people even further down the social scale and have more than a little to do with the rise of a more independent spirit. The continuing requirements of the monarchy for more money, this time from Edward III for his wars in France fuelled these sentiments further. It is perhaps no coincidence that during this time Parliamentary change again moved on apace. In 1343 the role

---

[38] see Davies the Isles p.356. He quotes a description of the plague by a Welsh poet, Ieuan Gethin, who wrote "We see death coming into our midst like black smoke, a plague which cuts off the young, a rootless phenomenon which has no mercy for fair countenance...woe is me of the shilling of the armpit   it is of the form of an apple, like the head of an onion, a small boil that spares no one. Great is the seething like a burning cinder, a grievous thing of ashy colour...". See also Churchill vol 2, chapter 6, History of the English Speaking Peoples for a description of the effect of the plague.

of Speaker of the House of Commons emerged for the first time – with the knights and burgesses meeting in the Painted Chamber at Westminster and the prelates and magnates in the White Chamber[39].

It was during the reign of Edward III (1327-1377) that we see the start of a proper labour market. With the population reduced by as much as a third by the plague, the ability of the magnates to have their land worked by the villeins was greatly reduced. There was an increase in the number of serfs who obtained a leasehold to their land.[40]

The wage inflation became so bad that by 1351 it was deemed necessary to pass the Statute of Labourers, which referenced prices back to the 20th year of the reign of Edward III and specified price capping[41]:

---

[39] Churchill, same chapter

[40] It was the time when the English language began to make serious headway against French among the upper classes, and the age of Wycliffe (1329-1384), Chaucer (1340-1400) and William Langland (1360-1399), who in his poem Piers Plowman wrote:

Labourers that have no land to live on but their hands,
Deigned not to dine a day, on night old wortes.
May no penny ale him pay, nor a piece of bacon,
But it be fresh flesh or fish, fried or baked,
And that chaud and plus-chaud, for chilling of their maw,
But he be highly hired else he will chide.

[41] "Whereas late against the malice of servants, which were idle, and not willing to serve after the pestilence, without taking excessive wages, it was ordained by our lord the king, and by the assent of the prelates, nobles, and other of his council, that such manner of servants, as well men as women, should be bound to serve, receiving salary and wages, accustomed in places where they ought to serve in the twentieth year of the reign of the king that now is, or five or six years before; and that the same servants refusing to serve in such manner should be punished by imprisonment of their bodies, as in the said statute is more plainly contained: whereupon

This shift in economic power led to popular ballads, whose words still resonate with us today, such as:

'when Adam delved and Eve span,
Who was then a gentleman?'

These social changes caused great resentment and unrest over the next 30 years, culminating in the Peasant's Revolt of 1381 in the reign of Richard II (1377-1399) which challenged the existing order.

The success of Richard II in facing down the Peasant's Revolt at the age of only 15 was not a precursor for a reign noted for its sureness of touch. The Peasant's Revolt led to Richard proposing the radical step (proposed but not taken) of abolishing serfdom. However his extravagant habits and arrogant treatment of some of the great nobles led to an open revolt in the late 1380's.

The role of parliament during the twists and turns of Richard II's reign is of some interest. Richard II summoned the 'Wonderful Parliament' in 1386 and demanded a large sum of money. Not only was this not granted, but parliament demanded the impeachment[42] of one of the king's favourites the Earl of Suffolk. This was not only an indication of the growing power of parliament, but also that it was an important forum in which to resolve disputes. This was reinforced a few years later in the 'Merciless Parliament' of 1389, when the much hated Chief Justice Tresilian was put on trial and subsequently executed, and others of the king's favourites were forced to flee to France.

---

commissions were made to divers people in every county to inquire and punish all them which offend against the same. "White, Albert Beebe and Wallace Notestein", eds. *Source Problems in English History*. New York: Harper and Brother Publishers, 1915.

[42] Impeachment had first been used ten years earlier in 1376, during the 'Good Parliament' in the closing years of Edward III's reign, when Peter de la Mare acted as the 'Speaker' on behalf of the 'commons'.

This series of events showed also the multiplicity of roles which parliament had at this time, as court of justice and council, as legislature and fund raiser. In their struggle with the monarchy the great nobles found the commons an important addition to their cause; but the commons could be swayed more than one way.

Richard II wanted revenge for the rebellion of powerful nobles in the late 1380's. He obviously subscribed to the Italian adage that revenge is a dish better eaten cold and bided his time. In 1397, nearly ten years after the events leading up to the Merciless Parliament he attacked the ringleaders. He declared the Earl of Arundel a traitor and had him executed, exiled the Earl of Warwick to the Isle of Man and had the Duke of Gloucester arrested, taken to Calais and murdered there. He then sought absolute power for the monarchy. The Parliament of the day did little to stop him. In January 1397 parliament was summoned, and not only did it relinquish many of its rights, but it ended by leaving the remainder of business that had not been dealt with to a committee of 18 people.[43]

These and other actions made the king unpopular among the nobility. He nevertheless raised an army and left for Ireland. Henry Bolingbroke (subsequently Henry IV) invaded in his absence and Richard's reign came to a precipitate end. It is perhaps a moot point as to whether the history of Britain would have been very different if Richard II had remained upon the throne; he was undoubtedly popular with the populace at large, but the events of the time demonstrate once again the vital inter-reaction of economic and political power, and the way in which parliament was increasingly becoming the forum of difficult decisions, be they political, legal or fiscal. What is more certain is that the deposition of Richard II led to substantial disunity in Britain as it was the immediate cause of the Wars of the Roses, and the energy with which Henry's son, Henry V, prosecuted his claim to the French

---

[43] Winston Churchill, History of the English Speaking Peoples, Volume 2, Chapter VII.

throne continued the Crown's dependency on parliament for the money to pay for it. The history of England's mediaeval monarchs is often one of continental ambition but insular resources.

The Wars of the Roses meant that constitutional progress largely lay in abeyance while more personal scores of influence and inheritance were settled by the great nobles[44]. The ascent of Henry Tudor (Henry VII) to the throne in 1485 resulted in the restoration of strong monarchy, a reduction of the power of the nobility, and a new stability enlivened by the early years of the Renaissance. Henry was an effective administrator, and a careful husbander of royal revenues and given his tenuous claim to throne doubtless he wanted to ensure that he did not become as dependent on parliament as some of his predecessors.[45]

Henry died in 1509 leaving a full treasury to his son Henry VIII, who some 25 years later had recourse to parliament for a different reason – the recognition of his divorce from Catherine of Aragon. The cleavage of Christianity between protestant and catholic, and the dilemma of a king whose wife was unable to bear him a son was the cause of a great

---

[44] However in about 1470 Sir John Fortescue, who had been Chief Justice of the court of King's Bench under Henry VI and who had followed him into exile after the Yorkist Edward IV had seized the throne in 1461 wrote a book entitled 'The Difference between an absolute and a limited monarchy'. This book contrasted the absolutist monarchy of France with the parliamentary style monarchy of England, and praised the latter. The book wasn't published until 1714, but was to receive a new lease of life and a wider audience in the nineteenth century when it was published under the title 'the governance of England' in 1885.

[45] He is one of the few monarchs whose tax collectors, Empson and Dudley, became (in)famous. His Chancellor , John Morton was the origin of the expression 'Morton's Fork' which described the view of the Chancellor that if you lived in luxury you were wealthy enough to pay taxes and that if you lived frugally you were saving enough money to be able to pay taxes.

constitutional crisis. The king was himself ambivalent (he had after all been granted the title of fidei defensor, defender of the faith, by the Pope), but the problem of succession was acute.

In the events that followed, the Papacy proved itself unwilling to accommodate Henry's need for an annulment. Since the religious route was blocked, the only alternative was the secular one. Cardinal Wolsey's failure to convince the Pope of Henry's case led to his fall and the stream of legislation passed through parliament to deal with the consequences of the new religious regime was ample testimony to the growing role of parliament as the ultimate arbiter of legitimacy.

As has been noted earlier Protestantism tended to be more open to the new ideas being formulated in Renaissance Europe. Although the early Renaissance flourished in Italy as soon as the new ideas moved from explaining received wisdom to challenging doctrine they were increasingly severely suppressed, as Galileo found. In its inception and in its practices protestants had much experience in defying authority and questioning orthodoxy[46]. This is not to say that they were doctrinally any more liberal or tolerant than their Catholic counterparts, but their churches were built on a willingness to flout established authority and, with the

---

[46] As has been noted earlier Henry VIII had been awarded the tile of Defender of the [Catholic] Faith by the Pope. Pope Leo X had awarded him this title in 1521 for his treatise on the seven sacraments and in repudiation of Luther's writings. Luther, by contrast, while praising the elegance of the writing referred to the king as 'a fool and an ass, a blasphemer and a liar.' Such was the regard the founder of Protestantism had for kings. An additional interesting fact is that the title was given to the king personally (tibi perpetuum et proprium – for you for ever and personally), but Henry retained it after the break with Rome and it was annexed to the crown in 1543 by Act of parliament, another instance of the perceived breadth of parliament's competence. See Davies, 'the Isles' , 'The Englished Isles' quoting Lingered.

anomalous exception of the Church of England,[47] they owed no allegiance to great prelates. It is therefore scarcely surprising that in the religious turmoil of the sixteenth century the attitude of those middling classes whose interests were represented in parliament should become more confident in their own abilities.

In addition partisanship in religion touched upon the security of the realm, and while Catholicism, a root cause for not only the Armada of 1588 but of the gunpowder plot of 1605, was beyond the pale (quite literally in the case of Ireland), the puritans were regarded with much suspicion – James I had a particular dislike of them. Religion continued to be a vital matter of secular concern.

A New Tune

By the middle of the seventeenth century when the monarchy was again falling into debt and increasingly reliant on parliament to bail it out, this new independence of spirit, bolstered by religious certitude, enabled parliament to contest the authority of the monarch in a way that would have been unimaginable at the end of the sixteenth century. In the previous centuries the monarchy and the nobility in their struggle for power had used the mechanism of parliament to aid their own side and institutionalised it. Although it was summoned at the monarch's pleasure, it provided the money and kept comprehensive records – it increasingly became the arbiter of legitimacy. By the reign of Charles I when the king in parliament no longer functioned effectively as a sovereign

---

[47] The Anglican Church saw no reason to forsake the authority of bishops when it parted from Rome, more for political than doctrinal reasons. It is one of the signs of curious compromise of the Anglican Church that the Creed in the Book of Common Prayer so beautifully written by Cranmer, should require belief in the 'holy catholic and apostolic church'. Whilst 'catholic' in this context may be deemed to mean universal it is an indication of a conservative reluctance to go the whole way down the protestant road.

body the question arose as to where sovereignty ultimately lay. There had been little doubt before: as Charles I remarked "A subject and a sovereign are clean different things". However the political and religious ferment of the times were to put this assumption to the test. The example of the northern Netherlands' successful revolt against the Spanish in the sixteenth century, and the establishment of republican government there as well as the example of Switzerland was perhaps a spur to the belief that monarchy was not essential to effective government.

It is perhaps notable that when King Charles I entered the Commons in 1642, it was the first time that any monarch had done so, and it was another telling sign that power had shifted dramatically away not only from the Crown, but also from the Lords.

Perhaps if Oliver Cromwell's sons had been more competent, or given more time or if Oliver Cromwell himself had lived longer Britain might have remained a republic. It is ironic that Cromwell found parliament as difficult to manage as King Charles before him, and he dismissed the Rump parliament in 1653, as well as a series of others in the following years. He ruled as a military dictator, and divided the country into ten then eleven regions governed by major generals. Parliament had achieved enough power to oust a king but not yet enough cohesiveness to rule in his place. In seventeenth century England, as in eighteenth century France, the transfer of power from monarchy to people was via a military dictatorship followed by a restoration of the monarchy, when the passions of principle were replaced by the pragmatism of compromise and accommodation.

After the restoration of the Stuart monarchs in 1660 there could be no doubt that the rules of the game had changed. In the Declaration of Breda in 1660 Charles II acknowledged that the government was constituted by 'King, Lords, and Commons'. When his brother James, who had converted to Catholicism, ascended the throne in 1685 his new religion made him unacceptable to a largely protestant aristocracy and gentry. The husband of James's daughter Mary, William of Orange, was invited to become king by a group of seven. William was not invited in by Parliament, but he was careful to call a parliament shortly after his arrival as the best way to legitimise his extremely tenuous claim to the throne.

The Glorious Revolution of 1688-1689 which brought William and Mary to the British throne marked the transfer of sovereignty from the monarchy to an oligarchy. It confirmed the upper middle classes as part of the governing mechanism of the country. After centuries of strife between the monarch and the nobility the gentry and wealthy merchants had ensured their place in the sun. The gentry had been able to use their importance in understanding local conditions and their influence in ensuring obedience to the laws and the raising of taxes as a way of obtaining a share in the power that they administered. Like modern day supermarkets the gentry were closest to the ordinary citizen customer, and by understanding their requirements were able to increasingly decide the terms on which the 'power supply' of monarchy and nobles reached its final destination. They had the added advantage that they also had an important influence on the price of that power, in the form of taxes.

However this new constitutional arrangement scarcely equated to any modern notion of democracy – it was merely recognition that real power was more widely dispersed. It would take nearly another hundred years and a tangled series of events before democracy would start to emerge in a society with its roots in Britain, but this would be in the New World, many thousands of miles away from William's landing place of Torbay in Devon.

Freer Rhythms

It is interesting to note in passing that the landowning classes in the United States, by taking exception to the interference of the British monarchy, had to raise their army not by coercion and simple payment as would have been the case in Europe, but by co-option and conviction. Indeed in some ways this paralleled the circumstances of the English Civil War[48]. Having no settled power base of their own, and relying on their persuasive powers and popular sentiment to win control of their continent the conditions were more favourable than in the old world for the sharing of power. This is not to say that there were not many landowners who were not imbued with the ideas of the writings of Tom Paine, Rousseau and Hume, as well as earlier influences such as Locke. However, power once acquired is not lightly given up, and doubtless for the many enlightened land owners there was a substantial number of their brethren who were not entirely convinced of the unalloyed benefits of democracy. The system of the U.S. Electoral College is a reflection of these concerns among an elite that had not yet become accustomed to exercising sovereign power.

Many of the Founding Fathers of the United States were wealthy landowners, but it is perhaps to Benjamin Franklin we should look as the archetypal inspiration of the democratic system in the United States, typifying as he did both self reliance and open-mindedness. A self made man, and a printer by profession, he was able to rise in American society in a way that would have been far more difficult in the more constrained societies of Europe. By creating a society that allowed such men to flourish the small communities on the eastern seaboard of North America were able to create a resilient and durable democratic structure following the American War of Independence. This was not always to be the case for other newly independent states in the western hemisphere, or elsewhere.

It was the free thinking of the Age of Enlightenment that would provide the bridge between oligarchy and democracy.

---

[48] Max Weber, The Protestant Ethic and the spirit of capitalism, Cromwell wrote to the Long Parliament after the battle of Dunbar in 1650 "Be pleased to reform the abuses of all professions; and if there be any one that makes many poor to make a few rich, that suits not a Commonwealth"

The absence of heavily entrenched interests and the necessity of co-operation, as well as self reliance bred from isolation were all factors in the American achievement. One of the ironies of the genesis of the United States of America is that it was catalysed by resentment of an over mighty corporation. That story is dealt with elsewhere in this book, but suffice it to say that the development of democracy in the United States was made easier by the absence of a lot of the historical baggage and vested interest which greatly constrained change in Europe. For much of Europe such change would come by a much more violent, revolutionary and ultimately more circuitous route.

A change of tempo

On the eastern seaboard of the Atlantic in the United Kingdom, where similar influences were at work, society was much more set in its ways. It required a far longer process for the voice of economic disenfranchisement to be heard and acceded to. The rising tide of independent businessmen of the growing new industrialising urban areas continued to push for political power to reflect their increasing economic power. The arguments that underpinned the demands for this class of people were prayed in aid for those even further down the economic scale, and movements such as the Chartists, so-called after the People's Charter of 1838, (only six years after the Great Reform Act of 1832) took up the call for universal suffrage.

In the 'Wealth of Nations' Adam Smith wrote "Wealth, as Mr. Hobbs says, is power. But the person who either acquires or succeeds to a great fortune does not necessarily acquire or succeed to any political power, either civil or military".[49] The key word here is 'necessarily' and even then is not fully correct historically. Leaving aside the question of military power (and in Smith's day commissions in the British Army had to be purchased, so that the absence of a modicum of wealth could certainly be a bar to significant military power in

---

[49] Wealth of Nations, Book I, Chapter V

that context, and as we have seen Pisistratus captured Athens with mercenaries) the feudal notion of society had been very different. Parliament was a forum for the sovereign to discuss vital issues of the day with the most important people of the country. In Smith's day, collectively, even more than individually, wealth and political power were closely connected.

As we have seen one of the most important functions of parliament, if not the most important, was the raising of money, certainly from the point of view of the monarch, and the MPs represented the moneyed classes of the time; it was they after all who would have to come up with the cash. If the wealth were large enough and the title grand enough the possessor was automatically a member of the House of Lords, representing no-one's interests but their own. They therefore automatically acceded to a measure of political power. There was indeed a direct linkage between wealth and power, despite Smith's protestations. As the source of wealth changed and broadened, the system adapted but the underlying linkage of wealth and power was clear – the wealthier you were the more political power you were entitled to. Indeed this was much more apparent at local level where justice was often a local affair meted out by the Lord of the Manor. In the absence of military power monetary power was an influential substitute.

As parliament evolved in the eighteenth century the House of Lords represented one of the two great pillars of society – the landowning classes. The House of Commons, represented by and large the squirearchy and the merchant classes in the towns. As we have seen they were a vital component since they were drawn from the class of people who as local magistrates and men of influence were essential in ensuring that the law was carried out, and who bore the brunt of the taxation required by the monarch.

The House of Lords existed since it made no sense to have the most powerful people in the land excluded from the law making process. The monarch clearly needed the nobles to be in the pavilion relieving themselves outside rather than vice versa[50]. The power of the House of Lords derived from the power that those entitled to sit there brought with them. These were the people who represented the landed interests that the eighteenth century economist Ricardo felt were such an impediment to economic growth.[51] Their presence was leavened by the Lords spiritual, who were important from a temporal point of view given the landholdings and taxation powers of the Church, and the fact that the Church had in reality been nationalised.

The Industrial Revolution gave rise to the problem that the newly enriched and more numerous commercial classes found themselves without adequate representation in this structure, (unless as individuals they became so successful that they were ennobled). The abolition of the Rotten Boroughs and the increase of the representation of the rapidly growing industrial centres in Britain rectified this imbalance over a period of years, with the commercial interest being largely identified with the Liberals and the landowning classes with the Conservatives.

The expansion of democracy in Victorian Britain is dealt with in another chapter, but by the time the Labour Party burst on the political scene at the beginning of the 20th Century to represent the interests of the working classes, the importance of the landowning classes, and hence of the House of Lords had significantly diminished. Not only had land become a much smaller part of the economy as a whole, but in addition much of that land was now held by corporations rather than individuals with titles, the Duke of Westminster constituting one of the more conspicuous exceptions. The Lords gradually ceased to represent anything of any great importance any more. Power followed wealth as it had done from the Middle Ages.

---

[50] Just as President Lyndon Johnson remarked of J. Edgar Hoover: "It's probably better to have him inside the tent pissing out, than outside the tent pissing in." New York Times 31st October 1971.

[51] See for example Heilbroner, the Worldly Philosophers Chapter iv

Given requirements of time and space it has not been possible to examine the routes to democracy in other countries, but in all cases democracies are dependent for their security on a significant dispersion of wealth across the population and are always vulnerable when real power lies outside.

Chapter III

What is a company?

Lord Thurlow, Lord Chancellor 1731 – 1806

"Did you ever expect a corporation to have a conscience when it has no soul to be damned, and no body to be kicked?"

A wealthy wisp

The demonstrations at Seattle, Genoa, Davos and more recently at the G8 meeting at Gleneagles and in nearby Edinburgh in Scotland in 2005 underline the deep malaise that is felt in Western countries as to the way in which corporate leviathans are distorting society and creating undesirable outcomes, some of them unintended, others deliberate. They also indicate dissatisfaction at the way in which popularly elected governments seem unable or unwilling to create policies that are capable of fundamentally changing the situation. However, as of yet, no coherent picture has emerged of a system that may replace the current one.

Democracy and corporate capitalism are strange bedfellows. The roots of democracy and capitalism are intertwined – one defending liberty, the other defending property. Indeed on an individual basis the more widespread the right to own property became the more supportive it was of democracy. Autocratic systems of power tend to restrict the individual right to own property. In pre-industrial societies land is the major source of wealth, and ownership is usually restricted to a small elite. Such societies prefer that the power that ownership gives be concentrated in a small number of hands. In the feudal system of landholding in England for example few people 'owned' land in the modern sense. The great nobles held their land from the sovereign, and the land was usually 'entailed' i.e. it could not be disposed of freely, but only in accordance with strict rules, which tried to ensure that the estate passed on intact to the next generation. In the same way the Church and the various monastic orders held land which was passed down the generations. In their way they were not unlike the corporations of today, with the same pretensions of immortality. Not much place within this framework for the sturdy yeoman farmer, stalwart of democratic liberties.

When capitalism meant the protection of personal property (as opposed to landed wealth) therefore, its interests paralleled those of democracy. The greater the degree to which wealth can be shared within a community the greater the likelihood of democracy working effectively. Corporate capitalism is of course an entirely different matter. Corporate capitalism, within its own sphere, tends to greater concentration of wealth, not less. Corporate wealth is now incomparably greater than individual wealth – even the mega rich of today achieve their wealth through a corporate structure. This concentration of wealth seems to be at work inside companies as well - witness the seemingly inexorable increase of the pay of senior executives as compared with the workforce in companies. Corporate capitalism does not provide any say to the members of the community[52] who are engaged in the joint economic endeavour – i.e. the business in which they work. In many ways corporate capitalism is the very antithesis of democracy. It is a fellow traveller, travelling under false colours. While capitalism is portrayed as an indicator of personal freedoms, corporate capitalism is in practice a denier of freedom, a depriver of economic independence.

Corporations do not feel, they do not touch, and they cannot be touched. Corporations do not cry. They do not laugh. Corporations have no soul. All their activities are ultimately soulless. In a number of science fiction futures humans are locked in a struggle with machines. In a sense this is already

---

[52] Except where the state or a level of government within a state is itself a shareholder, as in the case of nationalized or partly nationalized industries, or Volkswagen where the Land (State) of Lower Saxony is the largest shareholder.

happening today, but on a much more insidious basis. The word machine derives from the Greek word mekhane meaning contrivance. The word mechanism is derived from the same source and continues to convey the original meaning. Companies are mechanisms for aggregating capital, for maximising profit. If we were to imbue such mechanisms or machines with human attributes they would include ruthlessness, cunning, determination, obsessive focus, narrowness of interest, relentlessness and potentially immortality. They are dangerous enemies indeed. Their impact is everywhere yet they cannot be seen. They have many rights, but are adept at avoiding obligations. We have created them for our own uses, and they turn out to have acquired something akin to a life of their own.

The curious nature of corporations was well expressed in the case of Sutton's Hospital,[53] when it was commented "For a corporation aggregate of many invisible, immortal, and rests only in intendement and consideration of the law"

Democracy and other forms of government can be likened to a framework which moulds behaviour and the ways in which power can be exercised. A form of government can also be likened to a lens, which focuses the aims and ambitions, hopes and aspirations of the society to which it applies. Democracy acting for society as a whole is a multi-focal lens, trying to focus a multiplicity of different objectives from a myriad of sources. By definition it has limited ability to provide the clarity that all the sources require – the image that it casts is a melding of the many as they pass through the lens. The corporate mechanism is a highly powerful lens compared with the democratic one, focusing on a limited objective from a limited number of sources; it has the power to burn.

Decision making in human affairs necessarily involves the difficult subject of who is entitled to make decisions and on

---

[53] 10 Coke Reports 22b (1615). Quoted in A. B. Dubois "the English Business Company after the Bubble Act 1720-1800" 1938, the Commonwealth Fund, p.86

whose behalf. This is purely a matter of power; it may be the power of naked force or it may be the power of persuasion, but there has always been an ebb and flow of power from the one to the many, from monarchy through aristocracy to democracy. As has been noted the times and places when power has been exercised by the many rather than the few are the exception rather than the rule. Monarchy or oligarchy has been the norm, sometimes reinforced through religious structures with priest kings or powerful priesthoods.

It is not unusual for companies to be regarded merely as entities which have an influence over the state in which they are active, but they are, in addition, states in themselves, with their rules of governance affected not only by the strict legal framework within which they operate, but also by their scale and by their history, and the personalities of their senior management.

Community spirit

Although they clearly have more circumscribed goals as laid out in their own founding documents, companies are microcosms of society at large – as evidenced in a number of languages such as the French 'société anonyme', the German the use of the word 'Gesellschaft' or the Japanese 'kabushiki kaisha'[54]. The fundamental difference compared with democratic society is that the 'members' of the society are not those who work within it on a daily basis, but those whose participation is defined by their investment in it. It is as if in society at large voting rights were restricted to banks, corporations and wealthy individuals in proportion to their net assets. It is when we try to transfer the corporate model to the wider sphere that its ludicrous unfairness becomes most manifest. This is the framework for the delivery of power, not of justice. And yet we fail to question why it is right that

---

[54] The last word in Japanese constitutes two elements, 'kai', which connotes both meeting and society, and 'sha', which has the connotation of association.

in the sphere of politics and society at large one set of guiding principles should apply, but that in the sphere of commerce and business they should be noticeable by their absence.

The way in which corporates behave in practice reflects, rather imperfectly, the culture and value systems of which they form a part. This comes about because of the values of the people working in those corporations and in spite of their intrinsic structure. The way in which companies are run in countries such as Japan and Korea, is by no means as focused on the interests of the shareholders as compared with the United States or the United Kingdom. This reflects the difference in the social norms of those societies, rather than a substantial difference in the corporate structure itself. It is true that the structure of companies in a number of European countries has been altered to allow workers representatives on the boards, etc.; this ameliorates to some extent the influence of the shareholders, but it does not alter the fundamental nature of the corporate structure. As discussed elsewhere, this is more the influence of an older type of corporatism on modern day companies and even this variation is under attack as being less 'efficient' than the Anglo-Saxon corporate model.

The corporate mentality not only potentially reflects the values of the societies in which it operates but just as importantly it also affects the way of thinking of the societies in which it implants itself. It provides a benchmark against which previous attitudes are examined. The concept of capitalism is not, of course, limited to companies, but corporations provide a systematic and systemic vehicle through which it can be implemented and transmitted. Corporate capitalism is a distinct and different concept from individual capitalism. Companies intensely dislike the competitive nature of capitalism – all companies crave monopoly. Corporate capitalism is a very different creature from the capitalist society described by Adam Smith. The corporate structure can perhaps be found in its most virulent and original form in Anglo-Saxon countries. In addition their literalistic method of law-making and compliance, based on a precise interpretation of wording rather than the application of principles has probably led to a greater clarity of the implications of the classic corporate structure than elsewhere. The way in which company structure was conceived of in the United Kingdom and in the United States has had a significant impact on the way in which the corporate structure has developed around the globe, both as a result of direct influence, as in India, and in Japan after the Second World War, and also as a result of Anglo Saxon economic dominance which has perhaps existed for the best part of two centuries. Even today, in the waning years of US economic dominance, in both Japan and Germany we can see tendencies for the corporate model to become increasingly like that of the Anglo Saxon countries, rather than becoming more distinct.

It is for these reasons that the development of the Anglo Saxon company model from its European roots gives us an insight to some of the key generic characteristics of the company structure.

In the eyes of the law

The evolution of the company was a slow and uncertain one. The legal concept grew not so much out of commercial concerns, but out of charitable and administrative ones. An invention by the law to enable citizens to act as one body described as being a body 'only the law can see' - a 'corpus', the Latin word from which the English word corporation and indeed corps derives. It is perhaps worth noting that the potential implications of people acting together in this way were a matter of concern as far back as the second century AD, as this extract of correspondence between the Emperor Trajan and Pliny shows:

"Pliny: 'A great fire has devastated Nicomedia. Would it be in order to establish a society of 150 firemen?'

Trajan: 'No. Corporations, whatever they're called, are sure to become political associations'...'[55]

This exchange carries with it both the concept of corporations being bodies established for a public purpose, and betrays the similarity of origin of companies and trades unions – groups of people, working together for a limited purpose. It also captures the political dimension of corporations. Indeed in the guilds of the Middle Ages these two aspects of job protection and trade promotion were fused into one organisation.[56]

Even at the end of the eighteenth century, the sense of a corporation as being primarily a public body established for non commercial goals was dominant. In his work The Law of Corporations of 1793 Stewart Kyd, the British barrister described the development of the corporate form as "collective bodies of men" that formed as an outgrowth of existing communities: "At the first introduction, they were little more than an improvement on the communities which had grown up imperceptibly, without any positive institution . . . ." Kyd provides a definition of the corporate form as follows:

"A corporation then, or a body politic, or body incorporate, is a collection of many individuals, united into a body, under a *special denomination*, having a perpetual succession under an *artificial form*, and vested, by policy of the law, with the

---

[55] Quoted in 'Europe, A History' by Norman Davies, p.191

[56] See Sir Ernest Pooley, the Guilds of the City of London, 1945, who also points out the religious aspects of the guilds' activities. The guilds themselves were undoubtedly important organizations with their own interests (very often monopolistic) to protect. See pp 18-20 for examples of the way in which these various aspects were inter-woven. The monopolistic nature of guilds was also to be seen in Europe. See the conflict as late as 1666 between the French button makers and clothiers – who had dared to innovate with buttons made of cloth referred to in "The worldly philosophers" by Robert Heilbroner, Penguin 1991, p.31.

capacity of acting, in several respects, as an *individual*, particularly of taking and granting property, of contracting obligations, and of suing and being sued, of enjoying privileges and immunities in *common*, and of exercising a variety of political rights, more or less extensive, according to the design of its institution, or the powers conferred upon it, either at the time of its creation, or at any subsequent period of its existence."

The corporate form was thus defined by the attributes of perpetual succession combined with the powers to take and grant property, contract, and to sue and be sued, as well as to exercise those political rights defined in its charter. Although limited liability came to be a further defining feature and figured largely in the debates about the rights and obligations of the corporate entity, it was not at this stage such a prominent factor, reflecting no doubt the uncommercial nature of corporations at this stage. What is however clear is that in their origins corporations were described as 'a body politic' and capable of 'exercising a variety of political rights'.

The 1793 treatise also describes various classes and distinctions of then contemporary corporations. It classifies corporations into "corporations sole" and "corporations aggregate." Corporations sole were those that provided perpetual succession to an office held by one single individual; these corporations sole included "the King, archbishops, certain deans, and prebendaries, all archdeacons, parsons, and vicars . . . ." Corporations aggregate were those more currently familiar entities that consisted of a group of individuals banded together for a common purpose. Kyd further classifies corporations as either ecclesiastical or lay; ecclesiastical corporations being "those of which not only are the members spiritual persons, but of which the object of the institution is also spiritual."

All other corporations are lay corporations, which, Kyd, divides into two classes, *eleemosynary* (charitable) and *civil*. Eleemosynary corporations were those "constituted for the perpetual distribution of the free alms, or the bounty of the founder of them, to such purposes as he has directed." The chief examples Kyd provides of such eleemosynary corporations are hospitals for the poor and educational institutions. The treatise then describes by example the various purposes of the civil (non-eleemosynary) lay corporation.

Limited Purposes

Civil corporations were established for a variety of temporal purposes. In his work Kyd describes how a corporate capacity is given to the King, to prevent, in general, the possibility of an interregnum or vacancy of the throne, and 'to preserve entire the possessions of the Crown'. He mentions how other civil corporations are established for the purpose of local government, such as the corporations of cities and towns, under the names of Mayor and Commonalty, Bailiffs and Burgesses, and other familiar denominations and includes in this class the general corporate bodies of the two universities of England (Oxford and Cambridge). Kyd also refers to corporations which are established for the maintenance and regulation of some particular object of public policy, such as the Corporation of the Trinity House for regulating navigation, the Bank, and the different Insurance Companies in London, others for the regulation of trade, manufactures, and commerce, such as the East India Company, and the companies of trades in London and other towns. He also mentions other institutions for the improvement of science in general, or some particular branches if it, such as the Society of Antiquarians for promoting the study of antiquities and the Royal Academy of Arts for cultivating painting and sculpture.

What is notable about the list is the absence of anything that could be called an entirely commercial entity; there is of course 'the Bank' (the Bank of England) and the East India Company, but both of these, like the insurance companies, had been founded on a basis of public policy, either to facilitate trade and commerce within the country or in distant countries where the risks were considered great. Both the

Bank of England and the East India Company enjoyed the benefits of monopoly, precisely because when they were founded they were held to be special and one of a kind, serving the public interest.

It is therefore clear that the origin of corporations is by no means purely commercial. The origins (referred to later) and title of the Corporation of the City of London neatly illustrate this pedigree. Municipal corporations spring from the same source as commercial ones, but their evolution has followed a very different path. In essence the origins of these legal forms are just devolved structures of the general powers of a larger political entity for particular purposes, whether they be for local government, charitable and not for profit purposes, or for commercial purposes. The powers of corporations are ultimately delegated powers; they only exist because the state provides them with an artificial legal existence. Commercial corporations, no less than their municipal cousins, are states in miniature, albeit with different goals, yet despite their common heritage the evolution of their decision making structure could hardly have been more different.

A rather different business

It is fair to say that although the initial stirrings of the commercial corporate animal can be discerned in Italy, the modern corporate model was based on the Dutch and English approach in the 17th Century.[57] However the concept of a

---

[57] Overseas trade in often very difficult conditions resulted in the need to amass large amounts of money for hazardous undertakings, and usually with the privileges of monopoly. The Dutch East India Company (Verenigde Oost-Indische Compagnie (VOC)), was founded in 1602. The original paid up share capital was 6,424,588 Guilders, a huge sum at that time. The key to success in the raising of capital was the decision taken by the owners to open up access to a wide public and to accept shareholders as part-owners. The shares were tradable, and changes of ownership were noted by entries on the company's register, witnessed by two directors. In addition, the

body of people working together for commercial ends had much deeper roots, and is an intrinsic part of human society. In Europe much of early commercial activity was focussed around the Church, both through the activities of the monasteries and the great religious festivals which provided the backdrop for important fairs and markets.

During much of the 'Middle Ages' the Catholic church did not stoop to concern itself with commercialism; land owning was the great source of wealth and power in an increasingly feudal society and usury was left largely to the Jews. The missionary and crusading zeal of the church to convert the pagans of Eastern Europe, to reconquer Iberia and to claim the Holy Land for Christendom did however increase the requirements for a more effective money transmission system.

The rivalry between the Popes and the Holy Roman Emperors which greatly intensified from the 11th century onwards heightened the requirements of a money service that did not depend on the goodwill of princes. The military crusading orders of the Hospitallers and Templars (the Knights of the order of the hospital of St. John of Jerusalem, created in 1099, and the Poor Knights of Christ and the Temple of Solomon, created in 1118 respectively) with their far flung connections across Christendom were to partly fill this gap, particularly so in the case of the Templars. Unfortunately for the latter, so successful were they in their accumulation of wealth that Philip IV ('the Bel') of France, having exhausted the Jews of their treasure turned on the Templars in 1312 and suppressed the Order, burning its Grand master, Jacques de Molay, at the stake.

This rather robust banking regulatory regime may have achieved its immediate goal, but the King of France, and Pope

---

company raised money through the issue of bonds which did not confer rights of ownership. These and other Dutch financial techniques were adopted by England, a process made easier at the end of the 17th century by the accession of William of Orange to the British throne. See for example http://batavia.rug.ac.be/

Clement V who had co-operated in the suppression, were dead within a year and the Capetian dynasty which had ruled France for more than 300 years finished in less than a decade. Whether this turn of events was due to the curses reputedly uttered by Jacques de Molay at the stake, or the events which tempted the King of France to take such a high risk strategy in the first place, the fact remains that this venture into commerce by a Christian corporate entity did not spawn any comparable successors.

It was left to the wealthy merchant families in Lombardy to carry forward larger scale commercial transactions. It is no surprise that some of the earliest origins of collective commercial investment for profit, and indeed of financial institutions are to be found in Italy. The sack of Byzantium in 1204 by the fourth crusade (an enterprise that was both geographically as well as morally wayward) brought tremendous wealth (and the horses of St. Mark's cathedral) to Venice, making the city the major entrepôt for trade with the Levant.

The Italian commenda, which was used from the 13th century onwards, was one of the earliest methods of joint investment in a commercial adventure. It was a form of profit sharing under which an investor would bear the losses of the venture of a merchant in return for receiving three-quarters of the profit. Since a number of people could contribute to the same venture it was a form of joint investment. If the merchant invested his own money then he would share the profits proportionally for his amount. By allowing a number of people to share in the profits of a commercial enterprise it performed a not dissimilar function to the corporate structures of today.

During the fourteenth century the commenda was gradually replaced by the compagnia, which was centred on the assets of the family, and the family as a whole was liable for the obligations incurred. As the business of these families grew they started to borrow money from outsiders, and this required the introduction of limited liability as had been the case with the commenda, and by the fifteenth century Florentine law allowed for the co-existence of limited and unlimited liability. A Florentine law of 1408 regulated the *accomandita*, allowing for the co-existence of unlimited and limited liability partners

Another origin of the road towards a framework for collective commerce and finance can be found in the banking sphere in Italy. There was a technique used in the Middle Ages called *compera delle imposte,* which was a mechanism through which loans could be raised by states or cities against the assignment of tax revenues – essentially a purchase of tax receivables. There was a register to show the holdings of the creditors, and the loans were divided up into a number of equal parts which were freely transferable. The holders of the loans formed organisations (societas comperarum) to collect the receivables, although these only lasted while the loan was outstanding. However one of the organisations (which were generally called mons or maona (mountain)), called the maona dei Giustiniani, founded in Genoa to finance the acquisition of 29 ships to conquer the island of Chios and a part of Turkey (Foca), lasted from 1346 until 1566, as the Giustiniani managed to hold on to their possessions. This could be described as colonisation by joint stock enterprise and was in some senses the trailblazer for the English and Dutch East India companies.

The Banco di San Giorgio was founded in Genoa in 1407 in order to consolidate a number of state debts secured by tax receivables. By the middle of the 15th century it administered the great majority of Genoese public debt. Dividends were paid to investors deriving from the collection of taxes, and income from the Genoese colonies, such as Corsica. The Banco di San Giorgio was therefore regarded as a sovereign entity 'dominius et status' as it called itself; a state within a state. This again exemplifies that the dividing line between public and private corporations is by no means as clear cut as we assume it to be today.

The investment participations ('loca') in the institution were registered in public books, and certificates issued, for which there was a market. There was a management board of eight 'protectors', with at least 100 loca each, and a Great Council of 480 'stockholders' with at least 10 loca each. Since the bank was in essence a sovereign entity the protectors had both civil and criminal jurisdiction, and their role in part was similar to that of the Genoese magistrates.[58]

It can therefore be seen that from the very early days the nature of collective commercial enterprises was by no means divorced from society as a whole. On the contrary, the role of the commercial entity was interwoven with the interests of the state, and the thinking behind the division between the management board of the protectors and the Great Council perhaps not so very different from the division of the Houses of Parliament into the House of Commons and the House of Lords.

Coming of Age

As the trading role of northern Europe became more prominent, and particularly that of the Netherlands, these early innovations of corporate commercial activity were to be superseded by the monopolist entities created in the Netherlands and in England to further their overseas commercial activities, although the Banco di San Giorgio survived until the invasion of Genoa by Napoleon. In one of those interesting sidenotes of history, the bank even has an American connection - Christopher Columbus left a tenth of his possessions with the bank for the benefit of the people of Genoa, an early case of the New World benefiting the Old.

The guilds of London were also complex commercial animals. They were both trade unions and commercial

---

[58] Much of this information comes from a paper by Guido Ferrarini, at the Centre for Law and Finance University of Genoa, entitled "Origins Of Limited Liability Companies And Company Law Modernization In Italy: A Historical Outline". http://www.estig.ipbeja.pt/~ac_direito/Ferrarini3.pdf

enterprises as well as monopolists, usually associated with particular churches, and played a role in protecting law and order. Their commercial importance had become attenuated by the time of the rise of the forebears of the modern corporation, such as the Russia Company (founded in 1555) and the East India Company (founded in 1600)[59].

As early as the thirteenth century the guilds controlled the government of the City of London, and elected a mayor. Again the intimate connection between the political sphere and the commercial sphere can be seen, and the multiplicity of roles that the institutions carried out (including charitable ones) reflect these interwoven interests.

The wealth of the guilds, like that of the Templars before them caught the eye of a monarchy in constant need of revenue. The English monarchs started to call in the charters for the guilds to be renewed, in order to generate income out of renewal fees, and they also started to grant monopolies to court favourites and others which impinged on the rights of the guilds. In 1623 Parliament passed the Statute of Monopolies, intended to halt the practice, but Charles I exploited loopholes in the act and managed to raise £100,000 per year from selling monopolies, although given the limitations of the economy, this was inevitably a process of diminishing returns.

In the meantime some of the guilds turned to overseas enterprise and in 1505 the Mercers' Guild sponsored the "Guild or Fraternity of St. Thomas à Becket," also known as the Merchant Adventurers, organized to conduct trade with Holland and Germany. Although the merchants continued to

---

[59] The former continues in existence to this day and has recently celebrated its 450th anniversary. Since 1917 it has operated principally as a charity; a number of the members of the current 'court' are direct descendants of the families which traded in the British Factory in St. Petersburg, where it moved in 1723, thus testifying to the longevity of the corporate structure and its importance to the lives of its active participants.

operate independently, they nevertheless started sharing infrastructure and pooling capital. It was this company, together with the Dutch East India Company, which was the forebear of the British East India Company which was such a seminal influence in the development of the modern corporation.

The British East India Company was founded as *The Governor and Company of Merchants of London Trading into the East Indies* on 31st December 1600. Although the British East India company started by raising capital one voyage at a time, it subsequently raised capital for limited periods of up to 15 years, and in 1613 issued its first permanent stock. This pooling of capital on a permanent basis was essential in creating an identity for the company separate from its individual shareholders. It also came to enjoy limited liability. It became the ultimate in a monopolist corporation; having been granted a monopoly of all trade to the east of the Cape of Good Hope, and after a shaky start trying to compete with the Dutch East India company for the spice trade, its dominance over India grew so great that it became the de facto ruler of the sub continent and was still administering India 250 years after its foundation.

The East India Company acted as an imperial power in its own right; waging war, annexing territory, and acting in a civil and criminal jurisdictional capacity. Indeed the role and history of the East India Company illustrates for us the intimate relationship between commercial and political interests, and the parallels and similarities of corporate and political structures.

It was the 1773 Tea Act which was passed to relieve the company's financial difficulties by exempting it from the obligation to pay colonial tax which was an important catalyst of the American Revolution. There was a terrible famine in Bengal in 1772 during which a third of the population lost their lives. Adam Smith estimated perhaps 'three or four hundred thousand people' had died of hunger in a single year and the corruption of the company had reached such a pitch that the British government had intervened by sending out

Warren Hastings as Governor General to reform its legal and financial systems. Smith had previously commented on the thriving nature of the economy of the North American colonies and commented "the difference between the genius of the British constitution which protects and governs North America, and that of the mercantile company which oppresses and dominates in the East Indies, cannot perhaps be better illustrated than by the different state of those countries.[60] This background was undoubtedly a factor in Adam Smith's attack on the company's monopoly position. Smith commented "Since the establishment of the English East India Company, for example, the other inhabitants of England, over and above being excluded from the trade, must have paid in the price of the East India goods which they have consumed not only for the extraordinary profits which the company may have made upon those goods in consequence of their monopoly, but for all the extraordinary waste which the fraud and abuse, inseparable from the management of the affairs of so great a company, must necessarily have occasioned."[61]

The East India Company was however by no means the only corporation trading in the seventeenth century. There was a considerable expansion of business activity throughout the period. The scandals which attended the fevered speculation around Exchange Alley in London (where many of the shares of many of these enterprises were sold to an eager if gullible public) by the early part of the 18th Century culminated with the South Sea Bubble[62] and the subsequent passing of the

---

[60] Book I. Chapter viii, Wealth of Nations

[61] Book IV. Chapter vii, Wealth of Nations

[62] Huge amounts of money were invested at the time not only in the shares of the South Sea Company, which had been granted a trade monopoly in the south seas, but also in a myriad of other companies with little or no hope of turning a profit. Even Sir Isaac Newton, who had initially made money by selling his South Sea Company shares, was tempted to purchase some more as they continued to rise. When the company finally collapsed he was faced with a loss of some £20,000, and was said to have remarked "I can calculate the motions of heavenly bodies, but not the madness of people".

Bubble Act in 1720[63]. This Act, entitled "An Act to Restrain the Extravagant and Unwarrantable Practice of Raising Money by Voluntary Subscriptions for Carrying on Projects Dangerous to the Trade and Subjects of this Kingdom", was rather ambiguous, a product of a speculative crisis. In order to remedy the situation it provided "that acting or presuming to act as a corporate Body or Bodies, the raising or pretending to raise transferable Stock or Stocks, the transferring or pretending to transfer or assign any Share or Shares in such Stock or Stocks without Legal Authority either by Act of Parliament or by any Charter from the Crown to warrant such acting as a body Corporate shall for ever be deemed to be illegal and void."

Although comparatively few cases were brought under this draconian legislation[64], which provided for criminal penalties, it was to act as a serious constraint of the growth of the corporation as a way of doing business for a century or more, only being finally repealed in 1825. Obtaining incorporation by royal charter or by Act of Parliament was extremely difficult, and the development of the commercial corporation was immensely retarded during many of those hundred years. Business ventures had by necessity to use the unincorporated structure. This was well illustrated by the application of the Equitable Life Assurance Company in 1757 for a royal charter for incorporation (albeit on a mutual basis). The already established insurance companies, such as the Royal Exchange, objected to the potential for additional competition, and four years later the Attorney General, C. Yorke advised against the application, stating:

---

[63] 6 George I, Chapter 18 (1720)

[64] Some of the earliest were against existing chartered corporations, such as the Royal Lutestring Company, for Making and Dressing of Allamodes, Ranforces and Lutestrings in England, incorporated by royal charter in 1693, the Governor and Company of Copper Miners in England, incorporated by royal charter in 1692, and the Governor and Company of Copper Miners in the Principality of Wales, incorporated by Royal Charter in 1695.

"The Crown has very wisely been always cautious of incorporating traders because such bodies will either grow too great and by overwhelming Individuals become Monopolies or else by failing will involve themselves in the Ruin intendent upon a Corporate Bankruptcy. As Trade seldom requires the Aid of such Combinations but thrives better when left open to the free speculation of private Men, such measures are only expedient when the Trade is impracticable on any other basis than a joint Stock, as was thought the case in East Indies, South Sea, Hudson's Bay, Herring Fishery and in some others erected upon that Principle, but there does not appear to be any necessity in the present Case because the Business of insuring Lives is carried on not only by the two great Companies already named, but such Policies are duly underwritten by numbers of private Men."[65]

The dangers inherent in over mighty corporates were therefore well understood some 250 years ago, and perhaps the corporate structure might have been somewhat different if it had evolved during the Age of Enlightenment rather than spewing out in the heat of the Industrial Revolution.

By the end of the eighteenth century commercial corporations were still regarded with suspicion, both with regard to their utility and in respect of their motives. However change was in the air; the perceived advantages of canal transport resulted in more than 100 canal acts receiving royal assent by 1800, and the largest part of the English canal system was constructed before the turn of the century.[66] But it was not until the advent of the nineteenth century and the pressing funding requirements of the industrial revolution that something similar to the companies that we know today started to evolve, and they were to be a child of their time.

---

[65] Quoted in A. B. Dubois "the English Business Company after the Bubble Act 1720-1800" 1938, the Commonwealth Fund, p.29

[66] The Development of the Business Corporation in England 1800-1867, Bishop Carleton Hunt, Harvard University Press, 1936, p.10.

Chapter IV

The Magic Cauldron of the 19th Century

A New Beginning

So at last we arrive at the late eighteenth century, with burgeoning economic growth in Europe which does not automatically fall into the lap of the landed classes because it is the product of a revolution – the industrial revolution, which not only revolutionised technology but also the balance of power. At the same time we are in the age of the Enlightenment, where there is a deep questioning about philosophy, about the rights of kings to rule, and in Britain the degree to which such a tiny proportion of the wealthy should be the only ones allowed to vote, while the growing industrial powerhouses of the Midlands and the north of England, of Scotland and of Wales remain under-represented, or not represented at all.

There was therefore an extremely fortunate conjunction of events – at the very time that there was a massive change in the distribution of economic power, there was both an enquiry into the principles by which societies should be governed, and in Britain at least a sharing of power between the monarchy, the nobility and the wealthy upper classes. The skirmishes between the Crown and the aristocracy in their continuing struggle for power took place in Parliament rather than on the battlefield. Both the aristocracy and the Crown looked to parliament to legitimise their respective positions.

It was perhaps unsurprising that the first manifestation of real democracy should be in North America. Geographical distance made it difficult to control from Europe, while its strong protestant traditions meant that the population, particularly in New England, was accustomed to the idea that salvation lay in its own hands. The comparative freedom of expression as well as the self reliant nature of the American way of life were both inimical to a feeling of dependency, in either political or economic terms. The comparative lack of large fortunes, and the greater equality of income in North America doubtless also fed a certain feeling of greater social equality than existed in Europe, with its established aristocracy and great landed wealth in the midst of widespread poverty.

This is not to say that the American Revolution started out as a 'popular' movement supported by the people at large. On the contrary, many of the principal protagonists were, in American terms, wealthy men, who felt that their interests were being injured by the British state, and who saw their counterparts on the other side of the Atlantic having a say in the running of the affairs of state which they themselves were denied.

One of the most significant triggers of the American Revolution was the famous Boston Tea Party of December 16th 1773. The turn of events is well described in 'Gangs of America' by Ted Nace[67]. The incident was intimately connected to powers of corporate monopoly given to the East India Company, and the actions taken to service the company's interests by the British government was pivotal in arousing the ire of America's elite of the day, and in particular that of John Hancock, the Boston merchant whose signature was to be the first and largest on the Declaration of Independence..

The East India Company was going through a bad patch in the 1770s, with shareholders requiring higher dividends while there was a famine in Bengal (for which the Company bore considerable responsibility), and a depression in the European markets, resulting in plunging prices for tea. The company had some three years' worth of British tea in their warehouses, and after considering dumping it in Europe decided to dump it on the American market, where the vast majority of tea consumption was of tea smuggled in from the Netherlands.

---

[67] p. 52 et seq. Berrett-Koehler, 2003

To assist the Company the British parliament passed the Tea Act, in May 1773 which exempted the tea from export duty in the UK, but did not exempt the American colonists from paying import duties. In addition the company decided to sell its tea through specially commissioned local consignees – the new cheaper tea would therefore not only undercut other tea merchants, but the Company was going to distribute it through their own agents. In effect there was great apprehension that the Company would act like a modern day supermarket; control the supply chain and put local merchants out of business, as this pamphlet shown in Mr. Nace's book makes clear[68]:

To the Tradesmen, Mechanics, &c. of the Province of Pennsylvania

Hereafter, if they succeed, they will send their own Factors and Creatures, establish Houses amongst us. Ship us all other *East-India* goods; and in order to full freight their Ships, take in other kind of Goods at under Freight, or (more probably) ship them on their own Accounts to their own Factors, and undersell our Merchants, till they monopolize the whole Trade. Thus our Merchants are ruined, Ship Building ceases. They will then sell Goods at any exorbitant price. Our Artificers will be unemployed, and every Tradesman will groan under the dire Oppression. The *East India* Company, if once they get Footing in this (once) happy country, will leave no Stone unturned to become your Masters. They are an opulent Body, and Money or Credit is not wanting amongst them They have a designing, depraved, and despotic Ministry to assist and support them. They themselves are well versed In TYRANNY, PLUNDER, OPPRESSION and BLOODSHED. Whole Provinces labouring under the Distresses of Oppression, Slavery, Famine, and the Sword, are familiar to them. Thus they have enriched themselves, thus they are become the most
powerful Trading Company in the Universe....

---

[68] p.56. excerpts from a broadside signed "A Mechanic," Philadelphia, December 4, 1773

The governor of Massachusetts was unwise enough to appoint the Boston consignees of the Company from among his friends and family, and failed to include John Hancock one of the wealthiest merchants in the city. The economic arrogance of the Company with the help of Parliament had galvanised the merchants and the well-to-do, who saw their livelihoods clearly threatened, to support the more radical elements of Massachusetts society. The colonists demanded that the tea shipment aboard *The Dartmouth* be returned whence it came, but the authorities refused to provide the necessary permit for the ship to leave harbour, so some 150 colonists boarded the ship and sent its cargo to a different destination. According to Nace the 120,000 pounds of tea dumped into the harbour was about 10% of annual American consumption, and about 50% of the amount of legally imported (as opposed to smuggled) tea.

In 1774 Parliament passed what became known as the 'Intolerable Acts', closing Boston Harbour until compensation had been paid for the tea, depriving the Massachusetts legislature of its powers and making the governor a virtual dictator. This in turn led to the convening of the First Continental Congress in Philadelphia from September 5th to October 26th 1774, attended by George Washington among others, and by then the die was cast.

As the war developed and freedom was won, the question necessarily arose as to how to establish the legitimacy of the new governmental framework. It was here, in the work of the continental congresses, and in the deliberations during and after the War of Independence that the effect of the works of such free thinkers as Thomas Paine, which had been widely distributed, really came to the fore, and influenced the thinking of the Founding Fathers.[69]

---

[69] Paine's works 'Commonsense' and the 'Crisis' papers published in 1776 were hugely influential, and he knew and corresponded with such leading men as Benjamin Franklin. However when he published 'Age of Reason' some 20 years later, his commentary on

"We hold these truths to be self-evident, that all men are created equal, that they are endowed by their Creator with certain unalienable Rights, that among these are Life, Liberty and the pursuit of Happiness. - That to secure these rights, Governments are instituted among Men, deriving their just powers from the consent of the governed, - That whenever any Form of Government becomes destructive of these ends, it is the Right of the People to alter or to abolish it, and to institute new Government, laying its foundation on such principles and organizing its powers in such form, as to them shall seem most likely to effect their Safety and Happiness."

Thomas Jefferson's words in the Declaration of Independence of July 4th 1776 are a stirring reminder of the aspirations of humanity, and how eloquently they can be expressed in a society on the cusp of change and unencumbered with too many special and entrenched interests.

Another New Beginning

However, in one of those curious twists of history, in the same year that the Declaration of Independence was signed, a worthy Scottish professor was making a declaration of another, wordier, kind, a declaration also destined to have far reaching consequences for it was also in 1776 that Adam Smith published his 'Wealth of Nations'[70]. In it he proclaimed the virtues of the market, remarked upon the amazing productivity of a pin factory where all the work was segmented into simple repetitive operations, and extolled the virtues of competition.[71]

When people pray in aid Adam Smith as a founder of capitalism, they seldom mention at the same time his dislike

---

religion, Paine caused such offence in America that when he returned there from Europe he was ostracised and abandoned.

[70] More properly "An Inquiry into the Nature and Causes of the Wealth of Nations".

[71] Ibid. Book I, Chapter I

of corporations. The corporate mechanism of responsibility itself is inefficient and has exacerbated hugely the problems of agency identified by Adam Smith i.e. the problem for the proprietors keeping control of the management[72]. In the many debates in the 1820s about corporations which are dealt with elsewhere, Smith's antagonism to corporations was acknowledged, although it was acknowledged that he was less against such a mechanism in the field of insurance where the perils might overwhelm individual capital. Smith was also severely critical of the East India Company, although this was as much to do with its monopoly as its corporate nature[73].

The fact remains that in 1720, three years before Smith's birth, Parliament had passed the 'Bubble Act' which severely restricted the ability to form joint stock companies, and introduced draconian penalties on those entities that purported to act as if they were incorporated, and pretended to such privileges as transferable shares which companies incorporated by royal Charter or created by Act of Parliament could enjoy. This Act was not repealed until 1825, so that for the entirety of Smith's life the joint-stock company was a very rare business entity, tinged with the whiff of speculation, peculation and monopoly. Smith may well have been one of the founders of capitalism, but he was no friend of corporatism. His view of the hidden hand envisaged the inter-action of many different and independent agents, where competition would ensure improvement and accumulation of wealth would be on an individual scale. The corporate behemoths of the modern age, operating complex monopolies do not belong in Smith's world.

The 'Wealth of Nations' is a long book, and in it Smith makes a number of remarks which look at the consequences of manufacturing efficiencies, such as the dehumanising effect of repetitive labour[74], and he was sharply critical of that

---

[72] Ibid. Book V, Chapter i, Part Third, Article I

[73] Ibid. Book IV, Chapter vii, Part Third

[74] "In the progress of the division of labour, the employment of the far greater part of those who live by labour, that is, of the greater

corporate monopoly known as the East India Company, which as we have seen was one of the catalysts of the American Revolution.

Many of the leaders of the American Revolution were comparatively wealthy men. They were, as has been shown above, far from being anti-business. However they were profoundly suspicious of corporations[75]. After independence the power of chartering corporations which had previously been exercised by the sovereign and by Parliament was given to state legislatures. Many states were wary of granting incorporating powers to the federal authority, fearing a clone of the East India Company on American soil. Such dissent meant that the constitution was silent on corporates, but in the ratification process of the constitution five states recommended adding an amendment prohibiting the federal government from granting any charters that would grant "any exclusive advantages of commerce."[76]

---

body of the people, comes to be confined to a few very simple operations; frequently to one or two. But the understandings of the greater part of men are necessarily formed by their ordinary employments. The man whose whole life is spent in performing a few simple operations, of which the effects too are, perhaps, always the same, or very nearly the same, has no occasion to exert his understanding, or to exercise his invention in finding out expedients for removing difficulties which never occur. He naturally loses, therefore, the habit of such exertion, and generally becomes as stupid and ignorant as it is possible for a human creature to become. The torpor of his mind renders him, not only incapable of relishing or bearing a part in any rational conversation, but of conceiving any generous, noble or tender sentiment, and consequently of forming any just judgment concerning many even of the ordinary duties of private life." Wealth of Nations, Book V, Chapter i, Part Third, Article II.

[75] As a result of silver bank and land schemes in Massachusetts in 1740, an Act of Parliament had been passed in 1741 which expressly extended the Bubble Act to the American colonies; 14 George II, Chapter 37.

[76] Gangs of America, p.59 and seq.

Companies or corporations of the modern kind were as unfamiliar to the Americans as they were to the British as a result of the Bubble Act of 1720. Thomas Jefferson was certainly no fan when he wrote in 1816:

"I hope we shall crush in its birth the aristocracy of our monied corporations which dare already to challenge our government to a trial of strength, and bid defiance to the laws of our country."[77]

At the time of the American Revolution there were no commercial corporations of any size. The activities and influence of the British East India Company did not endear the young American state with affection for the corporate form. Indeed to the contrary, corporations were for many years regarded with suspicion, and their powers greatly circumscribed; it was only the constant application of their focussed self-interest during the course of the nineteenth century, and the enormous wealth available to them as the American economy grew at a phenomenal rate that enabled them to gradually acquire their body armour of legal rights.

An amazing impersonation

In truth, both in the United Kingdom and in the United States the corporate form enabled the elite to achieve by stealthy influence what they could not acquire by overt claim. In the United States the separation of the powers made this a slightly more intriguing exercise, since all three branches of government (the legislature, the judiciary and the executive) had to be influenced. This was not as difficult as it first appeared.

---

[77] Letter to Tom Logan, November 1816, in Paul Leicester Ford, *The Writings of Thomas Jefferson, Vol. 10* (New York, 1892–99), 69., quoted in Gangs of America, p.59

One part of the United States legislature, the Senate, as mentioned earlier, was not originally directly elected; the senators for each state were chosen by the State Legislature. It was a comparatively easy (if not necessarily cheap) matter for the wealthier businessmen to 'encourage' members of the legislature to see the advantages of their candidature. This gave rise to Mark Twain's remark "I think that I can say and say with some pride that we have legislatures that bring higher prices than any in the world."[78] In the second half of the nineteenth century the business world was already well placed to ensure that the Senate could block anti-business legislation.

It was not until the beginning of the 20th Century that the strain on the system to contain the interests of a moneyed elite on the one hand and the policy platforms of a popularly elected President and House of Representatives on the other led to the passage of the Seventeenth Amendment and the popular election of senators.

The judiciary in the United States was drawn, at least in part, from the same section of the population that was anxious to protect and extend its wealth. In part, but not entirely, and there was a lengthy tussle with more enlightened occupants of the bench for whom the protection of property was not their over-riding aim. However in 1883 Judge Stephen Field in the Santa Clara case in the US Circuit Court district of California decided that corporations had legal 'personhood' for the purposes of the 14th Amendment of the US Constitution.

---

[78] In "After-Dinner Speech," *Sketches, New and Old* (vol. 19 of *The Writings of Mark Twain*), p. 235 (1875), apparently as part of a speech prepared for a Fourth of July speech to a party of Americans in London, which was not given as General Schenck, the American ambassador, decided to dispense with further oratory after his own speech. Mark Twain (Samuel Langhorne Clemens), lived between 1835 and 1910 and therefore did not live to see the system changed.

In the appeal of the case to the Supreme Court[79] in 1886, before any argument was heard Mr. Chief Justice Waite announced: "The court does not wish to hear argument on the question whether the provision in the Fourteenth Amendment to the Constitution, which forbids a State to deny to any person within its jurisdiction the equal protection of the laws, applies to these corporations. We are all of opinion that it does."

The question of whether a corporation was a person for the purposes of the 14th Amendment was not deemed necessary to decide the case, and this vital precedent hangs only on the summary of the law reporter. Thus it was that corporations became the beneficiaries of a constitutional amendment whose purpose was to ensure that freed slaves would be entitled to 'equal treatment under the law'. The law of unintended consequences was also undoubtedly at work when the Fourteenth Amendment was passed.

The stage was thus set for the creation of a separate class of citizen which could act as a citadel of non-democratic control. As the corporations got larger, it was clear that power increasingly belonged to those who controlled these new non-democratic juggernauts, and less to those who depended on the whim of public opinion for the continuing exercise of their power.

The influence of big business on the presidency, and particularly on presidential candidates was also clear by the second half of the nineteenth century. The 'Compromise of 1877', under which the Republican candidate, Rutherford Hayes, became president of the United States despite receiving a lower number of votes than his Democratic rival, Samuel Tilden is rather reminiscent of the election of President Bush in 2000 about a century and a quarter later. Then, as now, the influence of big business was on the rise,

---

[79] SANTA CLARA COUNTY v. SOUTHERN PACIFIC RAILROAD COMPANY118 U.S. 394 Error to the Circuit Court of the United States for the District of California 1886

and it was symbolic that Hayes received the news of his election while travelling in the private railway carriage of Tom Scott, the mogul of the Pennsylvania Railroad Company.[80] Scott and the railroad interests had been actively involved in the negotiations of who should become president.

The second half of the nineteenth century was an important time for the development of the corporation in the United States. Since independence state charters with strict limitations had restricted what corporations could do. These often limited the lifespan of corporations, but not the liability of the shareholders, or provided that the shareholders would be liable to twice the amount of their investment. They also prohibited corporations from investing in one other.[81] Tom Scott was one of the leading players in expanding the influence and powers of companies, and in particular the railroads. He came to prominence at the Pennsylvania Railroad company, starting in 1850 as a station agent and rising to being a vice president of the company by 1860, with Andrew Carnegie as his protégé. As a lobbyist for the company he had managed to persuade the Pennsylvania legislature to repeal tonnage tax on the railway. The repeal of this legislation was immensely unpopular, but proved very difficult to reverse. However in 1861 the American Civil War called him to other duties. Scott was appointed an assistant secretary of war for railroads and transportation, and was raised to the rank of colonel. He was indefatigable during the war in arranging troop movements for the Union and returned a hero.

Scott came to wield a great deal of influence over the Pennsylvania State legislature, and in furtherance of his ambitions to extend his railroad interests into the southern

---

[80] Re-Assessing Tom Scott, the 'Railroad Prince', A Paper for the Mid-America Conference on History, September 16 1995, Dr. T. Lloyd Benson and Trina Rossman, Furman University Re-assessing Tom Scott, the 'Railroad Prince' http://alpha.furman.edu/~benson/col-tom.html.

[81] See Appendix I, taken from Gangs of America by Ted Nace

United States persuaded them to grant him a charter for a company that could revise its own name and purposes. This became the Southern Railway Security Company, with the ability to invest in the shares of other companies. This creation of a holding company structure was a revolutionary step forward. It would ultimately enable companies to circumvent state restrictions, and go jurisdiction shopping for the most accommodating legal framework[82], it would enable the construction of corporate structures of immense size and complexity, free from many of the disadvantages of the cumbersome trust structures being erected by the likes of John D. Rockefeller.

As the decades wore on American corporations freed themselves from the restrictions that had previously bound them, acquiring the benefits of limited liability and great flexibility, as well as a gift that evaded their human creators – immortality. Companies also acquired that hitherto peculiarly human trait, a personality, albeit a legal one.

Pressure of business

On the other side of the Atlantic in the United Kingdom there was also continuing mistrust of the corporation, paralleled by an increasing demand for the reform of the voting system. As the century wore on both electorate and companies were to become increasingly empowered in very different ways, and with radically different consequences.

The role of the corporation was rather more advanced in the United Kingdom at the beginning of the 19th century than it

---

[82] Tom Scott died in 1881 and only shortly after jurisdiction shopping became the norm. In 1888 and 1889 the revision of New Jersey's statutes made it the state of choice for incorporation, and by 1901 75% of corporations with assets of more than $25 million were using it as their home base, to be subsequently overtaken by Delaware when the New Jersey provisions were made more restrictive. See Gangs of America, p.83.

was in the United States, where there were only six corporations, excluding banks, at the time of the constitutional convention of 1787.[83]

To the extent that business was not conducted by individual wealthy men, joint-stock companies were used. Unless they were incorporated by Act of Parliament or by royal Charter, they had none of the privileges of modern day companies, and functioned far more like ordinary partnerships; the investors had unlimited liability for all the engagements of the company, the shares could not be bought and sold freely, and the company could not sue or be sued in its own name.

Those companies who had gone through the extremely arduous process of becoming incorporated through a royal charter, or by Act of Parliament were strictly limited to the activities laid down in their founding charter. The privileges of incorporation caused them to be viewed with considerable mistrust, but for the promoters of companies incorporation had a number of attractions – not only did it enable them to take legal action in the name of the company, rather than in the name of all the individual shareholders, and provide for the transferability and divisibility of shares but it also provided the potential (not always given) for limited liability. Without such protection shareholders were in the same position as the individual "Names" of Lloyds of London in modern times – liable as the saying at the time went 'to their last shilling and acre'. As the capital requirements and scale of business grew more and more people invested in businesses about which they knew less and less, and for which they were fully financially liable.

As the scale of business undertakings grew with the industrial revolution and as technology advanced, it became increasingly necessary to raise capital from a larger number of people, who found it ever more difficult to monitor the management of the company, and thus opened themselves up to considerable risk. There was therefore a burgeoning need

---

[83] Gangs of America, p. 59-60

for corporations with limited liability etc. to meet the growing calls for capital as the impact of the industrial revolution made itself felt, firstly for the construction of canals and later on with the construction of railways.

In 1803 the first price list for the London Stock Exchange was published, and by 1811 the number of stocks had doubled[84]. However the number of incorporated companies was tiny. There was therefore a considerable temptation to get round the provisions of the Bubble Act, even though there were draconian penalties. In 1808 a case was brought against the London Paper company and the London Distillery for a breach of the Act[85]. It was dismissed on the basis that it was the first case for 87 years, but the court declared for future reference that the Bubble Act was not obsolete. In the case Lord Ellenborough, the presiding judge condemned limited liability as 'a mischievous delusion calculated to ensnare the unwary public'.[86] In the previous year on 5th November the Morning Chronicle had remarked that all great companies were similar in social consequences to "the monopolies and exclusive privileges sold by the Stuarts".[87]

Even in the earliest days of the formation of the modern company therefore, and although looking through the prism of the past, the potential problems that might be created by the powers granted to corporations were being avidly debated.

When the Bubble Act was finally repealed in 1825, the Monthly Review magazine commented:

"But the proper occasion for such associations [companies] are comparatively rare and the principle degenerates into a pestilential abuse when it is applied to an ignorant and

---

[84] The Development of the Business Corporation in England 1800-1867, Bishop Carleton Hunt, Harvard University Press, 1936, p.14.
[85] Rex v. Dodd, 9 East 516-27 (1808)
[86] Quoted in The Development of the Business Corporation in England, p.19
[87] Ibid, p.17

impertinent interference with the smaller details of trade, endeavouring to crush the humbler industry of individuals by the overwhelming power of capital alone"[88]

It was perhaps ironic that in the same year of 1825 the Stockton & Darlington Railway commenced operations, since the railways, both in the United Kingdom and the United States were to prove to be an immensely important influence on the development of corporations in the nineteenth century. As the economy expanded and demand for capital grew banks and insurance companies in particular became more insistent in their demands for the privileges of incorporation. A committee on insurance was set up in 1810. The spokesman for the Lloyds insurance market in the House of Commons, Joseph Marryat[89], did not welcome this potential competition. He declared that the Bubble Act legislation "recognised as a general principle that *all* joint stock companies tended to the common grievance". It was to be some time before companies got their wish. Until 1824 only two companies, the Royal Exchange and the London Assurance company had the legal right to underwrite marine insurance.[90]

One of the problems of not being incorporated was that legal action, either by or against a company was difficult, since all the members had to be joined – the company could not sue or be sued in its own name. For example the Globe Insurance Company applied in 1806 for incorporation by Act of Parliament. Although it failed to receive this, the more limited right of suing and being sued in its own name was granted to five insurance companies in 1807, but progress was not hugely swift – by 1815 this privilege had been granted to another fifteen insurance companies and one copper mining company[91]

---

[88] Monthly Review III, 1826, p.26 et seq.

[89] Father of the Victorian novelist Captain Marryat of 'Mr. Midshipman Easy' and 'Children of the New Forest' fame

[90] The Development of the Business Corporation in England 1800-1867, Bishop Carleton Hunt, Harvard University Press, 1936, p. 23

[91] Ibid., p.23

However the ending of the long Napoleonic wars in 1815 resulted in a new surge of growth and prosperity by the early 1820s. Money was in plentiful supply and by February 1825 government bills (called 'Consols', because in 1749 Henry Pelham, the then Chancellor of the Exchequer had 'consolidated' the various debts of the British government into a consistent series of perpetual interest bearing bonds) were trading substantially over par even though they only carried an interest rate of 2¼%[92]. Investors inevitably turned to riskier investments – such as South American loans. In 1824 and 1825 £17.5 million was invested in South American loans. Risky though these were, at least the maximum loss was the amount of the loan; the lack of incorporation meant full personal liability for those investing in speculative ventures in domestic joint-stock companies. The search for higher investment returns with limited liability led to Parliament being inundated with requests for incorporation in these years[93]. By April, according to the Gentleman's Magazine[94] there were 250 private bills for incorporation before the House of Commons. One MP concerned about the degree of speculation advised "gentlemen to keep their money against a rainy day rather than invest in companies to bring salt water from Bognor, air from Heaven and blasts from Hell"[95].

There was also concern about the ability of shareholders to freely transfer stock in unincorporated companies, since they functioned essentially like partnerships. The supremely conservative (with both a large and a small 'c') Lord Chancellor of the time, Lord Eldon, was viscerally opposed to allowing incorporation except by charter or by an Act of Parliament. Indeed, far from agreeing to the repeal of the Bubble Act he announced his intention of introducing a bill to

---

[92] Baring in House of Commons, Hansard XIV, col. 222

[93] Incorporation did not necessarily mean that a company would obtain limited liability, but it was the only way it could be obtained.

[94] 1824, volume 94, p.364

[95] Hansard XII, col. 613, 1825, Sir J. Yorke during a debate on the St. Catherine's Docks Bill.

prevent the sale and transfer of the shares of any joint stock company which had not either received a charter or been created by Act of Parliament. However, such was the scale of speculation and concern about share transfers that the Bubble Act was repealed in 1825[96]. Under this legislation it was still not the case that companies enjoyed limited liability, and it was left to the Crown to decide the degree of shareholder responsibility. The actual status of an unincorporated joint-stock company remained uncertain for a number of years.

Then, as now, speculative frenzy was followed by collapse. Several estimates were made of the number of new enterprises. A pamphlet published by one Henry English in 1827[97] claimed that a total of 624 companies had been floated with a total capitalisation of over £372 million, and that of these only 127 were still in existence by 1827, with few of the canal or railway companies surviving, although English noted that some 156 companies formed before 1824 survived, including 63 canal companies and 25 insurance companies.

The mania of 1825 was debated in a House of Commons that contained many of the proponents and opponents of the Great Reform Act of 1832, whose time was yet to come. Huskisson, whose precipitate demise through being one of the earliest victims of a railway accident[98] significantly changed the political geometry of the House of Commons, defended companies, saying "if there was any one circumstance to which, more than any other, this country owed its wealth and commercial advantages, it was the existence of joint stock companies". However, it should perhaps be noted that since he was also the president of the British-Irish & Colonial Silk Company, established by charter in 1825 he may also be

---

[96] 6 George IV, chapter 91

[97] A complete View of the Joint Stock companies formed in 1824 and 1825, published in 1827.

[98] He was a passenger on the inaugural train journey of the Liverpool and Manchester Railway in September 1830. He died from being struck by the train, after he had alighted to speak to the Duke of Wellington who was in a different carriage.

considered as one of the earliest company lobbyists as well as one of the earliest railway victims.

In a debate of 1826, Matthias Attwood, (the brother of Thomas Attwood, who was to be such a seminal influence in the passing of the Great Reform Act, and led the Birmingham Political Union) announced that "there was no more harm in buying a share than in buying a shawl"[99]. However, his brother Thomas was, some nine years later, the sole dissenting voice against further corporate privileges being granted in the Trading Companies Act, as he "objected altogether to joint stock companies for purposes to which individual industry was competent".[100] Support for the advance of corporate privileges was full of nuance and reservation.

The slippery slope

In 1826 Huskisson introduced an Act permitting the establishment of joint stock banks more than 65 miles from London (so as not to impinge too closely on the activities of the Bank of England); there were already a number of Scottish joint stock banks and these had survived the crisis well. He would have agreed to limited liability, but the Bank of England among others objected.

---

[99] 1826, Hansard XVI, col.266.

[100] Thomas Attwood was a truly remarkable man. He founded the Birmingham Political Union to advance the cause of electoral reform, and was one of the first MPs for Birmingham after the passage of the Great Reform Act. He was a banker and actively proposed reform of the currency and its removal from the gold standard, and argued for the increase of the money supply at times of economic difficulties as a prescient precursor of Keynes. He also was active in the Chartist movement. His brother Matthias on the other hand not only represented a different part of the country (initially London, then Whitehaven), but also a different party – the Tories.

The difficult times following 1825 resulted in a very substantial reduction in the number of applications for incorporation; of the some 30 applications for incorporation by charter that were made to the Board of Trade (acting on behalf of the Crown) some privileges of incorporation were granted in about half a dozen cases, but limited liability was only given to one company - the Nova Scotia Mining company in 1831, although another company was chartered with 'single responsibility' (liability of up to the amount invested) and three with 'double liability' (double the amount invested) respectively.[101]

In the spring of 1834 there was a resurgence of speculative activity. The previous frenzy had focussed significantly on banks. On this occasion interest also extended to the rapid expansion of the insurance business and the first railway boom.

In 1833 Lord Althorp the Lord Chancellor[102], who had been one of the prime movers of the Great Reform Act, introduced a Bill for the renewal of the Bank of England's charter, suggesting in his speech[103] the granting of 'limited responsibility' to joint stock banks of deposit. His proposal was not carried.

The Times remarked:

"Every man in this country who chooses to take advantage of a joint stock company should be liable for its losses. If his name on the list of subscribers invites the public to confidence, his fortune thrown into the common stock ought to give the public security against mis-management, and if as

---

[101] The Development of the Business Corporation in England 1800-1867, Bishop Carleton Hunt, Harvard University Press, 1936, pp.58-59

[102] A member of the Spencer family and an ancestor of Diana, Princess of Wales

[103] 1833, Hansard XVIII, cols. 183-184

a *sleeping partner* he chooses to be robbed, the public ought not to be robbed because he chooses to *sleep.* "[104]

By March 1836, when William Clay moved for a select committee to enquire into joint stock banking 61 such banks with 472 branches had already been established, with another 38 due to be founded in that year alone. Clay favoured "limited liability; paid up capital; perfect publicity"[105] as the appropriate balance to be struck between corporate efficiency and protection of the public.

The Times had not changed its tune on this matter:

"Once let shareholders be pronounced only partially liable, and they will scarcely remember the existence of the bank, except when they occasionally receive some interest for their investment."[106]

So in the very earliest times of the modern corporation the dangers were well understood; the dangers to individual traders and small business of powerful corporations, and the dangers of lack of oversight of management that went with limited liability. John Ramsey McCulloch, editor of the Edinburgh Review[107], thought that claiming limited liability, companies would "substitute carelessness for attention [and] open a wide door for the commission of fraud." He went on to comment:

"It astonishes us that anyone living in London and having intercourse with practical men should have been found to lay the least stress on the publication of balance sheets, or accounts of assets and obligations. These are worse than worthless, being eminently calculated to deceive and

---

[104] The Development of the Business Corporation in England 1800-1867, Bishop Carleton Hunt, Harvard University Press, 1936, p.67
[105] Hansard, XXXIII, col.857
[106] 14th May 1836
[107] He also edited the 1828 edition of 'The Wealth of Nations'.

mislead…even though the parties were perfectly honest, the publication of a balance sheet would be good for nothing."[108]

By this stage banks in some states of the US did enjoy limited liability. McCulloch, who also authored a 'commercial dictionary'[109] commented that this had resulted in "an infinity of regulations for the prevention of fraud; but as might have been anticipated, these have proved quite ineffectual for their object." He referred to the scandal of the Sutton joint stock bank "incorporated in the moral and religious city of Boston in 1828." He did not consider "the swindlers of Boston more dextrous than those of London".[110]

These concerns were also echoed by the radical and reforming Lord Chancellor, Lord Brougham,[111] who commented that limited liability was "contrary to the whole genius and spirit of English law, contrary to the whole genius and spirit of the Constitution" and that it would "relax that care and vigilance which every partner ought to keep over his associates"

The railway boom of 1836-1837 was to inspire further legislation nearly a decade later and the Joint Stock Companies Registration and Regulations Act of 1844 was passed, following the report of a parliamentary committee under the Chairmanship of Gladstone, who was President of the Board of Trade at the time. The key focus of this committee was how to ensure companies did not defraud their investors. As a subsequent commentator described the committee as pointed out the findings of the committee were rather colourful, referred to the Report as "having conducted its deliberations in a state of mental perturbation…" and found that "the headings of the different sections "Form and Destination of the Plunder", "Circumstances of the Victims", "Impunity of the Offenders" and the like" as well as the

---

[108] The Development of the Business Corporation in England, p.70

[109] A Dictionary, Practical, Theoretical and Historical of Commerce and Commercial Navigation, 1832.

[110] The Development of the Business Corporation in England 1800-1867, Bishop Carleton Hunt, Harvard University Press, 1936, p. 71.

[111] Ibid p. 84

contents "might make a man fancy he was reading a novel instead of a blue book.[112] However the Act still did not provide for limited liability.

It was not until the passage of the 1856 Companies Act that the structure for the modern corporation was laid down. Indeed it required that partnerships for profit of over 20 people to be incorporated. It provided that the privileges of incorporation should be available to any seven people, upon registration of the Memorandum and Articles of Association, and the word 'limited' being attached to the company's name. The Act provided a model set of articles unless companies wished to substitute their own. Robert Lowe, the then President of the Board of Trade, commented "We leave companies to form their own constitutions as they please. The management we leave to the companies themselves. Having given them a pattern the State leaves them to manage their own affairs and has no desire to force on these little republics any particular constitution."[113]

In describing companies as 'little republics' Lowe was perhaps being more accurate than he realised.

The Silent Majority

By the beginning of the twentieth century therefore the structure of the modern corporation had already been firmly laid, freed from the restraints of an earlier era it was to rapidly assume a dominant position in the economic activity of both the United States and the United Kingdom as well as many other countries.

However the progress of companies had been in the context of concerns over property – investors being deprived of their

---

[112] Robert Lowe President of the Board of Trade, in his speech to the House of Commons preceding the 1856 Companies Act, Hansard 1856 CXL, col. 117

[113] Hansard 1856 CXL, col. 133-134

property without limited liability, investors being duped by fraud, the effects of corporations on the property of other businessmen. The rights and obligations of people in the nineteenth century and before were intimately entwined with the concept of property. The cry of the American colonists may have been "No taxation without representation", but there was also a subtext in the minds of many of "No representation without taxation".

Despite the glowing words of the Declaration of Independence, penned by Jefferson and quoted earlier on, the fact remained that for many, even in the United States, the question of property affected whether you could vote or not. It was an important indicator of one's worthiness to participate in an election. The right to vote in the United States was a matter for the states, and a number of them insisted on property qualifications. North Carolina, the last state to do so, only abandoned a property test in 1856. In addition of course neither slaves nor women had the right to vote. The classically educated could no doubt point to the precedents of Greece and Rome for justification of this situation. Indeed the problem of slaves having no vote was one of the reasons for the curious mechanism of the Electoral College for US presidents. Since a substantial part of the population of the South could not vote, any direct election of US presidents would inevitably favour the North, but for Electoral College purposes prior to the Fourteenth Amendment slaves were counted as three fifths of a person in terms of calculating the number of representatives. Ex slaves were given the vote under the Fifteenth Amendment in 1869.

It was understandable then that during the formative years of corporations concern about them should have been focussed on their economic and commercial impact, and how property rights could be secured and protected, rather than on their internal decision making structure. Added to this was the potential liability of shareholders over and above their investment. The advance of the corporation therefore was the protection and empowerment of money.

What then of the empowerment of the citizen? In the United Kingdom the way in which parliamentary government worked was very far from current ideas of democracy. Parliament was a forum for the trading off of various vested interests. It was dominated by landed wealth, both in the House of Lords and in the House of Commons. The aristocracy had two bites of this particular cherry in that not only did they sit in the upper chamber as of right, but they had considerable influence and powers of patronage in nominating people to seats in the House of Commons.

The amount of money that the French expended in loosening the British grip over North America was one of the factors in destabilising the ancient regime in France, but the French situation was very different from that of the colonies in North America, and notwithstanding the noble sentiments expressed, the aftermath was much bloodier, and the consequences far more disruptive than in the United States. In some ways the French Revolution was counter-productive in promoting the cause of universal suffrage and greater democracy. The United Kingdom's war with France meant then, as now, liberty was the servant of security, and the Tory government of William Pitt the Younger was by no means averse to the most drastic measures to ensure that the contagion of the French revolution's ideas, as well as its military forces should not infect Britain's shores, including the suspension of Habeus Corpus in 1793.

The early nineteenth century saw a mixture of radical unrest and popular conservatism, which ebbed and flowed with economic and social factors. Successive Tory governments introduced legislation to suppress the unrest that was also provoked by the effects of the long war with France which only ended in 1815 with the Battle of Waterloo. The end of the war saw an economic downturn and the demobilisation of perhaps up to half a million men from the army. The increased consequential unrest resulted in further oppressive legislation, such as the Coercion Act of 1816. For some the concept of Parliament was to represent interests (in particular property interests) rather than people, but even for these the rise of the great industrial towns which were wholly unrepresented, indicated that some change to the system was necessary.

It was natural that many in the new industrial cities should seek representation to protect their interests. On such meeting was held in Manchester on Monday the 16th of August 1819. The meeting was held in St. Peter's Fields and was attended by a crowd of some 50,000 people including many women and children. One of the main speakers at this meeting was Henry Hunt. Henry Hunt (1773-1835), was one of the key, if unlikely, radicals of the time, being a wealthy squire with extensive estates in Wiltshire and Somerset. His public speaking skills had earner him the sobriquet of 'Orator' Hunt, and he had the affectation of wearing a white top hat so that he would stand out.

The meeting had hardly begun when overly fearful local magistrates sent in the local yeomanry to break up the crowd and arrest the speakers. The Manchester yeomanry were recruited from the families of local businessmen, and were virtually untrained. They inflicted terrible damage on the crowd, and unlike the regular troops did not just use the flat of their blade, but the edge as well, resulting in an estimated 11 deaths, and many hundreds injured. The event was extremely well reported, not least because The Times reporter, John Tyas, had requested a seat on the speakers' platform, in order to hear and report the speeches better, and he too was arrested and held in custody for a short period[114]. A full report of the events appeared in The Times of the 19th August, which pointed out the entirely peaceful nature of the crowd prior to the attack of the yeomanry.

---

[114] Tyas was not exactly sympathetic with Hunt's radical views however. As he wrote in his article in The Times on the 19th August "As to espousing the political principles or espousing the wild doctrines of radical reform, supported by Mr. Hunt, it is the very last thing….[your correspondent] should ever be induced to do; he holds them in as utter abhorrence as the most loyal subject of his Majesty possibly can hold them…"

One commentator compared it to the Battle of Waterloo, and in the outrage that followed the incident was referred to as the Peterloo massacre. However, it was not until some 13 years had elapsed and the Tory administration and last replaced by the Whigs that reform was possible. In the meantime in 1820 Shelley had written a poem in Italy called 'the Mask of Anarchy' to commemorate the event, but it was not to be published until 1832[115]

Although therefore the need to change the political system in the UK was widely discussed at the end of the eighteenth century, it was not until well into the nineteenth century, and the return of the Whigs – the nascent Liberal Party – to power that any real potential for change existed.

The backdrop of the events leading up to the Great Reform Act of 1832, and the minimal nature of the reforms that the Act introduced illustrate clearly the way in which the landed classes understood that their position was under threat.

---

[115] The second, third and fourth verses are:

> "I met Murder on the way -
> He had a mask like Castlereagh -
> Very smooth he looked, yet grim;
> Seven blood-hounds followed him:
>
> All were fat; and well they might
> Be in admirable plight,
> For one by one, and two by two,
> He tossed the human hearts to chew
> Which from his wide cloak he drew.
>
> Next came Fraud, and he had on,
> Like Eldon, an ermined gown;
> His big tears, for he wept well,
> Turned to mill-stones as they fell.

Castlereagh and Eldon were both part of the Tory administration.

Beneath the discussion of lofty principles was the reality that power was slipping away from the monarchy and the landed classes: how it should be shared out among the incumbents and the emerging industrial wealthy and middle classes was the sub-plot. Land was losing its status as virtually the unique source of wealth generation and repository of wealth accumulation. The wealth of the rising industrial classes needed to be accommodated within the power structure. In fact the Great Reform Act expanded the right to vote very little, and actually deprived a number of people of their right to vote – it was far more about expanding the circle of power to accommodate new wealth than it was about the concept of wide democracy.

On the contrary, the right to vote was based on wealth, and the idea that ordinary people without property should be allowed to vote was as repugnant to many of the aristocratic Liberal Reformers (although not their Radical allies) as it was to their aristocratic Tory opponents. Lord John Russell one of the most indefatigable of the reformers was known as 'Finality Jack', one explanation of which is that he wanted the Great Reform Act to be a final settlement of who should have the right to vote in the UK.

In the years preceding the Great Reform Act 90 commoners could guarantee, through their patronage, the return of 137 Members of Parliament, while 87 peers could ensure the return of 213 MPs to the House of Commons.[116]

---

[116] EML Thompson 'English Landed Society in the Nineteenth Century, quoted in 'Reform! The fight for the 1832 Reform Act' Edward Pearce, p.30. Pearce on pp.27, 28 gives the example of Sir James Lowther, who sent a minimum of nine MPs to parliament (occasionally 11), who as a result of their servility to his wishes became known as 'the ninepins'. Such was the usefulness of these members that Sir James had been raised to the lofty heights of being Earl of Lonsdale by a grateful Pitt ministry (Lowther had found Pitt his first seat of Appleby). James Boswell worked for him as a recorder of Carlisle, one of his tasks being to decide who to admit as

There is perhaps a degree of irony that in February 1832, a month before the introduction of the Great Reform Bill into the House of Commons, the subscribers to a fund to erect a monument to the memory of the celebrated John Locke (1632-1704) should resolve to erect a statute to the great philosopher in London University, since although the subscription had been open since 1806, it amounted only to £846; this was insufficient to defray the expense of a monument in St. Paul's or Westminster Abbey. John Locke in his Second Treatise of Government[117] had done much to caste the argument for democracy in the context of the protection of property[118]. In Locke's work, which seeks to justify non-monarchical forms of government from first principles, his definition of property is quite wide[119] but this subtlety may not have communicated itself to all the propertied classes, as the debates on the Great Reform Bill were to show.

Even in the time of Locke the imperfections of the system were well understood:

"…it often comes to pass, that in governments, where part of the legislative consists of *representatives* chosen by the people, that in tract of time this *representation* becomes very

---

'honorary freemen' and allowed to vote. His duty was to consider the evidence and then decide in Lonsdale's favour.

[117] Published in 1690

[118] Ibid, §88 "And thus the commonwealth comes by a power to set down what punishment shall belong to the several transgressions which they think worthy of it, committed amongst the members of that society, (which is the *power of making laws*) as well as it has the power to punish any injury done unto any of its members, by anyone that is not of it, (*which is the power of war and peace;*) and all this for the preservation of the property of all the members of that society, as far as is possible., and in §124 The great and *chief end,* therefore, of men's uniting into common-wealths, and putting themselves under government, *is the preservation of their property.*"

[119] Ibid § 173…(By *property* I must be understood here, as in other places, to mean that property which men have in their persons as well as goods)

unequal and disproportionate to the reasons it was at first established upon. To what gross absurdities the following of custom, when reason has left it, may lead, we may be satisfied, when we see the bare name of a town, of which there remains not so much as the ruins, where scarce so much housing as a sheepcote, or more inhabitants than a shepherd is to be found, sends *as many representatives* to the grand assembly of law-makers as a whole county numerous in people and powerful in riches"[120]

However such was the power of entrenched interests that nearly a century and a half had to elapse and a revolution of a different kind from the one which enabled Locke to return to Britain[121] take place before the reforming process would even begin.

Re-jigging the constitution

It was the industrial revolution that was to make the case for reform so overwhelming. The massive growth of population in the newly industrialised areas of the Midlands and the North of England as well as Scotland and Wales made the absurdities of the system increasingly difficult to justify. Power, influence and patronage, not democracy, were the order of the day, and it was not a coincidence that the county of Cornwall, with a population of 192,000, and where the Crown had extensive landholdings through the Duchy of Cornwall, sent 44[122] members to Parliament in 1831. As Sir

---

[120] Ibid, §157

[121] Locke was initially the personal physician and subsequently the political confidant of the first Earl of Shaftesbury, who was instrumental in trying to persuade Charles II to exclude his brother, James, Duke of York, who had become a Catholic, from the succession to the throne. Locke had to flee to Holland in 1683, where he stayed until the 'Glorious Revolution' of 1688 when William of Orange invaded England and James II fled to France.

[122] Edward Pearce in 'Reform!' referring to Edward and Annie Porritt's 'the Unreformed House of Commons, p.92, claims there

Robert Inglis pointed out in a debate on the first Reform Bill 'The fact is that as the House of Commons rose in importance, the Crown felt it necessary to have its own prerogative guarded here.'[123]   By contrast Manchester (population 182,000), Birmingham (144,000), Leeds (123,000) and Sheffield (92,000) had not a single MP between them, and the whole of Lancashire with a population of more than 1.3 million only two MPs.

Even the constituencies which did have a vote often did not bother. The 11 electors of the Rotten Borough of Old Sarum, slightly north of Salisbury had, prior to the Great Reform Act not voted since 1715.

The general picture is alarmingly laid out in "The Great Reform Act" by Eric Evans. The number of people entitled to vote did not rise as fast as that of the population as a whole, but this was perhaps the least of the problems. Parliamentary elections which were fixed at every three years in the reign of Queen Ann were subsequently contested every seven years under the Septennial Act of 1716. "No more than 190 out of England's 489 seats (39 per cent) were contested at any one general election during the period 1734-1832. The general election of 1761 witnessed the nadir of English political quiescence when only four English counties and 40 boroughs polled.   No general election in the half century before the Reform Act saw more than 11 county contests or more than 82 borough contests.[124]

The patronage of the two seats of Appleby in Cumbria was shared by the Earls of Lonsdale and Thanet.   Sir Philip Francis described his selection there in 1802 as follows:

---

were 48 seats in Cornwall "eighteen of them within 'a stretch of 28 miles long by twelve miles deep around Liskeard.'"

[123] Hansard's Parliamentary Debates, Volume 2, 1st March, column 1104

[124] The Great Reform Act of 1832, Eric J. Evans, Routledge, p.10

"I was unanimously elected by one elector to represent this ancient borough in Parliament...there was no other candidate, no Opposition, no Poll demanded... So I had nothing to do but to thank the said elector for the Unanimous Voice with which I was chosen...On Friday I shall quit this triumphant Scene with flying Colours and a noble determination not to see it again in less than seven years."[125]

The qualifications for voting in England and Wales were historically arbitrary, ranging from those where any adult male paying local poor rates could vote ('scot and lot' boroughs), or where any adult male resident for at least six months and not a pauper could vote ('potwalloper' boroughs), through 'freemen' boroughs where the right to vote depended on different definitions of being a 'freeman', and 'corporation boroughs' where only the members of the (municipal) corporation could vote to 'burgage boroughs', where voting rights were inherited almost like a piece of property[126]. In Scotland voting rights were much more restricted – only owners of property of £100 or more were qualified to vote, with the result that in 1831, when Scotland's population was over 2.3 million the total electorate was about 4,500.[127]

As Thomas Paine pointed out in 'The Rights of Man', "Can anything be more limited, and at the same time more capricious, than the qualifications of electors are in England? Limited – because not one man in an hundred (I speak much within compass) is admitted to vote. Capricious – because the lowest character that can be supposed to exist, and who has

---

[125] Quoted in 'The Great Reform Act, p.8

[126] In his speech during the debate of the first Reform Bill, O'Connell, recalled that at the time of the Union of Ireland with Britain a number of towns had been disfranchised: 'the borough of Askeaton was one of the boroughs thus disfranchised and £13,000 was given by the Parliament to Massey Dawson as compensation for the loss he had sustained by the disfranchisement of it'. Hansard col 1084, quoted in 'Reform!'

[127] See 'The Great Reform Act, pp.5-6

not so much as the visible means of an honest livelihood, is an elector in some places: while in other places, the man who pays very large taxes, and has a known fair character, and the farmer who rents to the amount of three or four hundred pounds a year, with a property on that farm to three or four times that amount, is not admitted to be an elector."[128]

Yet as he had pointed out in his previous sentence "The Constitution of France says, *That every man who pays a tax of sixty sous per annum* (2s. 6d English) *is an elector.*" So even after the convulsions in France the linkage of property and electoral rights had not entirely disappeared.

As a consequence of the Industrial Revolution there was an increasing proportion of wealthy people, in the newly industrialised areas, whose property was not represented in Parliament. There was, of course, very considerable agitation for reform, but the concepts of universal suffrage supported by some of the Radicals were very far from the minds of the Whig administration that was swept into office in 1830. It followed a succession of Tory governments which had been in power for nigh on 50 years, and which had stoutly resisted change to the system.

Much of the discussions in respect of the Reform Bills would centre on the value of the property level that would be appropriate to permit people to vote, and the way in which it should be calculated. Lord John Russell, the government minister responsible for presenting the legislation to the House of Commons, wished to allay fear that the measure could be considered 'democratic', and he denied 'that the measure would have the effect of rendering the House a democratic assemblage in that sense of the word.[129]:

The Prime Minister, Earl Grey, told the House of Lords in 1831:

---

[128] Thomas Paine 'The Rights of Man', March 1791, Part I.
[129] Hansard, Third Series, volume 2, 1st March, col. 310, 311

"The principle of my reform is, to prevent the necessity for revolution....there is no one more dedicated against annual parliaments, universal suffrage and the ballot, than I am"[130]

In addition voting was not by secret ballot, but took place over a long period of time, providing the occasion for both bribery of votes and blackmail where voters were the tenants of a powerful landlord.   Prior to the Whig administration coming into office Russell made a speech in the House of Commons in which he declared "Universal suffrage and vote by ballot are measures that, in my opinion, are incompatible with the Constitution of this country."[131]

Thomas Macauley, the historian and MP for Calne, pointed out that the intention was merely 'to admit the middle classes to a large and direct share in the Representation without any violent shock to the institutions of our country'.[132]   Although Macauley was prepared to concede that "Universal Suffrage exists in the United States without producing any very frightful consequences", he was not a proponent of allowing voting to what he called 'the lower orders':

"We know what effect distress produces even on people more intelligent than the great body of the labouring classes can possibly be....It is therefore no reflection on the lower orders of Englishmen who are not and cannot in the order of things, be highly educated, to say that distress produces on them its natural effects...it blunts their judgement, inflames their passions, that it makes them prone to believe those who flatter them and distrust those who would serve them."[133]

---

[130] Quoted in 'The Great Reform Act', p.58

[131] Ibid. p.51. this should be contrasted with the experience of Henry Hunt, who when he was an MP informed the House of Commons that he remembered the time when he had stood unsuccessfully for Preston shortly after the Peterloo massacre and '400 families were afterwards in the year 1820 expelled from their homes in consequence of voting for him' Hansard, vol II, 1st March 1831, col. 1215.

[132] Hansard, vol. II, 1st March, 1831, col. 1191

[133] Hansard, vol. II, 1st March, 1831, col. 1192

Some with literary tastes sought refuge in quoting Shakespeare. Lord Stormont was moved to quote from Coriolanus:

"...Let deeds express
what's like to be their words: We did request it,
We are the greater poll, and in true fear
They gave us our demands.' Thus we debase
The nature of our seats, and make the rabble
Call our cares fears, which will in time
Break ope the locks o'th' senate, and bring in
The crows to peck the eagles."[134]

There were those arguing for a more participatory democracy influenced by the US experience, such as Henry Hunt MP, a radical member of the gentry, who had been to prison for his beliefs and who commented that he was sorry to hear Macauley say 'that we ought to give Representatives to the middle classes to prevent the lower classes from having Representatives'. Hunt contended 'that every man who paid taxes to the State was entitled to a vote in the choice of his representation and that taxation and Representation should go hand in hand. Was he then to be told by the honourable member for Calne [Macauley] that those who fought in the army and the navy of their country – who paid the greatest portion of the taxes...by taxes levied on almost every article of human subsistence...were unfit to choose their Representatives..?'[135]

---

[134] Hansard, vol. II, 1st March, 1831, col. 1183. Lord Stormont might well have quoted Coriolanus's next speech which includes the words 'Where one part does disdain with cause, the other, Insult without all reason, where gentry, title, wisdom, Cannot conclude but by the yea and no, Of general ignorance   '. However referring to the views of the mythic figure of Coriolanus, reputedly from the 5th century BC was surely not a good historical precedent. This was a man who turned against Rome in his dislike of the plebs, and the ensuing 500 years as a Republic were remarkably successful.

[135] Hansard, VII, 4th October 1831, col. 1209

The first Reform Bill, and its successors, which made a stab at creating constituencies of similar population and reducing a number of constituencies from two members (then the norm) to one, as well as the abolition of 'rotten boroughs' was considered rather radical and only passed its second reading in the House of Commons by one vote. Earl Grey the Prime Minister decided on early elections in April/May 1831, which was a triumph for the Whigs, and which, even under the unreformed system, gave them a majority of over 130 seats in the Commons.

The House of Lords remained obdurately opposed to reform, dominated as it was by class interest even more than the House of Commons. Ultimately it was only the threats of a flood of new peerages that persuaded the House of Lords that it would have to give way. Even this happened only after the Duke of Wellington had tried and failed to form an alternative government, and public outrage had reached such a pitch that there was real fear of civil unrest and a run on the banks as one of the major radicals of the day had coined the slogan 'to defeat the Duke [of Wellington] go for gold.'

The Duke of Wellington foresaw dire consequences if the Reform legislation were passed: "Throughout the whole of the empire, persons in the lowest condition of life, liable to and even existing under the most pernicious of influences, are liable to become voters, or in other words, to exercise political power...what must we expect when these lower classes preponderate everywhere?"[136] He went on to answer his own question, saying that a democracy had never been established ' without a war upon property and the public debt' and would 'continue in the same course till you passed through the miseries of a revolution and thence to a military despotism.'[137] Indeed Wellington had already made the point "It is only by the influence of property over the elections of members of the House of Commons... that the great powers

---

[136] Hansard, vol VII 4th October 1831, col. 1197
[137] Hansard, vol VII 4th October 1831, col. 1201

of such a body as the House of Commons can be exercised with discretion and safety."[138]

The essence of the arguments can perhaps be summed up by the response of Lord Wynford to a speech made by Lord Plunkett an Irish peer and sometime Chief Justice. Plunkett had asked "Are not the people of England to be trusted?", to which Warnford replied that "God forbid that [I] should characterize them – taking them as a body – in any other way than describing that there was not a more respectable people on the face of the earth, but…they ought only to be invested with additional rights in proportion to their capacity for comprehending them. [I] would not entrust them with rights which they were not capable of exercising."[139]

Lord Wynford suggested that Lord Plunkett's arguments could lead to universal suffrage. Lord Plunkett (on the side of reform) thought this an outrageous suggestion: "I not only did not use the words "Universal Suffrage" but I have all along declared myself openly against such an absurd and mischievous idea,"[140]

The arguments are as familiar to us today as they were then. Entrenched interest, then as now, considers itself uniquely well qualified to make decisions on behalf of those not so fortunate.

A little under the influence

It is important to place the 1832 Reform Act in context. It probably increased the electorate from under 13% of the adult male population to about 18% of the male population.[141] The length of parliament of up to seven years was to remain

---

[138] Hansard, vol VII 4th October 1831, col. 1200

[139] Hansard, vol VIII, 7th October 1831, col. 196

[140] Hansard, vol VIII, 7th October 1831, col. 199

[141] Figures based on research quoted by Frank O'Gorman, quoted in The Great Reform Act, Appendix 2

unchanged until 1911, and the secret ballot was only introduced in 1872. The British electorate had to wait for nearly 100 years before universal suffrage for men and women became a reality[142]. This was not in retrospect an immensely radical measure. It was, however, viewed as the thin end of the wedge, and it gave rein to arguments of principle as to how society should be represented and by whom.

Nevertheless it was not the finely honed arguments within the palace of Westminster that ultimately won the day, but the tens of thousands, and hundreds of thousands of protestors, brought out into the streets by the likes of Thomas Attwood of unrepresented Birmingham, and his Birmingham Political Union, and the extra-parliamentary activities of those such as Francis Place, the 'tailor of Charing Cross Road' who went on to become one of the founders of Chartism. The 'Reform riots' in Bristol and widespread unrest elsewhere, after the defeat of the second Reform Bill in the House of Lords were also doubtless persuasive as an indication of the strength of feeling in respect of the Lords' intransigence.

As can be seen from the above, at the critical moment when corporations were starting to take shape in their modern form, democracy was starting to have real meaning for the first time in nearly two millennia. In Britain, the privileged classes, who were so reluctant to make anything more than the most minimal of concessions to the rest of the population in the political sphere were scarcely likely to welcome a further breach to the defences of their position by considering the rights of their workforces in a commercial context. On the contrary, they were unwilling to concede to the vast majority

---

[142] Women were eventually given the vote in the United Kingdom in 1918, after the First World War. However only women who were householders or married to householders and over the age of 30 could vote under the 1918 Act, whereas all men got the vote at 21. It was not until 1928 that women could vote on the same basis and at the same age as men.

of the population any voting rights even in a political context; it would have been inconceivable for them to have entertained the idea in a commercial context, buttressed as they were by the laws of master and servant and inviolable property rights.

It was this attachment to the concept of property as the marker of being entitled to make decisions that was to inform the development of the corporation at the same time. In the political world all were affected by the decisions of government, but it was a long time before the interests of people were put above the interests of wealth. In the world of the corporation the interests of the people working in a company were never really considered when laying the first few stones of the architecture of the modern corporation. It was accepted that wealth was the essential and indeed only criterion on which decision making could be based. The concerns of the shareholders in companies was focused on how their wealth could be preserved through limited liability when things went wrong, and how they could control the management of the companies to ensure that their investments prospered. In both the political and the business sphere property was the defining characteristic of who should be entitled to a say. It was the effect on property which gave a right to be involved in making a decision, not the effect on people.

In the United States the transfer of power to the people largely preceded the rise of the corporations. The fact that the corporations caught up so quickly to dominate the American economy, given the initial antipathy to their very existence should give some pause for thought. The segregation of powers and a wider electorate did little to halt the march of corporations. Indeed the very openness of American society may well have assisted their rise – in Europe the vested interests of title, land and privilege realised that their position was threatened by the rise of wealthy business – there were no such impediments in the United States. The direct election of the Presidency meant that the President had to be as mindful of the popular votes as of the influential business interests.

The Civil War convulsions, and the expansion of the country to the West ensured that there were concerns other than just the economy, while the Progressive and Populist movements which were such a force to be reckoned with at the end of the nineteenth and the beginning of the twentieth century had an important influence on the political platforms of presidential candidates.

However even this was only a stay of execution. The anti-trust Sherman Act of 1890 was a political acknowledgment that the growth of corporate power was both highly visible and a matter of serious public discontent. As the twentieth century dawned, and corporate influence waxed, as the cost of courting the media and running for office grew, it necessarily followed that money would be more and more influential in securing the success of candidates. As the politicians clawed their way up the system to a greater and greater extent it was inevitable that they would not only be increasingly beholden to the very wealthy, and those who controlled wealth, but that they would be wealthy themselves, or at least drawn from among their numbers.

In the United Kingdom, with its unwritten constitution, the defence of elitism throughout the nineteenth century was redoubtable. The elite were against change and resented upstart companies almost as much as upstart would-be voters, but the former could be accommodated and converted more easily than the latter. For the entire century the people entitled to vote were a significant minority of the population, and for much of the time government was either run from, or heavily influenced by, those sitting in the House of Lords. The system was certainly open to talented outsiders, whether gifted lawyers like Lord Brougham or gifted politicians like Benjamin Disraeli, but in their willingness to get involved in making money out of the industrial revolution (unlike many of their counterparts on the continent) and to take enough of the rising industrialists into their ranks to make ennoblement a reasonable aspiration, the British aristocracy fought an extremely effective rearguard action against the rising tide of democracy and also the more robust attitudes of corporatism.[143]

Under the British constitution the aristocracy controlled a significant part of the government, a blocking chamber of the legislature, and the appointment of the judiciary was in the gift of the Lord Chancellor who sat in the House of Lords. It was not until the 20th Century, and the arrival of Asquith and Lloyd George to high office that their grip faltered.

Nevertheless, during the nineteenth century through a number of Company Acts the position of the corporation was strengthened and its formation made easier. It took more than 100 years for the corporation to escape the strictures of the Bubble Act. Under a series of Companies Acts of the mid nineteenth century, of 1844, 1856, 1862 and 1867, their formation became a mere administrative process, while the liabilities of their shareholders were limited to the investment and no more. Parliament had fully capitulated to commercial convenience, but had yet to pay the cost.

What had not been noticed when the shareholders were given limited liability was that their right to be described as the 'members' of the company had also been limited. They were, as they had been before, investors in the company, but now, as the Times had intimated, they could sleep easier in their beds knowing the full extent and limit of their involvement in the company.

The investors might have investments in 50 companies and have little knowledge of any of them. As companies grew larger, and investors more numerous, their connexion with the

---

[143] These attitudes lingered long. When the 'Big Bang' came to the London investment banking, jobbing and broking markets in the mid 80's, throwing open the market to all comers, and removing barriers between different parts of the market, it was possible for one of the participants moved to write a book about it to describe it as "The death of gentlemanly capitalism" (Philip Augur, Penguin 2000)

company became ever more tenuous. Their position was in considerable contrast to that of the employees of the company, whether management or ordinary worker, who were the real members of the company. In the labour struggles of the twentieth century these two sides sought to establish their own constitutional arrangements within the corporate structure without any assistance from corporate law, which seldom looked beyond the relationship between the owner shareholders and their management delegates. Since management represented the money, they were necessarily thrown into a position of potential conflict with the employees.

The evolution of the relationship of these parties is somewhat reminiscent of that of the Crown Nobles and Commons of previous centuries. The shareholders can be compared to the monarchy, the absolute owner and sovereign of the corporate enterprise, the directors the great nobles, serving the interests of their master, but having an agenda of their own (and potentially able to supplant the shareholders through a management buy-out), while the middle management are the gentry aspiring to greater office and holding sway over their junior colleagues. The workforce are the people at large, now, as then, without a voice.

Chapter V

Is there a problem?

Wider still and wider, shall thy bounds be set

We have traced the rise of the corporation in previous chapters. How it had difficult early years and was deeply unpopular during the 18th century. How it grew rapidly in the nineteenth century and acquired new rights. The pace of growth did not slacken in the 20th century. On the contrary, governments grew ever more reliant on companies, and particularly large companies to deliver their increasingly ambitious plans in both war and peace. The size and scale of companies has, to some extent crept up on us unawares. The market capitalisation of General Electric, for example, was not far short of $400 billion at the end of 2004, Exxon and Microsoft some $325 billion. Just those three companies alone therefore had a market value of more than $1 trillion, an unimaginable number, and about one tenth of the total Gross Domestic Product of the United States, by far the largest economy in the world. This was equivalent to well over half of the entire GDP of the United Kingdom, the sixth largest economy in the world, and more than the GDP of Canada. General Electric alone was capitalised at a value larger than all but the 25 largest economies in the world. BP, with a market capitalisation of some £120 billion has assets equalling nearly 15% of the British economy, while UBS, the Swiss bank, with a market capitalisation of some $90 billion, is valued at over one third of the total GDP of Switzerland.

One could replicate the examples, but there is perhaps no need. It is clear that the multinational companies of today are extremely large, and therefore have the ability to wield enormous influence over the societies in which they operate. If they have substantial resources in comparison with the industrial economies which they call home it can be well imagined what influence they can bring to bear in the poorer countries of the world where their corporate wealth is a large multiple of the GDP of those countries.

When one speaks of globalisation, it is in fact a short form for commercial globalisation. If the nineteenth century saw the creation of political empires, the twentieth century saw their decline and replacement with commercial empires. The eighteenth and nineteenth centuries saw the growth of colonisation by people, the twentieth century colonisation by companies.

How have they used their influence, both in terms of the way in which they treat their own workforce and the way in which they influence those outside the company? Since the sole goal of any company is profit, and a company's electorate is based on money rather than people, it is not perhaps surprising that the actions of companies have reflected this.

Although corporate capitalism has hitched a ride on democracy's locomotive it is travelling under false colours – it is autocratic by design and in practice. Corporate capitalism by distancing the ownership from the management as well as the workforce has managed at the same time to distance social values and commercial concerns. This has been a gradual process; the world of trade and business was historically bound by the values of the societies in which it operated, now increasingly it is shaping them.

The effect of companies can be seen on a number of levels. They have an impact on the global economy. The dominance of a rather small number of 'multinational' companies has an impact on the world economy and on the economies of individual countries across the world. Companies have an impact on the communities in which they operate and the political systems with which they come into contact. They have an impact on such various matters as the environment and sport. Companies have an influence on the people they employ and their families, on the people they might employ, on the people they decide not to employ and on those they stop employing. Companies have an influence on the people they contract with. Companies affect the values of all those that come into contact with them, and whose behaviour is changed to a greater or lesser extent to accommodate the needs of companies, and the priorities of the corporate framework. In short the influence of companies is pervasive in our society, and like the proverbial iceberg much of their influence lurks beneath the surface, unseen, but none the less powerful for that.

The direct impact of corporate behaviour has received a huge amount of publicity over the last few years. The way in which Enron manipulated the energy markets in the United States, and engaged in very elaborate off-balance sheet financing, at a time when it was one of the top ten companies in the United States, resulting in the collapse of the company and extensive misery for its employees and pensioners (not to mention the overcharging of their customers) was just a part of the litany of corporate misbehaviour which included Tyco International and Worldcom in the United States and companies such as Ahold, Vivendi and Parmalat in Europe.

We would, no doubt, prefer corporations to act more responsibly, such as the corporation described in Joel Bakan's 'the Corporation':

"Each year the company produced a Corporate Responsibility Annual Report; the most recent one, unfortunately its last, vowed to cut greenhouse-gas emissions and support multilateral agreements to help stop climate change. The company pledged further to put human rights, the environment, health and safety issues, biodiversity, indigenous rights, and transparency at the core of its business operations, and it created a well-staffed corporate social responsibility task force to monitor and implement its social responsibility programs. The company boasted of its development of alternative energy sources and the fact that it had helped start the Business Council for Sustainable Energy. It apologized for a 29,000-barrel oil spill in South America, promised that it would never happen again and reported that it had formed partnerships with environmental NGOs to help monitor its operations. It described the generous support it had provided communities in the cities where it operated, funding arts organizations, museums, educational institutions, environmental groups, and various causes throughout the world. The company, which was consistently ranked as one of the best places to work in America, strongly promoted diversity in the workplace. "We believe"' said the report, "that corporate leadership should set the example for community service."[144]

Unfortunately, as Mr. Bakan pointed out, this paragon of corporate good governance was Enron. It demonstrates that whatever the veneer of social values that may be painted on a company's surface, (either voluntarily or imposed from the outside) a company's goal remains the same – to make money for the shareholders, and its framework is one within which management have very large scope to manage the company in their interests as well as or instead of those of the shareholders.

A Mean Affair

The way in which companies have put the interests of their shareholders above the interests of their employees is hardly a new story – indeed it is an intrinsic part of the communist view that labour is exploited by capital. However to some extent this has tended to be viewed by many as a tale from the past – of vicious Victorian mill owners, and non-unionised workforces, powerless in the face of the greed of their masters, and in a world where the political as well as the economic reins were held by the moneyed class - a Dickensian world which is now thankfully behind us in the caring and sharing world of the 21st century. Such relative complacency is sadly misplaced. It is true that many of the exceptionally harsh workplace practices have been curbed, but often enough they have just been transferred – either to the Third World or, closer to home, to factories employing

---

[144] Joel Bakan, the Corporation, p.57

people from the Third World in the developed world. A number of books have been written in the comparatively recent past outlining the way in which the actions of corporations have been deeply disturbing from a social and ethical point of view. The examples set out below from these and other sources are to illustrate the ways in which the corporate model has provided a framework which enables some of the least desirable human traits to be harnessed to a level unknown before, and the impact that this has on individuals and societies.

In his book 'Fast Food Nation' Eric Schlosser paints a very depressing picture of the way in which in so many aspects of the food industry in the United States, human dignity and decency has been sacrificed to the relentless pursuit of profit.

One of the industries which Schlosser highlights is the meat packing industry. At the beginning of the last century this was firmly associated in the United States with Chicago. Upton Sinclair in his book 'The Jungle' described Chicago's Packingtown as 'the greatest aggregation of labour and capital ever gathered in one place', and some 40,000 people were employed in the area. Sinclair's book, which exposed the harsh employment practices of the time, resulted in Congress passing food safety legislation in 1906.

This, one would assume, is the first of perhaps a series of pieces of legislation ensuring that working conditions in the meat packing industry over the years would improve, in line with higher standards of living generally, and greater concern about injury at work and the necessity of increasing skills in an ever more demanding market environment. The reality is otherwise. Schlosser contrasts an improving pay scale in the industry until the early 60's with the trends that have developed since. He tells how in 1960 Currier J. Holman and A. D. Anderson started their own meatpacking company – Iowa Beef Packers, and a trend towards the de-skilling of the meat packing industry. In some ways the Adam Smith of 'the Wealth of Nations' would perhaps have applauded as the two men sought to introduce the lessons of his pin factory to meat processing; the Adam Smith of 'the Theory of Moral Sentiments'[145], would perhaps have been less impressed with Holman's involvement in 1970 with Moe Steinman, who had close ties with the Cosa Nostra. Holman and IBP were convicted in 1974 for bribing union leaders and meat wholesalers. Holman was not punished with a prison sentence or a fine, and IBP was fined just $7,000. Steinman's son-in-law had been made a group vice president of IBP, although, according to the judge in the case he "knew virtually nothing about the meat business".

Given their attitude towards labour relations IBP probably wondered what all the fuss was about. This was illustrated by an exchange between counsel and Arden Walker, the head of labour relations at IBP during a federal hearing in the 1980s:

"Counsel: With regard to [employee] turnover, since you [IBP] are obviously experiencing it, does that bother you?
Mr. Walker: Not really
Counsel: Why not?
Mr. Walker: We found very little correlation between turnover and profitability. For instance, insurance, as you know, is very costly. Insurance is not available to new employees until they've worked there for a period of a year or, in some cases, six months. Vacations don't accrue until the second year. There are some economies, frankly, that result from hiring new employees".

And what of Iowa Beef Packers today? They have now been taken over by Tyson Foods, the world's largest chicken processor. It has not only taken on board the advantages of a

---

[145] 'The Theory of Moral Sentiments', by Adam Smith was published in 1759, prior to his being appointed as the tutor of the Duke of Buccleuch. It opens with the lines: "How selfish soever man may be supposed, there are evidently some principles in his nature, which interest him in the fortune of others, and render their happiness necessary to him, though he derives nothing from it, except the pleasure of seeing it." It should not be supposed that Smith ascribed the same sentiments to companies.

lean manufacturing process, but also the virtues of outsourcing. It leaves the raising of the birds to contractors, while retaining their ownership. The company supplies the feed, veterinary services and technical support. Schlosser explains their system as follows:

"The chicken grower provides the land, the labour, the poultry houses, and the fuel. Most growers must borrow money to build the houses, which cost about $150,000 each and hold about 25,000 birds. A 1995 survey by Louisiana Tech University found that the typical grower had been raising chicken for fifteen years, owned three poultry houses, remained deeply in debt, and earned perhaps $12,000 a year. About half of the nation's chicken growers leave the business after just three years, either selling out or losing everything. The back roads of rural Arkansas are now littered with abandoned poultry houses."

Although one company's attitude might be regarded as exceptional, it seems that the actions of other companies in the meat processing industries are not as public spirited as one might wish. Mr. Schlosser reviews the record of ConAgra, the largest food service supplier in north America. In 1989 in the case of Braswell v. ConAgra Inc., ConAgra was found guilty of cheating chicken growers in Alabama. During an eight year period over 45,000 lorry loads of chickens were deliberately underweighed at a ConAgra processing plant. In 1995 ConAgra agreed to pay $13.6 million to settle a class action lawsuit that accused the company of having conspired with seven other firms to fix prices in the catfish industry. In 1997 ConAgra paid $8.3 million in fines and pleaded guilty to charges involving wire fraud, the misgrading of crops, and the addition of water to grain. According to the Justice Department, ConAgra cheated farmers in Indiana for at least three years by doctoring samples of their crops, making grain seem of a lower quality in order to pay less for it. After buying the grain at an unfair price, ConAgra employees sprayed water on it and thereby fraudulently increased its weight, then sold it and cheated customers."

Schlosser looks at the ConAgra abattoir in Greely, Colorado in his book. He points out that some two-thirds of the workers there cannot speak English and that during one eighteen month period more than five thousand different people were employed there – an annual turnover rate of about 400 percent. Many of the workers are Mexican immigrants, who receive a wage which, according to Schlosser, at $9.25 per hour adjusted for inflation, is more than a third lower than what was paid when the plant opened over 40 years ago. This large turnover in employees is not perhaps a surprising situation for an industry with the view of labour relations mentioned above.

Schlosser has much to say about other aspects of the American food industry and the way in which it has tried to make its workforce a commodity. His image of the industry would not be an unsuitable background for a Dickens novel.

Lest it be thought that the American food industry is a case apart, George Monbiot in his book 'Captive State' gives the example of the actions of a British supermarket, Safeway (now taken over by Morrisons) in 1999. In November 1999 Safeway sent the farmers who supplied it a notice entitled 'Good News from Safeway', touting a promotional strategy and requesting a £20,000 contribution per product line, adding "We look forward to you joining us in this campaign, and anticipating a favourable response, we will take the liberty of sending you an invoice on Friday of this week. Thank you in advance for your support"[146]. Monbiot continues with this description of the supermarkets' behaviour pattern:

---

[146] George Monbiot, Captive State, Pan 2000, Chapter 5. This incident is also quoted in 'Shopped', by Joanna Blythman, Harper Perennial 2005. On page 151 Blythman also points out the UK supermarkets' commitment to fair trade on the same page. In 2003 Tesco wrote to its primary suppliers asking them to pay £69.50 per quarter per supplying site to cover its costs in respect of the Ethical Trading Initiative (an alliance of organisations promoting fair trade).

"At the end of the year, both bakers and fruit growers supplying the superstores may be forced to pay a 'rebate' to the chain they supply; if they refuse they will not be asked to sell their produce to that company again. The chairman of La Forneia, a firm that sells bread to one of the superstores, has revealed that when the chain he sells to is asked to make a donation to charity, it will turn to him or one of its other suppliers and instruct them to hand over the money in the superstore's name. The charity takes it in the belief that it had been provided by the superstore, and the grateful disabled children, cancer patients or injured pets are pictured in the local papers with the superstore's beaming manager."[147]

Monbiot describes how the supermarket owes nothing to the farmers, farmers often find themselves locked into selling food to the supermarket, simply because the collapsing wholesale market has left them with no choice. The supermarket can gradually reduce the price it pays until the farmer's business folds, whereupon it switches to a new supplier, who is less aware of the hidden cost of the relationship. A survey by the *Daily Mail* newspaper revealed that apples in the superstores were marked up by as much as 198 per cent, while eggs commanded prices up to 439 percent higher than were paid to farmers. Some of the big chains ensure that the producer's options remain limited: in some cases manufacturers have been warned that if they also supply their goods to the discount clubs they will lose their trade with the superstore.

Monbiot quotes John Breach of the Fruit Growers' Association who pointed out, 'farmers who dare to raise objections to terms and conditions run a very real risk of being de-listed'.[148]

Monbiot goes on to point out that workers in the developing world have even less defence against the imposition of the superstores than those in the developed world. One of the

---

[147] George Monbiot, Captive State, Chapter 5
[148] Ibid. p.184

British superstores, ASDA, was taken over by Walmart the US giant in 1999. A week after Walmart took over ASDA the US National Labour Committee reported that the American company's contractors in Bangladesh were paying workers as little as 5p an hour, a quarter of the Bangladeshi minimum wage. They were expected to work for up to 80 hours a week.

The UK supermarkets appear little better. In her book 'Shopped', Joanna Blythman quotes a grower of vegetables in Kenya, who among many complaints pointed out that a supermarket rejected 50% of the baby carrots which they supplied. He commented:

"We never get to see our rejected produce, because it goes into their systems as sliced carrots – free to them at our expense. When we said that we could not afford to grow baby carrots, we were labelled as difficult. Over the last five years we have found that their packers have increased the proportion of our vegetables that they reject from 10 per cent up to 30 per cent, so eroding any gains we might have made by scaling up our production.

While these conditions have been imposed, prices for our produce have been slashed. When I first started supplying UK supermarkets in 1997, the price we were paid for beans was around fifty pence a kilo for something retailing at around £4 a kilo. Now in 2004, we are being paid twenty-six pence a kilo, a reduction of nearly half on a product retailing at no less than £5.30 a kilo on supermarket shelves.....Air freight is around £1 or so, but who is taking the rest?"[149]

He also commented:

"The obvious thing to do is stop growing for supermarkets...however, we have around 600 people working here...as there is no social security here, what will our workers do? Some have worked on flower farms and seem to us to have been weakened by the chemicals inhaled while in

---

[149] 'Shopped', Joanna Blythman, Harper Perennial 2005, p.174

greenhouses. Others are in varying stages of infection by HIV. They cannot get work anywhere else....Our policy is to give them jobs that they can do easily. Most can manage weeding or picking peas. We employ two teachers for the local school where the student-teacher ratio is 100 to 1."[150]

Even with any progress which may result from the promises for debt relief and fairer trade for Africa, the day to day reality on the ground is likely to be little changed while there remains such inequality of bargaining power. Given the experience of UK suppliers, who can doubt that even if trade barriers are reduced, little of the benefit will flow to the producers of the goods in developing countries.

The Daily Grind

The effects of these labour practices have widespread repercussions and cause huge social problems. This is also true in the developed world. Polly Toynbee in her book 'Hard Work: Life in Low-Pay Britain'[151] outlined some of the social consequences and reality of this situation in the UK. Many people are trapped into poverty whatever their aspirations and capabilities – there is no ladder for promotion. Much of the work in the public sector is outsourced to private companies, and often one stage further to agencies. Each degree of contracting out means that there is another profit margin that has to be met, that has to be extracted out of the system.

In very service oriented jobs such as cleaning or portering in a hospital or providing school dinners there are, in reality, very few efficiency savings that can be brought to bear, so the profit has to come from the difference of what the company is paid, and what it pays its staff. It therefore cannot be any surprise to anyone that there is enormous pressure to keep staff wages as low as possible where work is outsourced in these areas. The system has other consequences as well. The

---

[150] Ibid., p.174-175
[151] Bloomsbury, 2003.

managers within the public sector are therefore often not in a position to manage the staff in their institutions, since they are not employed by them, but by other companies. The managers also lose the expertise of understanding the nature of the jobs, and what time and skills are required to do them.[152] The people actually doing the job are, by the nature of their employment, divorced from any public sector ethos.

The results are often staff paid at very low wages, with little capacity for improvement, very high staff turnover, little if any training, and huge inefficiencies since staff from one outsourced company will not do the work of another outsourced company or even help with it, or indeed help with the work of those lucky enough to be directly employed in the public sector, unless it is written into the contract. This contractual demarcation inevitably reduces flexibility in the system as well as reducing staff initiative.

Notwithstanding the nice theories of economists, as Polly Toynbee points out, given inadequate child care facilities, the cost of travel etc., many people and particularly women in low paid employment need to find very local work, and with hours that suit school hours. This often results in very low pay because not only are the hourly rates low but the number of hours worked in a job may also be low. Even for those families lucky to have more than one wage earner these low wages often result in long working days to try and make ends meet, and huge worries about leaving older children on their own.

Polly Toynbee also contrasted the pay she worked in a cake factory in 1970 with the pay she received in a cake factory in 2002. In 1970 she received £14.25 for a 40 hour week. The Institute for Fiscal Studies calculated for her that this would

---

[152] The decision by Network Rail, the body responsible for the British railway infrastructure to bring some of the engineering work 'in-house' was recognition that the more work is outsourced, the more difficult it is to monitor in the absence of relevant benchmarks that the management are familiar with and understand.

be worth £239.45. She worked in a cake factory in 2002, which advertised paying the minimum wage. A forty hour week there would be £164 per week; this represents a huge drop in wages over those years, and at a time when the prosperity of the United Kingdom generally has risen very substantially.

Those on low pay are getting significantly less of the national cake, and the way in which the corporate mentality has expanded its influence is undoubtedly a significant factor in this. This is not an isolated phenomenon.

For unto every one who hath shall be given, and he shall have abundance

In his book 'Wealth and Democracy', Kevin Phillips shows that the problem of unequal income distribution in the United States is getting worse not better. He calculated[153] that the 'chasm' between America's single largest fortune and the median family income widened from about 4000:1 to 1,416,000:1 between 1790 and early 2000. It is certainly true that there were very large increases and decreases of this ratio in the intervening years according to Phillips, but in 1982 the ratio was some 60,000:1, and has risen substantially ever since.

The CIA, on the US section of its website, cheerfully points out that "Since 1975, practically all the gains in household income have gone to the top 20% of households."[154] The inequality is even greater than these figures imply. Phillips[155] used figures from the Congressional Budget Office to show that the percentage increase in after tax income between 1977 and 1994 was minus 16% for the lowest 20%, and a massive positive 72% for the top 1% of the population.

---

[153] p. 38

[154] http://www.cia.gov/cia/publications/factbook/geos/us.html#Econ

[155] Wealth and Democracy, a political history of the American rich, by Kevin Phillips, Broadway Books, 2002, p.136

The United Kingdom is following the lead of the United States. In the BBC Panorama programme 'Winner takes all', broadcast on 7th November 2004 it estimated that in 1979 under 6% of UK national income went to the top 1% of the population, while by the end of the 1980's 9% went to the top 1%, and that this had since risen to 13%. It claimed that two decades ago America's top executives earned some 40 times worker's pay, while the level is now 300 times worker's pay, and that the highest paid US chief executive in 2003 earned $148 million, including stock options.

According to Dr. Edward Wolff, director of the Income Studies Project at the Jerome Levy Institute of New York, quoted by Greg Palast in his book 'The best democracy money can buy' between 1983 and 1997, 85.5% of the increase in America's wealth was captured by the richest 1%, and as acknowledged by the CIA above, 80%of the American population benefited not at all. According to Wolff 1% of the American population own $2.9 trillion out of an estimated $3.5 trillion stock and bond assets held by the population as a whole.[156]

The income disparities seem in line with the estimate of Kevin J. Murphy, Morgan Stanley Chair in Business Administration, Marshall School of Business, University of Southern California: 'Since 1970, cash compensation for CEOs has gone from 25 times the pay of the average worker to about 90 times the pay of the average worker. Total compensation, including stock options measured at grant value, went from just over 25 times average worker pay in 1970 to a peak of almost 600 times average worker pay in 2000, and has now dropped down to about 360 times average worker pay.'[157]

---

[156] The Best Democracy Money Can Buy.' By Greg Palast, Robinson, p.319

[157] Quoted in –http://www.finfacts.com/comment/comment9.htm, 10th May 2004

Research published in the British Medical Journal in April 2005 highlighted the fact that disparities of life expectancy between the wealthiest and poorest parts of the United Kingdom are widening rather than narrowing. The health editor of the Independent newspaper commented as follows[158]:

"Thousands of people are dying prematurely in deprived inner cities as the gap between rich and poor in Britain widens. The difference in life expectancy between the poorest and most affluent parts of the country has grown to 11 years and is now more pronounced than in Victorian times, researchers say.

In February 2001, the Government announced national targets to raise life expectancy in the most disadvantaged areas faster than elsewhere by 2010.

The target, from a baseline of 2001, is outlined as: 'Starting with local authorities, by 2010 to reduce by at least 10 per cent the gap between the fifth of areas with the lowest life expectancy at birth and the population as a whole.'
More recent figures show the trends so far are moving in the wrong direction. The increase in life expectancy in the most advantaged areas is outrunning that in the poorest areas. Among men, the gap between the local authority with the lowest life expectancy - Glasgow - and the one with the highest - East Dorset - rose from 10 to 11 years over the period from 1995-97 to 2001-03. Among women, the gap increased from 7.8 to 8.4 years. George Davey Smith, professor of clinical epidemiology at the University of Bristol, who led the study, said in the British Medical Journal: 'In a relatively short period, that is a substantial increase.'

The health gap remained stable between 1992-94 and 1995-97 but has been widening since. It is now wider than it has been since Victorian times, the authors say, and reflects increases in the gap between rich and poor."

---

[158] "Thousands die as health gap widens", Jeremy Laurence, Health Editor, Independent Newspaper, April 29th 2005

There can be little doubt that companies have greatly facilitated this trend towards unequal pay distribution and greater inequalities of wealth. The control that managers have on workforce pay is a great deal more direct and effective than the control shareholders exercise on management pay, and this is perhaps particularly the case now that the influence of trade unions in both the United States and Europe is less powerful than it was before. In addition the sheer scale of the giant corporations of today makes it possible for executives to be paid fabulous amounts of money, since it is still a small percentage of corporate revenues.

This was commented on by the United States Federal Reserve chairman Alan Greenspan in his testimony to a Senate banking committee in Washington on 16th July 2002[159] that "infectious greed" had gripped the business community during the 1990s and that "too many corporate executives sought ways to 'harvest' some of those stockmarket gains".

He added that the "spread of shareholding and options among business managers perversely created incentives to artificially inflate reported earnings in order to keep stock prices high and rising. The incentives they created overcame the good judgment of too many corporate managers."

Mr Greenspan concluded that:

"It is not that humans have become any more greedy than in generations past. It is that the avenues to express greed had grown so enormously"

It is therefore clear that the corporate requirement for profits and the opportunity for executive enrichment have had a significant effect on wage disparity in the US, both in inflating executive pay and in depressing the pay of ordinary employees.

---

[159]

http://www.federalreserve.gov/boarddocs/hh/2002/july/testimony.htm

A venture into the Unknown

The requirement for profits and the potential gain for executives of profitable companies also manifests itself in other areas; the squeezing of farmers (which is leading to a fundamental change in the nature of rural communities) by the supermarkets has already been referred to above. In addition the quest for the industrialisation of the agricultural sector has led to the promotion of genetically modified crops and animals. This has caused very considerable controversy, and although the European Union has tried to resist the demands of the United States in promoting the interests of its agribusiness companies, it has already given permission for some genetically modified crops to be grown in the EU.

Yet the business of genetically modified food, with all its attendant risks and unknown factors does not meet some exceptional need that cannot be met in any other way; in her book on genetic engineering 'GE Genetic Engineering and You' Moyra Bremner quotes Richard Powell of Novartis in 1999[160] as saying that 'At present GE crops are of no benefit to consumers whatsoever'. Their development is purely a reflection of the corporate desire to increase profitability, even though the ramifications may be very serious, long term and irreversible.

A comparison may be made between the requirements for the introduction of new medicines and those for the introduction of newly engineered foods. New medicines in the United States or Europe have to be tested for many years, and numerous trials have to be carried out to assess their suitability for human use. These medicines are then prescribed by trained medical practitioners to meet a specific medical need. Often they are required to be taken for only a short period of time. Even then mistakes occur, such as the tragic case of thalidomide, which resulted in the birth of babies with incompletely formed limbs. However such

---

[160] 'GE Genetic Engineering and You', Moyra Bremner, Harper Collins, 1999, p. 26

medicines can be withdrawn from circulation and the damage limited.

However the degree to which the public can have confidence in the regulatory authorities has been severely dented recently. An article appeared in the Independent newspaper on the 12th June 2005, referring to work done by its sister publication, the Independent on Sunday. The first part of the article read as follows:

"Vital data on prescription medicines found in millions of British homes has been suppressed by the powerful US drug regulators, even though the information could potentially save lives.

An investigation by The Independent on Sunday shows that, under pressure from the pharmaceutical industry, the American Food and Drug Administration routinely conceals information it considers commercially sensitive, leaving medical specialists unable to assess the true risks.
One team of investigators found that 28 pages of data had been removed from the FDA files on one of a new family of painkillers because of confidentiality

Last week a major research study led by Professor Julia Hippisley-Cox at Nottingham University, revealed that ibuprofen, the supposedly "safe" painkiller, increases the risk of heart attack by almost a quarter. The finding was a particular blow to thousands of users who have already switched from the best-selling drug Vioxx, which was withdrawn last year after evidence that it too could increase the risk of heart attacks

Key information about Vioxx and other drugs that form part of the new generation of painkillers called Cox-2 inhibitors had been suppressed, it emerged. Now researchers are questioning the reliability of the data about other drugs, including the full range of painkillers.

Dr Peter Juni, one of the team of Swiss investigators who helped to expose the risk of the new-generation drugs, claims his efforts were obstructed by the FDA.

"As part of the Freedom of Information Act, the agency is required to make available its reports on all drugs that are approved. Unfortunately, these reports are not as useful as they could be," he and his team say in an editorial in the British Medical Journal.

"For example, only 16 out of at least 27 trials of celecoxib that were performed up to 2002 in patients with musculoskeletal pain were included in the relevant reports... In the case of valdecoxib, we found that many pages and paragraphs had been deleted because they contained trade secret and/or confidential information that is not disclosable."

Dr Juni, senior research fellow in clinical epidemiology at the University of Berne, is demanding that drug companies be legally required to make public any adverse effects as soon as they become available. Researchers also want more independent research, with financial firewalls between drug companies and doctors carrying out clinical trials.

Last year The Lancet published trial results that showed that unacceptable heart risks linked to the drug rofecoxib (sold as Vioxx) were evident four years before it was finally withdrawn by its maker.

The Lancet's editor, Richard Horton, said at the time that the discovery pointed to lethal weaknesses in the FDA's approach. He said: "Too often the FDA saw and continues to see the pharmaceutical industry as its customers, a vital source of funding for its activities, and not as a sector of society in need of strong regulation."

The increasing lack of independent expertise as a result of the role that pharmaceutical companies play ion research has also been highlighted recently by the case of Dr Aubrey Blumsohn, senior lecturer and bone metabolism specialist at Sheffield University. Dr. Blumsohn told The Observer that he became highly concerned about the analysis of data collected as part of a study he was conducting on drugs manufactured by Procter and Gamble. The research was into the effect the osteoporosis drug Actonel had on women at risk of fractures.[161] As the newspaper reported:

"Blumsohn claims that for nearly a year he was prevented from seeing the full data, despite being named as the lead author on the study, and having two reports published in his name. Two years after raising his concerns about research conduct, he was suspended from his university post after he threatened to speak to medical journalists about the issue."

The newspaper also reported that the drug in question, Actonel, is known to be a safe and effective drug, and the issues raised by Blumsohn do not suggest otherwise. Procter and Gamble strongly denied his claims, and said that it was 'standard industry practice' not to hand over all data to academics, and that the ghost writer, Mary Royer, was familiar with the 'key messages' they wanted to convey about the drug.

As mentioned in the article:

"There are increasing concerns among medical ethicists about the relationship between the major drugs companies and the academic institutions that are paid millions of pounds each year to carry out research on their behalf. Pharmaceutical companies gain more credibility for their studies if they bear the name of independent academics holding university posts even if they haven't actually written the report."

It must be a matter for considerable concern that pharmaceutical researchers appear to be under such great commercial pressure, and the revelation that it is 'standard industry practice' to withhold data from the academic researchers whose name is on the research document must give rise to very considerable concerns as to what faith the

---

[161] "Doctor accuses drugs giant of 'unethical secrecy', by Jo Revill, Health Editor, The Observer newspaper (U.K.), 4th December, 2005.

public can have in the objectivity of such a practice if it even happens when the effectiveness of the medicine appears not to be in question.

If the law were commercialized in the same way, it is perhaps analogous to a barrister being expected to sign off legal opinions, even though not in full possession of all the facts. It seems difficult to see how objective professionalism can flourish in such an environment.

So even in the case of pharmaceuticals, with all the checks and balances in place there is reason to believe that the profit motive and commercial gain are capable of overcoming many of the protections instituted for the benefit of the public.

The public is far less protected from genetically modified crops. No such similar trials have been conducted to ensure that they are safe for humans to eat, and yet they can be bought freely (indeed unknowingly), without any requirement for a prescription, and eaten over a very long period of time, with no medical condition to be dealt with in the first place. The implications of their use are potentially much wider than pharmaceuticals. Their potential impact on the environment has quite properly received a lot of publicity, but the very limited safeguards that exist in respect of their effect on human health has perhaps received less attention. Safeguards comparable to those for medicines are not in place, and the influence of corporations in ensuring that public health concerns do not obstruct profit goals is potentially even greater. In his book 'Captive State' George Monbiot explored[162] the connexion that existed between Monsanto and the FDA, and the way in which rBST (recombinant bovine somatatropin, an artificial hormone which stimulates milk production in cows) was approved by the FDA.

It is interesting to note in the light of the recent article in the Independent that he quotes a Dr. Richard Burroughs, who was

---

[162] Chapter 7 – Monsanto's Magic Potion

sacked by the FDA in 1988, who explained his sacking as follows:

"I was told that I was slowing down the approval process. It used to be that we had a review process at the FDA. Now we have an approval process. I don't think the FDA is doing good, honest reviews any more. They've become an extension of the drug industry"[163]

It is claimed that there is no evidence to show that genetically modified food has caused any harm to anyone, but given the great difficulty in establishing causation, one is tempted to quote Dorothy Parker on hearing of the death of President Calvin Coolidge (who was famously taciturn) 'How can they tell?' The rise of some medical conditions such as asthma and allergies could be attributable to any number of factors; without any benchmarks who can tell, in the absence of an instantaneous and violent reaction, what may be the long term consequences of such genetic manipulation?

In her book, Moyra Bremner does however instance one example which should give pause for thought[164]

In the late 1980's the company Showa Denko K.K. decided to use genetic engineering to accelerate and increase the efficiency of producing tryptophan, a food substance. They genetically engineered bacteria by inserting several genes that caused the bacteria to express certain enzymes at much higher levels than normal and to express other enzymes that are not normally present in the original bacteria.

The enzymes expressed in these bacteria through genetic engineering altered cellular metabolism substantially, leading to greatly increased production of tryptophan. These genetically engineered bacteria were immediately used in commercial production of tryptophan, and the product placed on the market in the USA in 1988.

---

[163] ibid. p. 238

[164] p. 28 et seq.

Showa Denko was allowed to sell the tryptophan produced in genetically engineered bacteria without safety testing because they and other companies had been selling tryptophan produced in non-genetically engineered bacteria for years without ill effects. It was considered that the method of production (whether via natural or genetically engineered bacteria) was immaterial and that, since tryptophan had already been shown to be safe, the new material needed no testing. In effect they considered it substantially equivalent to the tryptophan that had been sold for many years.

Within a few months of its introduction 37 people who used it were dead and some 1,500 permanently disabled. It took months to discover that the poisoning was due to toxin present in the tryptophan produced using Showa Denko's genetically engineered bacteria. One factor that contributed to this time delay was the fact that the product was not labeled to distinguish it from tryptophan produced through conventional methods.

Independent research showed that the tryptophan produced by genetically engineered bacteria contained several highly poisonous substances, one of which could kill, even at less than one part in a thousand.

Mistakes can of course happen in any walk of life. The point here is that given the force of the profit motive companies are prepared to take risks which have wide social cost which they will not necessarily be asked to bear. The manufacturer in the above case denied liability, although it did pay out of court compensation. But for the wider question of the genetic engineering industry as a whole, legal liability is likely to be very much harder to prove, and if we seriously damage our environment monetary compensation will in any event scarcely be an adequate or appropriate remedy.

Careful Calculation

Companies can also be more calculating with regard to the risk reward ratio. In his book 'the Corporation' Joel Bakan cites[165] the case of the Chevrolet Malibu produced by General Motors, the petrol tank of which was prone to burst into flames. Patricia Anderson was driving home with her three children after attending midnight mass on Christmas day in 1993, when a car drove into the back of her Chevrolet Malibu, causing it to burst into flames and resulting in terrible burn and other injuries to the family. At the resulting trial the jury decided that the placement of the fuel tank at the rear of the car had not been changed to a more secure position in the Malibu model due to cost considerations.

More chilling still was the revelation in the case that Mrs Anderson brought against GM that the company had previously asked one of its engineers to analyse fuel fed fires in GM vehicles. The report "Value Analysis of Auto Fuel Fed Fire Related Fatalities" calculated that:

1.   each year GM on average had 500 fuel fed fatalities
2.   each fatality cost GM an estimated $200,000 on average
3.   There were some 41 million GM vehicles on the road.

The author concluded that the cost per vehicle was therefore $2.40 ($100 million divided by 41 million vehicles). The cost to General Motors ensuring that the fuel tank did not explode in crashes was put at $8.59 per vehicle. Therefore the cost saving of not doing this was $6.19 per vehicle. Leaving aside the obvious logical fallacy that designing a car in this way might well result in an increased number of fuel fed fatalities and that the cost per accident might well go up, it displays a sharp divergence between the corporate mentality and the values of American society in which GM operates. In the US juries set damages, and this unacceptably clinical approach to the financial cost of human injury was demonstrated by the

---

[165] pp. 61-65

jury in the Anderson case in awarding her and her family compensatory damages of $107 million and punitive damages of $4.2 billion. The punitive damages were later reduced to $1.2 billion, but the Los Angeles Superior Court Judge upheld the verdict, saying "the Court finds that clear and convincing evidence demonstrated that defendants' fuel tank was placed behind the axle on automobiles....in order to maximise profits – to the disregard of public safety."

General Motors filed an appeal to the California Court of Appeal. The US Chamber of Commerce made a submission in that appeal claiming that jurors are 'not well positioned to make accurate risk utility assessments in cases involving complex engineering issues'.

The Appeal court took a very different view from the lower courts.[166] They found that the entire jury verdict was impermissibly tainted by passion and prejudice, and that a new trial was necessary. The Court of Appeal decided that it was perfectly reasonable for General Motors to undertake a risk-utility test, quoting as follows:

"If the analysis is sound and indicates that the costs of a safety measure exceed the value of the safety benefits it produces, then the firm is not negligent" — much less reckless or malicious — "for foregoing the measure." Viscusi, *Corporate Risk Analysis, supra*, 52 STAN. L. REV. at 568

Though this rule is straightforward and the logic underlying it is unimpeachable, its application is complicated by the fact that juries are not well-positioned to make accurate risk-utility assessments in cases involving complex engineering issues."[167]

As the intervention of the Chamber of Commerce and the decision by the Court of Appeal shows there is a serious

---

[166] California Court of Appeal for the second appellate district - division four no. B135147

[167] p.10 of the judgement

divergence between the corporate approach and social attitudes. It was interesting that the Court of Appeal's words echoed those of the Chamber of Commerce. The Court did not say how it would calculate 'the value of the safety benefits'. Like the expression 'collateral damage' the phraseology fails to communicate the human suffering implied by the statement. It is also slightly self-referential: the less compensation paid to any family injured, the more the 'costs of the safety measures' are likely to exceed the 'safety benefits'. The reductio ad absurdam of this argument is that if families were not entitled to receive any compensation, then the 'value' of the safety benefits would be nil, the costs of any safety measures would always be higher, and a company never negligent for not implementing them.

The case was not about "risk utility assessments"; it was about the jury valuing life while the company sought to put a price tag on it. It is clear that from the Court of Appeal's judgement that the language of counsel for the plaintiffs was highly emotive, and there is no doubt that the damages were enormous. However this case exposed the gulf that divides the corporate viewpoint and its cold calculation of commercial acceptability on the one hand, and the individual citizen's view of what constitutes acceptable behaviour on the other. The Court of Appeal clearly shared the corporate view of the world. It quoted an article in the New York Times as follows:

"Not surprisingly, the jurors forsook their duty to conduct their own risk-utility test, and instead slammed General Motors with an unprecedented $4.8 billion punitive exaction that made clear that they would not countenance any attempt to place a dollar value on human life. *See* Andrew Pollack, *4.9 Billion Jury Verdict in G.M. Fuel Tank Case: Penalty Highlights Cracks in Legal System*, N.Y. TIMES, July 10, 1999, at A7 (explaining that "[t]he jurors wanted to send a message to General Motors that human life is more important than profits" and quoting juror as saying "[w]e're just like numbers, I feel, to them * * * statistics. That's something that is wrong").["168]

The Court of Appeal also took exception to the fact that counsel for the plaintiffs described the plaintiffs as ordinary people, whereas General Motors was portrayed as "one of the largest corporations in the world," a "mindless and soulless corporation" with "no conscience" and "no blood running through [its] veins."[169] The Court proclaimed that:

"Rhetoric emphasizing the difference between corporations and individuals in this way has long been condemned as an incitement to prejudice against corporate defendants."

This is somewhat remarkable, since although the language may indeed be colourful it is also literally true. It therefore appears to be the case that the words of Lord Chancellor Thurlow quoted at the beginning of Chapter III are to be condemned even though they are true, because they are an incitement to prejudice against corporations according to the Californian Supreme Court. The Court of Appeal decided that the counsel's 'elicitation of jury passion and prejudice' had been 'grossly improper' and decided to send the case back for a re-trial.

General Motors is not unique. On the contrary the GM case appeared to be something of a re-run of Ford's production of the Pinto some 20 years earlier. Again the cost of improving the safety of the petrol tank was thought to be more important than the risk to human life, a cost benefit analysis was done on the number of estimated burn deaths and injuries, and ultimately in 1978 there was a trial where damages of $128 million were awarded in similar circumstances.

As the Ford and GM cases (and the intervention of the Chamber of Commerce) show these corporate policies are not one-off renegade strategies of maverick management. They

---

[168] p. 11 of the judgement.
[169] p. 33 of the judgement.

are the natural outcome of the profit goals that companies and their employees have been set.

It is clear that the viewpoint of companies has been winning. In 2003 The Supreme Court reversed a judgement of the Utah State Court which imposed punitive damages which were 145 times the compensatory damages.[170] This was on the basis of the 14th Amendment, and that the punitive damages constituted grossly excessive or arbitrary punishment on the corporate tortfeasor.

In the case, the Supreme Court reiterated its disdain for evidence of out-of-state conduct resulting from a broad corporate policy. "As a general rule, a State [does not] have a legitimate concern in imposing punitive damages to punish a defendant for unlawful acts committed outside the State's jurisdiction ... A basic principle of federalism is that each State may make its own reasoned judgment about what conduct is permitted or proscribed within its borders, and each State alone can determine what measure of punishment, if any, to impose on a defendant who acts within its jurisdiction."[171]

This inevitably means that the scope to impose punitive damages on corporations is being even further whittled away. The ability of companies to calculate their potential liability for any given amount of malfeasance has been made much more accurate, and the cost of such malfeasance greatly reduced. It will be no surprise, given the attitude of business

---

[170] *State Farm Mutual Automobile Insurance Co. v. Campbell*, 123 S.Ct. 1513 (2003)

[171] Ibid. p. 11 of the judgement. In addition in the GM case the Californian Court of Appeal went so far as to state that undue emphasis on the out of state origins of a corporate defendant could prejudice a fair trial. "Counsel's Repeated References To General Motors' Out-Of-State Location Were Grossly Improper.", p.39 of the judgement. It was felt that referring to the fact that General Motors was not based in California

so clearly displayed above, that companies will be even more willing to take risks with human life in the pursuit of profit than they were in the past.

At least however there are some legal remedies available to mere human beings in the US. The legal and other remedies for those affected by corporate activity are rather fewer in the developing world than those available to US citizens. In December 2004 one of the worst industrial accidents in history occurred in Bhopal in India. Highly poisonous methyl isocyanate (MIC) gas leaked from the plant, together with even more toxic reaction compounds. Some 7,000 people were killed instantly and contributed to the death of more than 20,000 others.[172]

Many still suffer from the long term effects of the poisoning, some blinded, some with chronic coughs, others in pain.

The foreman of the MIC plant said that he was supposed to get six months' safety training, but after just 15 days training he was told to take charge of the MIC sub-system. In the end they agreed to one month's training.

He claimed that the most vital safety instrument in the plant, the temperature indicator alarm, which could have warned of the disaster, was not working because of a design fault. It went wrong after just two weeks and never worked again. In the original design, there was supposed to be a back-up but it was never installed. He also claimed that there was a loud siren installed to warn the public of a leak, but four months before the disaster they changed it to a muted siren because there were so many leaks from the plant that they didn't want people to panic.

Dow Chemicals, the company which took over Union Carbide in a merger, refuses to clean up the site.

---

[172] See article in The Independent 2nd December 2004, 'Bhopal: A living legacy of corporate greed'.

The victims received just £300 in compensation from Union Carbide. This is as much the fault of the Indian government as of the American company. In 1986, the Indian government agreed a deal in which Union Carbide paid just $470m (£245m) in compensation, and less than half of this has been paid out to the victims. The influence of the ordinary citizen on such outrages seems pitifully small in the world's largest democracy.

In his book 'The Best Democracy Money Can Buy' Greg Palast cites numerous instances of the way in which companies have trampled over communities. In Alaska, for example, a native community was persuaded to part with valuable land at Valdez Harbor, which according to Palast was worth tens or possibly hundreds of millions of dollars, and was the only place on the Alaska coast that could support an oil terminal geologically, for the princely sum of $1. As a further twist the Chugach tribe, together with their villages of Chenega and Nanwalek, which also had land, were incorporated by their lawyer Clifford Groh, (who then went on to be a lawyer for an oil company), and became the Chugach Corporation, the Chenega Corporation and the English Bay (Nanwalek) Corporation, thus changing them for ever; the chiefs' powers taken over by CEOs and the tribal council by a board of directors.[173] Thus the communities have now become companies. It was on March 24th 1989 that the Exxon Valdez broke up and covered the Alaskan coast line with 11 million gallons of crude oil. In the case that followed the jury awarded punitive damages of $5 billion in 1994. But in 2001 the US court of Appeal ruled that the amount was excessive, and sent the case back to the trial court to adjust the damages (the mayor of the local community committed suicide after the news). Although the damages award was largely re-instated, not a penny of it has yet been paid out.[174]

---

[173] Greg Palast, the Best Democracy Money Can Buy, Robinson p. 268

[174] See article published in the Independent, 25th March 2004 by Andrew Gumbel

Getting to Know You

The inter-relationship between corporates and government exists at many levels. Corporations clearly have a substantial interest in the regulatory framework within which they operate – since this often has an important impact on their cost of doing business. At the local level, the obtaining of planning permission may make the difference as to whether they are able to do business at all in a particular locality. This can lead to some interesting relationships.

As Mr. Monbiot outlines in his book 'Captive State'[175], West Berkshire council in the UK, in order to fulfil requirements set by the UK government for additional housing in the south-east supported a scheme to build 1,700 new houses on 350 acres in a place called Sandleford Park, south of Newbury, the landscape of which was striking and may have been designed by the celebrated Capability Brown. This was part of the draft Local Plan intended to lay down future land use. At the public enquiry, held to investigate the appropriateness of the Plan it transpired that some of the council's fees (including that of the barrister and expert witnesses at the enquiry) were being paid for by a property developer interested in developing the site. On further investigation it turned out that three other property developers had helped meet the local council's expenditure.

The internal inquiry launched by the council to investigate the position, as a result of public disquiet in respect of these relationships appeared to endorse the decision of the officers of the council to accept this help from companies as it saved the council both time and money. It is difficult to see how such an arrangement could result in the council taking an objective view of the requirements of the developers; it is even more difficult to see how they thought that they would be perceived to be objective. In any event, when companies start paying the fees that would otherwise be paid by councils

---

[175] p. 134 et seq.

it exemplifies a very close working relationship which at the least may be open to misinterpretation.

It is, of course not just with the implementation of existing legislation that companies are concerned. They also have interests in either the enactment or repeal of legislation that may be advantageous or disadvantageous to them. They also have an interest in being exempted from certain legislation which will cost them money. Businessmen have always demanded protection from competition and complained about the cost of complying with government legislation throughout the ages, and the interests of property and power have always been intertwined; whether it be the creation of the East India Company to exploit the risky opportunities of the East or the interests of the southern planters of the United States being a major contribution to the Civil War, the tension between business and government is a constant one. The use of slaves, of child labour in factories, down mines and up chimneys was stopped, not as a result of corporate scruples, but because of legislative change forced on companies and businesses by changing social attitudes. Companies in this sense are no different from their individual proprietor precursors, except that the stakes are much higher.

Again, we like to think that the bad old days of the Victorian business are far behind us in these days of corporate social responsibility, but as noted above, the goals of the corporation have not changed, and consequently they still seek to influence the legislature to their advantage.

In his book Mr. Palast provides one example, from Texas, of how companies and politicians inter-react. As he says[176], "the power stations of Texas produce three things: electricity, pollution and political donations". He cites the example of the 'Big Brown' plant of TXU in Texas which is powered by lignite (brown coal). According to Mr. Palast TXU dumps 389,000 tons of contaminants into the air each year, making it the number one polluter in the state. President Bush when he

---

[176] p.123

was the governor of Texas, signed a 'grandfather' statute exempting some TXU plants from laws requiring scrubbers to clean their emissions. Another large power company, Reliant Energy, also benefited from this legislation. Both companies had been substantial donors to the Bush campaign to be elected as governor for Texas.

It is scarcely necessary to replicate examples of what is self-evident corporate behaviour – an interest in influencing the legislature of a country – indeed at face value it is a perfectly legitimate concern for a company. However it raises some very serious questions, some of them fundamental to the functioning of democracy. Companies and governments come into contact frequently in the modern world, and the potential for the formation of close and what might be viewed as 'cosy' relationships has increased - see George Monbiot's description of the close relationship between the government and a bio-tech company – to the extent that when a reporter from the Express newspaper contacted the company its call was returned by the Cabinet Office[177]; governments depend on companies for carrying out their policies, and will inevitably be open to companies' profit making concerns and their potential generosity.

Large international companies are of such a vast scale that they are able to deploy enormous resources over long periods of time to state their case through lobby groups. Companies can contribute to election campaigns in cash or in kind. In all these ways companies have a very significant potential influence over government and politicians for their agenda – which is to make more money. This influence is simply not matched by other interest groups. It is therefore increasingly difficult to expect politicians to be wholly objective when weighing up any given policy decision, when powerful corporations have an interest in the outcome.

The corporate agenda is also international. Mr. Monbiot refers in his book to the European Round Table of

---

[177] See Captive State, pp. 269-270

Industrialists, founded in 1983, which was an early and vital influence in the creation of a single European market. They have an exceptional access to government at the European level to put forward the business point of view. The view of the ERT is that 'Government and business need to share information, goals and cultures, and to pull together as a team'.

Its website claims that the ERT 'has contacts with the Commission, the Council of Ministers and the European Parliament. Every six months the ERT meets with the government that holds the EU presidency to discuss priorities. At national level each member has personal contacts with his own national government and parliament'.[178]

The influence of companies from the lowest to the very highest level of government, for whatever agenda they wish to pursue, is pervasive and unparalleled. One might even ascribe the acceptance by governments of the theories of 'trickle down' economics as showing the influence of corporates. After all, the concept is merely the liquid version of crumbs from the rich man's table. The only saving grace of this scenario is that companies do not, as yet, have the vote. Indeed they are not particularly loyal to the countries whose governments they seek to influence.

The actions of corporations may increasingly dictate the tax strategy of countries since they well equipped to avoid tax. Robert McIntyre, director of Citizens for Tax Justice (CTJ) analysed the tax payments of 275 Fortune 500 companies in 2002 and 2003. He found that the average rate was less than half the statutory 35% and 82 paid zero or less in federal income taxes. An investigation by John Plender of The Financial Times into tax payments by UK subsidiaries of multinationals uncovered a similar picture.[179] In a separate

---

[178] Ibid, p.320 et seq.
[179] See article by Vanessa Houlder, Financial Times, 22nd November 2004.

piece of research CTJ found that the situation was even worse in respect of state taxes for larger companies, with the 252 companies examined paying only about one third of expected state income tax payments, and some companies, such as Toys "R" Us and Boeing reported as paying no net state income tax over the 2001-2003 period. With globalisation such companies are rapidly moving towards becoming untaxable. This underpayment of tax by corporations is sometimes explained as a drive for greater shareholder value, but the shareholders may well be in another state or another country, and in the meantime smaller businesses and individuals have to pick up the shortfall.[180]

Companies are not partners with their communities; they are now unruly mistresses, ready to move to the next alluring prospect at the drop of the proverbial hat. They have no loyalty to the community where they grew up, except through the personal views of senior management[181]. Redmond, near Seattle may have benefited from Microsoft's growth, but it is notable that another company which grew up in Seattle,

---

[180] See http://www.ctj.org/pdf/corp0205an.pdf

[181] Indeed it is interesting to note the impact of companies on societies where their interests did not coincide. Although many other influences were also at work the effect of the East India Company on the relative manufacturing strengths of the UK and India was doubtless notable. As Paul Kennedy pointed in his book "The Rise and Fall of the Great Powers", there was a massive change in the economic importance of Britain and India (and others) from the latter half of the eighteenth century, as the following chart shows:

Relative Shares of World Manufacturing Output

	1750	1800	1830	1860	1880
Britain	1.9%	4.35	9.5%	19.9%	22.9%
India	24.5%	19.1%	17.6%	8.6%	2.8%

Boeing, saw fit to decide on Chicago as its headquarters in May 2001, having looked at Dallas Fort-Worth and Denver closely in the process as well.

For the communities that depend on a company plant the cost can be devastating if it closes. In management parlance the interests of the company and those of the community are not 'aligned'. This is another effect of large global companies. In the early days of the industrial revolution there was often such an alignment, or at least a better one, particularly where a company had only one plant or where it had its headquarters. This factor is still present today[182]

Even sporting teams are not resistant to this phenomenon. Given the importance of television rights the local fan base, once the bedrock of any team's success, financial and sporting, has become marginalised, and the location of a team's ground has itself become less important. Not only has the transfer of individual players in games such as soccer become commonplace, but whole teams now change their domicile to a different country, bribed away to new cities for their potential to create new business. In 2004 the Montreal Expos, a major league baseball club in Canada were lured to Washington DC in the United States. One of the carrots/conditions of the move was the construction of a new $440 million stadium, for which Washington DC Council arranged the funding.

It would, of course be possible to add numerous additional examples of the pervasive influence of companies, on the environment, on working practices, on health, on government and so on, but their influence is so wide ranging that it cannot be in doubt. The above examples show that very often their effect is very damaging as the profit motive drives out other considerations and encourages people to act in a callous and calculating way that is very different from the values of the

---

[182] See the contrasting attitudes of Pfizer in New York and Nortel in Joel Bakan's the Corporation, pp. 22 and 28.

ethical system in which they operate. The corporate structure also enables them to do this on a hitherto unimagined scale.

Misplaced Trust

The way in which companies operate has an insidious and indeed invidious effect on the values that we hold. The pursuit of profit is not value neutral. On the contrary it professes to put profit above other considerations. It implies that other values are less important, and it is only comprehensible in a context which places material values above moral ones. This is one of the key reasons why the attempt at engagement between western corporates and Islamic countries is inevitably full of tension: the driving force of corporate life, profit, is wholly at odds with religious priorities. At best this can breed incomprehension, at worst fanatical hostility. The struggles between business and religion in Europe and America were not painless, but they occurred within the same culture, at a time (in the seventeenth century) when religious certainty was on the wane and society was becoming more secular, and the struggles were largely between individual attitudes, not the imposition of corporate ones.

According to Francis Fukuyama in his book 'Trust: the social virtues and the creation of prosperity' the creation of trust is not only a very important social factor, but by lowering the cost of doing business, it is also a very important economic factor. Max Weber, in his book "The Protestant Ethic and the Spirit of Capitalism' foreshadowed this idea by pointing out in his '"Churches" and "Sects in North America"', the vital importance belonging to a 'sect' made in ensuring that people were trustworthy (and therefore a good credit risk). He relates this story from his own travels in America:

"'Sir', said an older gentleman who was a commercial traveller for **Undertakers' hardware** (iron tombstone lettering), with whom I spent some time in Oklahoma, 'as far as I am concerned, everyone can believe what he likes, but if I discover that a client doesn't go to church, then I wouldn't trust him to pay me fifty cents: **Why pay me, if he doesn't believe in anything?"**[183]

The focus on corporate profit to the virtual exclusion of everything else has an impact that is wider than the impact on the behaviour of company executives, serious though this is, or of seeking to ensure that costs are not borne by the company, but by society. Companies seek to ensnare everyday behaviour in order to maximise their profits. They institute campaigns for children to nag their parents to maximise their sales of toys and services. They ask actors to pretend to be bona fide passers by, and speak loudly about corporate products as if they were satisfied users, rather than merely promoters of the product. Taxi drivers are paid to venture opinions which appear to be their own, whereas they are in fact nothing more than paid endorsements.

Companies now try to exploit trust for commercial gain. Joel Bakan in his book 'the Corporation'[184], refers to 'undercover marketing'. He writes:

"Imagine that you are walking along an out of the way trail in a national park. A group of young hikers is standing at the side of the trail talking to one another in loud, excited voices. You cannot help but overhear them. "They would be talking about the great backpack they are wearing" says Jonathon Ressler, CEO of marketing firm Big Fat, "how [with other backpacks] your back hurts after you hike 84,000 miles…[but] with this backpack it has a special da-da-da-da…it's really comfortable. "Boom" says Ressler, "they have just delivered the message" to you – and you have no idea that you were just pitched a product by a group of professional actors working for Big Fat". As Bakan points out "undercover marketing, with deception at its core, is another example of how unrestrained corporations – not just Ressler's Big Fat, but the corporations that hire him as well – can be in

---

[183] Penguin, p.205
[184] p.132

their search for profit". More than that, however, undercover marketing demonstrates how deep the commercialisation of society runs.

In an ironic echo of Weber's insight he quotes Edison School's financier Michael Moe as saying 'The Corporation has essentially replaced the church in terms of who you are. It wants the same thing as the church…obedient constituents that…pay [their] dues and follow the rules'[185].

Companies through these actions are rapidly depleting the social capital that has eased their rise. Their message of motivation is materialism. This was exemplified by the speech of Gordon Gekko in respect of the fictional company Teldar in the film 'Wall Street' (1987):

"The point is, ladies and gentleman, is that greed -- for lack of a better word -- is good. Greed is right. Greed works. Greed clarifies, cuts through, and captures the essence of the evolutionary spirit. Greed, in all of its forms -- greed for life, for money, for love, knowledge -- has marked the upward surge of mankind. And greed -- you mark my words -- will not only save Teldar Paper, but that other malfunctioning corporation called the USA"

This speech was memorable, not because the sentiments were universally despised, but because on the contrary they reflected the materialism of much of American (and indeed Western) society. This attitude however was in stark contrast to the Christian values which play such a large role in American society, and which are a fundamental part of the Western heritage.[186]

---

[185] p.134.

[186] The problem of greed has been with us a long time. It is for example the theme of Chaucer's The Pardoner's Tale, where the Pardoner's motto is 'radix malorum est cupiditas', which can be translated as 'greed is the root of all evil'. Yet even the Pardoner freely admits that he wants to sell pardons of people's sins so that he can enjoy the good life, and that he is greedy himself.

A Changing Landscape

The role of the corporate in focusing on the purely commercial carries within it an implication of what we ought to be focusing on. As individuals we are increasingly seeing the world if not through corporate eyes, then at least through a pair of corporate spectacles. In the same way a coloured lens only lets through a certain wavelength of light, and everything is viewed in a particular tint, so too our perception of society is 'coloured' by the corporate lens. As more people wear corporate spectacles, as those who wear them become more important, and as we wear them for longer, our view of the world changes to a much more corporate orientated, materialistic one. It is a kind of indoctrination by implication, no less insidious because it often acts imperceptibly by an exclusion of information which it deems to be unimportant or secondary.

It is part of the very nature of humanity that there should be an intrinsic conflict between materialistic and spiritual and social values. However, in the past it has only been religious values which have been institutionalised, from Egyptian god kings to the Christian church. Through the corporation materialism has been institutionalised. For the first time in history there is a powerful entity which proselytises the importance of profit to the exclusion of other considerations.

It has become increasingly clear to politicians that the economic and material well-being of the electorate is the single most important factor in getting governments elected. There are, of course many other issues that are debated, but a government which gets elected when the economy is doing badly wins against the odds. "It's the economy, Stupid" was one of the key slogans of the 1992 Presidential election campaign of Bill Clinton, and continues to resonate today. The dominance of the Conservative Party in UK politics for much of the 20th Century owes a great deal to its pragmatic focus on economic issues, and it is notable that the current Labour government in the UK has made the 'prudent' running of the economy a touchstone of its success.

Companies have thus created a triangle of influence; the corporate structure and process provides a powerful framework for the propagation of materialism, the agenda of governments and political parties is heavily affected by this, and therefore the influence of companies over political parties and the understanding of their interests is increased. Governments also increasingly look to use companies to implement government policy, or to act as partners with government in achieving policy goals (e.g. the use of the Private Finance Initiative in the UK where companies effectively act as an arm of government in running prisons, hospitals and schools). These three influences of companies mutually reinforce the way in which the corporate structure shapes our society.

Since politicians have a limited number of hours in the days during which they can be influenced, it follows that if companies have an increasing influence over government, this must be at the expense of the influence of others. Whatever their concerns for the environment, or of the less fortunate in society, their perception of the problem is likely to be increasingly framed by the interests of the corporate sector – how much will policies in these areas cost the economy, what will be the effect on business, and to what extent could or would the corporate sector be willing to carry such policies out.[187]

---

[187] This 'business interest' has become increasingly pervasive in shaping society's priorities and identity. After Wales obtained its own separate Assembly in 1999, after a gap of some 600 years, the Welsh Assembly petitioned the UK government to make 1st March, St. David's Day, (the equivalent of St. Patrick's Day in Ireland), a national holiday in Wales. The UK government refused to allow a national holiday in Wales, largely on the basis of disruption to business. It has continued its stance. In a debate in the House of Commons on the 2nd March 2005, the Under-Secretary of State for Wales said: "It is estimated that it would cost about £2 billion to have an additional bank holiday in the UK...if a case were presented to the Government based on a full consultation with

So embedded has the corporation become in our way of life that it has become increasingly difficult to imagine society without corporations; to an increasing extent human relationships are conducted through the medium of the corporation, and our actions are moulded accordingly. As corporations become larger, and continually seek to make themselves more efficient this disintermediation of direct human contact and its replacement of contact through companies reduces even further the richness of human relationships.

The requirements of corporations affect our everyday activities. The act of shopping in a supermarket is a far more 'sterile' activity from the point of view of human relationships than shopping at a local store where you know the shopkeeper. It is far less likely to act as a focus for the exchange of information in the community. Indeed part of its efficiency comes from reducing human contact to a minimum. In the same way call centres reduce the effective interaction of human beings. By reducing the 'service' to a very narrow item of knowledge they may well be replicating Adam Smith's famous pin factory approach in the service sector, but something is inevitably lost in the process. We become increasingly aware of being part of a mechanistic, rather than a human process; when the mechanism fails it results in a mixture of irritation, frustration and helplessness.

There is an increasing feeling of dealing with the monolithic, where 'the system' is not and cannot be responsive, except to pre-programmed requirements, and where flexibility is draining out of the system. The standardised convenience delivered by corporations is delivered at a price. In the same way that it is more difficult to change the course of an oil tanker than a dinghy, so it requires a massive amount of effort to change the direction of the large behemoths of the corporate world. In 1969 the then Canadian Prime Minister,

---

business and industry…and taking account of the full impact on the economy and our essential services – we would consider the matter." It is clear that the wishes of industry count for more than the wishes of the citizens.

Pierre Trudeau remarked that for Canada having the US as a neighbour was not always easy:

'Living next to you is in some ways like sleeping with an elephant. No matter how friendly and even-tempered is the beast, if I can call it that, one is affected by every twitch and grunt.' For individuals today this is increasingly the case with our relationships with companies; even if they were totally benign their overpowering influence and their increasing scale dwarfs us by comparison.'

In addition there is the underlying assumption that conformity is a rather more desirable attribute than diversity. Many companies make a virtue out of necessity by proclaiming their ability to cater to different tastes, and indeed for some companies their success is dependent on their ability to service requirements of those not met by other companies, but for business as a whole efficiency would be better served if human beings were more alike.

In the interests of production runs business would prefer it if our colour preference for cars was the same. How much easier it would be for latter day Henry Fords if we could be persuaded that the colour we wanted really was black. As companies globalise they have a great incentive to encourage people to want the products they produce already – if successful this strategy is likely to be far cheaper than designing for the new market and setting up new production lines for its different requirements.

Companies have a great interest through advertising to create markets for their products and to change people's aspirations and attitudes. Since they rely on ever growing markets – whether this is by increasing their own market share at the expense of others or by a growth in the market as a whole, they have an interest in encouraging materialism. Without a continuing increase in consumerism they are unlikely to meet their own financial targets. Companies are therefore not just in the position of being neutral players in the value systems of communities. Their self interest dictates that they are the high priests of consumerism; their purpose in life is not just to satisfy demand, but to create it.

The corporate quest for higher profits and larger scale has inevitably led to a drive for globalisation as companies grow and look for new markets. Their ability to seek out new sources of supply and demand and the comparatively low cost of energy making it possible to ship goods across the globe economically has meant that the supply chain has become ever more inter-dependent. Large global companies have been able to take advantage of the enormous differences of wealth that exist in the world. In some cases it has helped to diminish them, as in the case of the China, but the benefits of globalisation are considerably less discernible in Africa, and the bargaining power of the large corporations does not necessarily lead to fair trade. It has however led to a significant transfer of manufacturing skills from the developed world to the developing world, and an increased dependency in the developed world on products made at some considerable distance.

Sense and Sensibility

In a stable political environment such a dependency may purely be a question of comparative cost, but the British experience during the Second World War highlighted the vulnerability of countries which depend on long supply chains for many of the articles that they need for every day use. The developed world is becoming increasingly dependent on the developing world. This renders them more vulnerable to disruption of their supply lines, and increasingly vulnerable to economic pressure even in times of peace. The dispute in late 2005/early 2006 between Russia and the Ukraine about gas prices resulted in a diminution of gas supply to Europe, and a very substantial increase in the cost of gas, particularly in the UK. It was a timely reminder of the potential consequences of energy dependence and the fragility of purely market arrangements.

In a few decades time it is likely that the size of the Chinese economy, will be comparable with that of the United States[188]. Should China at any stage decide to attack Taiwan then the potential of the disruption of supplies to the United States and other countries of the developed world would be considerable. In those circumstances comparative cost advantages would not be the prime consideration.

According to Kevin Phillips in his book 'Wealth and Democracy'[189] in 2000 Taiwan made 39 per cent of the world's disk drives, 54 per cent of its monitors and 93 per cent of its scanners as well as 53 per cent of its laptops and 25 percent of the personal computers. Since that time a significant part of that production will undoubtedly have been relocated to China where costs are considerably cheaper. It seems increasingly surprising that as the power of China grows concern over the transfer of technology should be largely limited to sales of military equipment. It is said that the Venetians were rather more concerned in guarding the secret of their glass making process, hiring assassins to deal with any glass master who might have the temerity to leave the Republic to use his craft elsewhere. It would seem that modern day corporations take a more profligate attitude to the dispersion of technology – they are after all indifferent to which country acquires it as long as their legal rights are secure. But the populations whose skill base advantages are being rapidly eroded cannot afford to be so sanguine.

However, by expanding the interdependence of the world economies corporations are also making the world increasingly vulnerable to systemic economic collapse. Not since the early decades of the last century, when international trade looked to the gold standard to facilitate international commerce have the major economies of the world been so interlinked. The Great Depression which spread its tentacles around the globe as a result of the collapse of the American

---

[188] Shortly after 2040 according to Goldman Sachs economist, Jim O'Neill

[189] p. 289

stock market, firstly in 1929, and subsequently to even lower levels in the early 1930's showed the downside of globalisation. Following that time the social dislocation in Europe and elsewhere reduced the international trading ties, and after the Second World War there were numerous constraints on the free movement of money and goods. Not until the Thatcher government of 1979 was exchange control abolished in the United Kingdom, allowing the pound to float freely against other currencies.

Perhaps the many economic actors in the world economy can be compared to grains of sand. If a great weight were to drop on part of the sand pile, a large number of the grains would be dislodged and displaced, but the shock of the impact would be absorbed without a great deal of damage to the vast majority of grains. However if these grains were fused by the miracle of technology into a sheet of glass, and the same weight dropped, the brittleness of the system would result in damage far removed from the point of impact. It is undoubtedly the case that with its many qualities, glass is a far more useful substance than sand, but it is also far more vulnerable.

In the same way we are creating a world trading system of marvellous sophistication and complexity, but also of greater inter-connectedness and fragility. The world economic system is becoming increasingly vulnerable as advanced countries become increasingly vulnerable to disruption of their supplies. The knowledge of self sufficiency of previous generations is being forgotten. Fewer and fewer people in the advanced countries are involved in essential industries. Our vulnerability to disruption of the corporate supply chain has increased greatly as a result of low transport costs enabling supply chains to become considerably lengthened and dependency increased on distant countries.

In the early 1970s the United Kingdom lost huge numbers of elm trees to Dutch elm disease. The impact of the fungus responsible (*Ophiostoma ulmi*) is rampant, because the elm tree is essentially sterile and propagates by sending out shoots or suckers. In this way, once a tree is infected, because it is often connected to a great many other trees, the potential for the fungus to affect other trees is exceptionally high. We are creating societies which are more vulnerable than they have ever been to systemic collapse. It is no part of the mission of companies to concern themselves with long term systemic collapse – they seek to influence governments to do this on their behalf and expect that the costs will be borne elsewhere. Companies merely calculate the risk reward ratio for possible political outcomes on their profitability.

A Tempting Prospect

Companies quite naturally seek low cost countries. A number of the countries which have newly joined the European Union have created low tax regimes to attract businesses. There is a new trend to so-called flat tax where the income, corporation and value added taxes are all harmonised at a single low rate. From a company's point of view it is an extremely desirable situation when countries compete on tax. The success of the Irish economy in becoming one of the most prosperous in the European Union from being one of the poorest is owed in part to its low rate of corporation tax, and its generally attractive fiscal treatment of certain kinds of businesses.

Tax subsidies and penalties have long existed to reflect countries' wishes in respect of what industries they wish to encourage, and which to discourage. However there is a substantial and entirely understandable temptation when countries belong to the same trading block, such as the European Union, for countries to use fiscal advantages to overcome their disadvantages, such as distance from market, lower technical proficiency and less developed infrastructure. This is particularly the case when so many other areas of policy may be decided elsewhere. To the extent that companies can bid one country against another for fiscal gain there will undoubtedly be an increasing shift of power from the state to the corporate sector. Whatever their sovereign status, governments bent on increasing their economic growth rates must take full account of the wishes of business as well as of their electorate and frame their fiscal legislation accordingly.

The tension between the profit motive and other considerations has long been evident in the health service. Corporations involved in providing health care whether to a nationalised health service, as in the UK, or in the context of a largely private health system as in the US quite properly wish to make a profit. However one of the key ways in which profitability can be improved in other sectors – reducing costs – is clearly fraught with difficulty. This is also true in respect of increasing productivity. Higher patient 'turnover' at the expense of clinical need is a constant temptation in a profit driven environment. Patients expect a tailor-made, bespoke medical service. The medical companies want to deliver a standardised high volume product. In addition it is worth noting that it is not enough for such a company to be profitable; it has to compete for funds in the marketplace with other companies in other sectors which do not labour under the same constraints. Its shareholders will put their money elsewhere if they can receive a higher return.

This same tension between the profit motive, and values which require judgement and considerations which cannot be translated into money is increasingly evident in the law as well. The United Kingdom is currently considering whether to allow legal practices to incorporate. This, of course, is highly likely to be disastrous in the long term. Solicitors and barristers in the United Kingdom are officers of the High Court of Justice and their obligations lie to the law and the professional standard of their calling. They are asked to make judgements about what is right, not only in respect of whether something is lawful, but also in respect of their clients' best interests. The law is not a business, and its main aim is not to make a profit; at its highest, the law should be the implementation of the principles of justice. There is little doubt that throughout the centuries it has often fallen far short of this aspiration, but as Browning said "Ah, but a man's reach should exceed his grasp. Or what's a heaven for?" Before its repeal in the 1967 Criminal Law Act, there was a common law offence of champerty under English law. It was both a crime and a tort for an unrelated third party to have a monetary interest in the outcome of a case. As Lord Denning explained it in *Trepca Mines Ltd (No.2)* [1963] 1 Ch 199 at p.219:

> "The reason why the common law condemns champerty is because of the abuses to which it may give rise. The common law fears that the champertous maintainer might be tempted, for his own personal gain, to inflame the damages, to suppress evidence, or even to suborn witnesses. These fears may be exaggerated, but, be that so or not, the law for centuries had declared champerty to be unlawful, and we cannot do otherwise than enforce the law; and I may observe that it has received statutory support, in the case of solicitors, in section 65 of the Solicitors Act 1957."

The law, as noted above, has now changed (it was also changed in Australia in the mid 1990s), and lawyers can now look to contingency fees to fund cases in the same way that they do in the United States. It is of course the case that allowing lawyers to base their fees on the outcome of a case enables less well off litigants to bring claims that, in the absence of state legal support, they would be unable to bring. However, as Lord Denning pointed out, for centuries the law feared lawyers having a pecuniary interest in the outcome of a case, and the degree to which objectivity and the duty to the court might be undermined. Likewise if lawyers are allowed to become companies and have their shares owned by the public, either directly or indirectly, they will inevitably face conflicts of interest. If a firm of lawyers is involved in a particularly large case where there is a large contingency fee and the outcome will affect their earnings, there will undoubtedly be important additional pressures on the lawyers conducting the case.

As another Master of the Rolls, Lord Phillips, remarked[190]:

"The greater the share of the spoils that the provider of legal services will receive, the greater the temptation to stray from the path of rectitude."

We are seriously in danger of becoming a society of cynics in the Wildean sense, knowing the price of everything and the value of nothing. This is perfectly in tune with corporate behaviour which does not concern itself with values (except to the extent that these are brought in by individuals) but with profits. As Anthony Sampson wrote:

"The respect now shown for wealth and money making rather than for professional conduct and moral values has been the most fundamental change in Britain over four decades."[191]

Whichever way one turns in modern society one can see the change in behaviour brought about by the influence of the corporate framework. The way in which we view the world has been changed; the way in which we act in a corporate setting is often different from the way in which we act as individuals. The mission of companies is to constantly minimise costs and increase profits in order to maximise returns to their shareholders. It is therefore entirely natural that they should want to shoulder the minimum number of their social obligations, since these, with few exceptions, result in additional costs for the company. These costs which are passed on by companies are sometimes referred to as 'externalities' in that they externalise the cost to the company of conducting what ever business they are in. However a reduction of cost for the company does not mean that it disappears, it merely means that the cost is shifted to society as a whole thereby increasing the profits for the shareholders.

---

[190] R. (Factortame) v. Secretary of State for Transport in 2002 [2002] EWCA Civ 932

[191] Anthony Sampson, Who Runs this Place? The Anatomy of Britain in the 21st Century, p.348

It is undoubtedly true that some companies provide jobs and opportunities where none existed before. However the question arises of whether such jobs and opportunities could not have been provided by non-corporate forms of business endeavour, or by corporate entities with different characteristics. The nineteenth century created an explosion of technological progress, but for large parts of the economy this was not done through the large, quoted corporate form. There was a tremendous growth in railways, steel and energy in the United States, but even in the United Kingdom many metalworking and coal and steel businesses were in smaller family companies rather than the larger conglomerates of the US and Germany. We should not therefore confuse business and trade with companies. It is still an open question as to whether the use of the corporate vehicle, convenient though it is, has resulted in a net benefit to society as a whole given its unique focus on financial outcome.

There is constant pressure in modern western society to consume more and more. People are inundated with requests to borrow by the banks, and to spend, spend, spend by innumerable adverts. It is hardly surprising that personal indebtedness is increasing and that personal savings are trending downwards. Although when economic conditions are tough individual consumers will save more and spend less, as a matter of necessity, notwithstanding the many blandishments to which they are subject, the question is whether there is a secular trend over a number of economic cycles towards greater indebtedness by consumers faced with this onslaught of the profit making imperative. In the last ten years or so the net savings ratio in both the US and the UK has come down to a level of about 1%, from a level of about 8% in the early 1990's. There is much to suggest a long term ratcheting up of spending at the expense of savings.[192]

---

[192] Report 239 of Smithers & Co. Ltd, April 2005, "The UK and the US have the same problems. (perception is skewed by data presentation.)".

Much less in evidence is the degree to which human beings in their role as producers suffer in order to provide for human beings as consumers and the degree of overlap between the two. At its most basic the 24 hour a day, seven days a week opening convenience of a hypermarket means longer or more inconvenient working hours for those who staff the stores. The fact that such stores seem suitable to their customers' lifestyles indicates also an increasing trend towards 24 hour seven day working. At a time when the Western world has never been as wealthy as it is today, how is it possible that increasing numbers of people are required to work in a way that is so detrimental to their health, and quite contrary to their biological clocks?

Companies are having a direct impact on the social values of the society they exist in, and often crowd out other values a result of being able to quantify more clearly the financial benefits of a proposed course of action, whereas the social costs are much less easy to quantify, are more diffuse, often evolve over a much longer period of time (and therefore are less of a priority) and are borne by a much wider number of proponents with differing agendas.

The flexibility of Anglo Saxon companies in respect of their workforces is little more than a cost transfer mechanism. The costs that they do not fully absorb internally have to be dealt with elsewhere within society. Historically this was the case for environmental damage. It is still the case for workforce reduction/relocation. It is, of course the case, depending on their economic circumstances, that companies will have no choice on occasion but to reduce their workforces, or otherwise go out of business, but it is also true that many of the decisions in respect of the workforce are made much easier because the company does not have to bear the full cost of the consequences. There is no equivalent of 'double entry accounting' between the corporate sphere and the social sphere.

The influence of the company assails us from all sides. Corporates are hard-wired by their corporate goals to be very hard-nosed about their attitudes. Their world does not revolve around people, but around profits, and they are gradually re-shaping the world around their agendas. Behaviour which in people would be reprehensible has somehow become acceptable in companies, and bit by bit they are seeking to change the attitudes and activities of human beings, not only inside companies but in society at large to meet their profit goal more effectively. What was a means to an end has become the sole goal of companies, and increasingly the key concern of the developed world.

Diminishing Returns

The corporate world is not a sustainable model for competition. It is, in fact, a form of systemic suicide. Companies are involved in ensuring the destruction of the system which provides their justification. If we assume that competition is a good thing and should be encouraged, then it is inevitably the case that some competitors will do well and some will do badly. In a stable system at a given point in time, or over a short period of time, this may well result in a satisfactory outcome. But over a long period of time there will emerge a number of dominant players who have the resources to overwhelm the competition. They can use their financial strength to destroy existing and would be competitors.

If we examine the world of Adam Smith it is clear that the market which he knew and envisaged is far from the situation in which we find ourselves today. Corporates are the 'accumulators' par excellence, and have consequently grown mightily since Smith's time. Since they are not imbued with any morality, and have but the one goal of profit, it is inevitable that they should seek to dominate markets in their quest to maximise profits. Monopoly is a far more congenial environment for the maximisation of profits than competition. Indeed monopoly has been a travelling companion to joint stock companies since their earliest days. Commercial companies in England were first permitted only when the perils of the market were such that a joint enterprise alone could meet the need, and the uncertainties so great that the grant of a monopoly required in order to raise the necessary capital. The East India Company was typical of this type of company, and for two hundred years and more after its foundation monopoly was considered a natural, if by no means automatic, attribute of a company. They are just returning to their roots.

Whilst competition may result in the market itself growing in the longer term, and thereby increasing a company's profits, in the shorter term competition acts to depress prices, and hence profit margins. Competition, and the hidden hand of the market may be desirable for society but it is a burden to be borne by companies. While society may strive to maintain the market, companies seek to dominate it, with the ultimate goal of monopoly. As Smith remarked 'People of the same trade seldom meet together, even for merriment and diversion, but the conversation ends in a conspiracy against the publick or in some contrivance to raise prices".[193]

As the number of market participants becomes fewer, as for example, in the case of the British supermarkets, the idea of the invisible hand becomes more and more difficult to sustain. On the contrary the relevant price comparisons become easier and easier the fewer participants there are. The potential for new market entrants of sufficient size becomes less and less, while the least competitive of the larger supermarkets becomes increasingly susceptible to takeover or going out of business. Anti trust legislation or similar measures are necessary to curb successful corporates' destruction of the market mechanism which they find so irksome.

Yet anti-trust legislation is manifestly failing as a means of controlling corporate expansion. The importance of size has become a mantra, scale is everything, and the politicians are reversing the protections of the earlier part of the last century,

---

[193] Adam Smith. The Wealth of Nations p.129, Book 1, chapter x, p.129 Oxford World Classics

as Eric Schlosser pointed out in his book 'Fast Food Nation'[194].

The Sherman Antitrust Act was passed in 1890, but was ineffective in the meatpacking industry so that by 1917 the five largest meatpacking companies, Armour, Swift, Morris, Wilson and Cudahy controlled about 55% of the market. Schlosser commented:

"In 1917 President Woodrow Wilson ordered the Federal Trade Commission to investigate the industry. The FTC inquiry concluded that the five major meatpacking firms had secretly fixed prices for years, had colluded to divide up markets, and had shared livestock information to guarantee that ranchers received the lowest possible price for their cattle. Afraid that an antitrust trial might end with an unfavourable verdict, the five meatpacking companies signed a consent decree in 1920 that forced them to sell off their stockyards, retail meat stores, railway interests and livestock journals....

For the next fifty years, ranchers sold their cattle in a relatively competitive marketplace. In 1970 the top four meatpacking firms slaughtered only 21% of the nation's cattle. A decade later the Reagan administration allowed these firms to merge and combine without fear of antitrust enforcement. Today the top four meatpacking firms – ConAgra, IBP, Excel, and national Beef – slaughter about 84 percent of the nation's cattle. Market concentration in the beef industry is now at the highest level since record keeping began in the early twentieth century."

The various anti-trust and anti-monopoly legal provisions are necessary, because corporate growth by its very nature is not self-regulating. It is a cancerous growth that will continue to grow at an accelerating pace until it overwhelms the organisms hosting it and kills them. The vigour of

---

[194] p. 136-9

corporations is not in doubt, but the ability to control these growth patterns is very much open to question.

There have been a number of ways in which companies have been able to mask the cancerous nature of their growth

- They have been able to redefine the market in which they operate, so that Tesco, the UK supermarket has been able to buy its way into the convenience store market, because the UK competition authorities have decided that this is a different market from selling food in a supermarket, where they already have over 30% of the market, nearly double that of their nearest rival Asda, a subsidiary of Walmart[195]. This means that Tesco have been able to buy up chains of small local neighbourhood shops and convert them to the Tesco format, and increase their market share even further through acquisition in a way that would not have been possible if the food market had been considered as a single market.

- Companies have expanded their geographical coverage as the restrictions on doing business in other countries have reduced. As companies have met constraints in their own domestic markets they have expanded their activities into other areas (for example food supermarkets moving into clothing retailing and pharmaceuticals) and into different geographical areas, creating large multinationals.

Not content with organic growth many large companies are continually engaged in looking at merger and acquisition targets. The fact that there is a great deal of evidence to show that as often as not mergers are undertaken at prices which destroy value in the acquiring company seems to have done little to reduce their attraction. It may well be that the appeal of a bigger and bigger empire to a chief executive may

---

[195] See article by Elizabeth Rigby, Financial Times 21st September 2005.

outweigh an objective analysis of the value of the company to be acquired. The result of both organic growth and merger and acquisition activity has resulted in a very substantial increase in the size of companies as outlined earlier.

In 1976 Anthony Sampson wrote a book about the global oil industry called "The Seven Sisters: the Great Oil Companies and the World They Made" about seven very large oil companies – Exxon, Shell, BP, Socal (Chevron), Mobil, Texaco and Gulf. Since that time the seven sisters have been reduced to four, with Gulf Oil and Texaco going to Chevron, and Mobil to Exxon. Further amalgamations, both by those companies and others, such as the merger of Total with Elf and Fina, have created an even smaller number of larger oil companies. Of course the opening up of Russia, China and India has created new opportunities, introduced further potential competitors and expanded the geographical market, but we are rapidly approaching the endgame when there will be no new geographical markets to aim at, and the large incumbents will slug it out between themselves until either there is only one company left or they carve up the world in a cosy oligopoly where competition has no real meaning.

In 2001 GlaxoWellcome merged with SmithKlineBeecham to become GlaxoSmithKline the largest pharmaceutical company in the world at the time. The merger was described in the Guardian newspaper as follows:

> "There were times not long ago that drug companies were merely the size of nations. Now, after a frenzied two-year period of pharmaceutical mega-mergers, they are behemoths, which outweigh entire continents. The combined worth of the world's top five drug companies is twice the combined GNP of all sub-Saharan Africa and their influence on the rules of world trade is many times stronger because they can bring their wealth to bear directly on the levers of western power."[196]

---

[196] Guardian, 26/06/2001

This surge of gigantism continues in virtually all industries, from steel to cars, from banking to brewing. Even the professions, such as the legal and accounting firms have become enormous, and have become increasingly like corporates in their structure. Their size has made them more autocratic and despite the absence of shareholders, it seems that their professionalism is vulnerable as never before to goals of profitability, as the fall of Arthur Anderson, entangled with Enron, so clearly illustrated.

A Question of Sport

Yet this impact of companies on competition has not gone unremarked. On the contrary, it appears that the American sporting world is clearly not wholly convinced of the merits of unalloyed market forces in producing, if one may use the term, a level playing field ensuring long term competition. The National Football League (and Major League Baseball) in the United States is organised on completely different lines from those which apply to the various European football (soccer) leagues. This difference in approach has been the subject of a very interesting paper.[197] The following extract from the introduction encapsulates the distinction:

"Introduction

'All schemes used in the United States punish excellence in one way or another. The European football approach punishes failure by promoting excellent minor league teams to the majors and demoting (relegating) poor performing major league teams back down to the minors. The revenue loss from a potential demotion to a lower class of play is severe punishment for low quality - severe enough that salary treaties, league sharing arrangements, and unified player

---

[197] Produced by Luigi Buzzacchi, of the University of Turin, and Stefan Szymanski and Tommaso M. Valletti of Imperial College London, "Equality of opportunity and equality of outcome: open leagues, closed leagues and Competitive Balance".

drafts are so far thought to be unnecessary, even though star salaries are enormous. It is an interesting economic question as to which system achieves better results.' *Rosen and Sanderson (2001)*

Since Superbowl I in 1967 the NFL has expanded from a league of 16 teams to one of 32. During this period seventeen different franchises have won the Superbowl. In Serie A, the top division of Italian soccer, 48 different teams have participated since 1967, but there have been only 11 different winners. Serie A has had more teams not because it is a larger league - in most seasons only 18 teams compete for the championship title. However, the institution of promotion and relegation permits new teams to enter the league each year. Nonetheless, despite having more competitors, fewer teams seem to have a chance of winning - less than a quarter of the teams in Serie A over the period have won, compared to half of the current NFL franchises. Moreover, a similar story emerges if any of the North American leagues are compared to the national soccer leagues of Europe. In other words, soccer leagues tend to be much less balanced than the major leagues. However, this is not true when measured in the way that has been conventionally adopted in the sports literature. This paper proposes a way of measuring competitive balance that permits comparison between the North American closed leagues and the open leagues of Europe."

One of their conclusions (p.12) was that 'despite the greater opportunity through promotion and relegation for teams to reach the highest rank, there seems to be relatively less turnover at the very top in open European leagues than in the closed North American leagues. 'On average over the last thirty years there have been 50% more teams achieving the highest rank in North America [as] compared [with] Europe.'

A table contained in the research highlighting the difference between the American and European approaches is provided in Appendix II. Continued competition over a period of years is a vital consideration to maintain the support of the fans, and indeed the sustained existence of sport as part of the entertainment industry. America, that bastion of corporate instincts, has clearly decided that untrammelled commercial competition is not the best way to achieve and sustain this goal. In 1922 the Supreme Court granted major league Baseball an exemption from anti-trust laws, thereby sanctioning this approach at the highest level.

It remains to be seen whether the less structured approach of relegation and promotion in Europe remains unaffected. Whereas fifty years ago the European soccer leagues were more balanced than their American counterparts (i.e. there was greater variety in the winning teams), the research shows an increasing tendency for a more limited number of teams to occupy the top spot in Europe. It remains to be seen how popular football will remain if there are only one or two teams who have any reasonable chance of winning national leagues. It is likely that fans will be asked to look at Europe wide competitions for their excitement, as the clubs, like other corporates, find their home market too small.

As mentioned in other chapters democracy is an historical peculiarity, and by diminishing the sphere within which democracy is applied we risk the system as a whole. The increase of scale is perhaps leading us to a "democracy" of corporates – i.e. revisiting the notions of neo-corporatism and sidelining real democracy.

An education in itself

There are social changes associated with the increase in very large employers. The number of independent business people is probably on the wane, and the degree of their independence is less. Many of the professionals, such as doctors and lawyers who used to work in smaller practices are now working in larger ones. The size of firms of solicitors seems to get ever larger, and in the large City of London firms further and further away from what might be described as anything resembling the original concept of a partnership.

Even barristers' chambers are amalgamating and becoming larger. Doctors' practices in the United Kingdom are becoming larger. Accounting practices have already become global. The relationships that people had with their professional adviser are now becoming more and more relationships with the institution, with the people becoming interchangeable. In short people are becoming commoditised, which is what corporations crave. Even though professionals do not necessarily work in a corporate structure, the way in which they work has increasingly been moulded by the mind set and priorities of the corporate world.

This supposedly independent class of people is being decimated by the encroachment of corpocracy, or perhaps to put it another way they are being recruited to its cause. As more and more of their number are now employees of corporations, or reliant on corporate customers their interests are becoming increasingly bound up with those of companies. The pool of potential dissent to current trends is drying up.

The very class therefore which in the nineteenth century was seminal in producing the demand for democracy in its own interests is now being increasingly neutered, as are the academic institutions whose primary function is the pursuit of knowledge and understanding regardless of profit. Whether in the agricultural, manufacturing or service industries there is an increasing tendency towards large scale enterprises, where individual independence, except when focussed on making more money, is generally not prized. Large organisations of any sort tend to value uniformity.

It has been suggested that the advent of the internet and the world wide web would be a great force for liberalisation and freedom of expression, with individuals being empowered by the web. Such hopes are misplaced. Although information can be turned into knowledge, and knowledge is a vital component of power, history teaches us that it is the aggregation of knowledge that is critical in establishing control.

In addition the web is not only a powerful tool for disseminating information, it is also an excellent place for disseminating disinformation. The web encyclopaedia Wikipedia has constantly to guard against contributors providing wrong information in its articles. Doubtless, many of these are well intentioned errors, but the quandary highlights the fact that the information sources on the web are not sifted. It would be possible to mount a disinformation campaign on the web relatively easily. A concerted infiltration of the relevant blog sites and manipulation of the Google algorithm system so that multiple cross-referencing web sites were boosted up the priority list could well achieve the equivalent of urban myth and uncertainty, without traceability. If companies like the marketing firm Big Fat referred to earlier are willing to plant stories by using actors pretending to be normal people there is no reason to suppose that companies will not be willing to subvert the information on the internet to achieve a commercial advantage.

It should not be supposed that anonymity on the internet is a level playing field. Where sufficient pressure has been applied the operators of the system have been willing to provide the information requested, or to remove the offending facility.

Up until now this pressure has been governmental. For example in April 2005 Shi Tao, a journalist working for a Chinese newspaper, was sentenced to 10 years in prison for "providing state secrets to foreign entities". He had passed details of a censorship order to the Asia Democracy Forum and the website Democracy News. He had posted these details using an anonymous Yahoo! Account.

The pressure group Reporters Without Borders (RSF) obtained a translation of the verdict, and found the answer. Mr. Tao's account information was "furnished by Yahoo Holdings". Yahoo!, the document says, gave the government his telephone number and the address of his office.

George Monbiot reported this in September 2005.[198] In his article he aptly quoted from Thomas Friedman's book The Lexus and the Olive Tree in which Friedman argues that two great democratising forces - global communications and global finance - will sweep away any regime which is not open, transparent and democratic. "Thanks to satellite dishes, the internet and television," he asserts, "we can now see through, hear through and look through almost every conceivable wall. ... no one owns the internet, it is totally decentralised, no one can turn it off ... China's going to have a free press."

It is greatly to be doubted that global finance is a democratising force – international bankers are hardly noted for their political radicalism, nor are the institutions they work for. As for international communications, the Chinese experience shows that they can be controlled. Perhaps not as effectively as shutting down newspapers, but they are not quite the democratising influence that they have been painted by Friedman and others.

It is not just in undemocratic China that the authorities seek to control the internet. There is a website of independent media called Indymedia.com. On the 7th October 2004 it issued a press release which started:

"Thursday morning, US authorities issued a federal order to Rackspace ordering them to hand over Indymedia web servers to the requesting agency. Rackspace, which provides hosting services for more that 20 Indymedia sites at its London facility, complied and turned over the requested servers, effectively removing those sites from the internet.

Since the subpoena was issued to Rackspace and not to Indymedia, the reasons for this action are still unknown to Indymedia. Talking to Indymedia volunteers, Rackspace stated that "they cannot provide Indymedia with any information regarding the order." ISPs [Internet Service

---

[198] The Guardian, 13th September 2005

Providers] have received gag orders in similar situations which prevent them from updating the concerned parties on what is happening.

It is unclear to Indymedia how and why a server that is outside the US jurisdiction can be seized by US authorities."

So even democratic governments can and do interfere with the functioning of the web. The influence of advertisers will also be crucial. Much web content is free because the business model is based on advertising income. If the major advertisers do not like the content of a website they can withdraw their advertising. A subtle and pernicious system of self censorship is one possible outcome – a very different position from the liberating effects claimed for the internet.

It is rather the large corporations and the large governments who are likely to capture and control the usage of the web over the long term. They will be able to aggregate the information available and sift it, manipulate it and ensure which parts of it receive the greatest prominence. In August 2005 The Justice Department of the United States served Yahoo!, AOL and Microsoft with subpoenas, requiring them to release information in respect of URL [Uniform resource Locators –essentially website addresses] and also search queries. They complied with the request.

Google also received the subpoena and chose to contest it. Whatever the outcome of the case, it demonstrates that huge new databases or people's behaviour are being created. Google, whose motto is famously 'Do no evil' may appear to be fighting intrusive government in this case. However the fact remains that it is the company which has the information, and the government which is trying to obtain it. Whatever the virtues of the company's founders, what possible long term guarantee can there be as to how the company chooses to use its data? To whom is it answerable? Perhaps in the future, shareholders will claim that the company will be doing evil unless it exploits its database to maximise profit. Compilation of such huge quantities of data, some of it no doubt sensitive, puts enormous potential power in the hands of those who control it.

Even in its daily operation the services provided by the internet further the process of turning people into commodities. Shopping in a supermarket is a more impersonal experience than shopping in a local shop. But shopping on the internet is even more so. It is often impossible to ask the questions you want to ask – only certain questions will be understood and catered for. Very often there isn't even the option to speak to someone at a call centre if there is a problem, however far away they may be. Emails can be generated from a supplier from an email address to which it is impossible to reply. If the system works well it can be extremely efficient, but when it works badly, there is little ability to complain or explain the circumstances.

The system is also open to fraud. A website which billed itself as "The UK's best source for digital video equipment" was shut down by US authorities, for the simple reason that although it purported to be in the UK and offered a London-based 0207 phone number, calls were routed through to a call centre abroad. In reality the site was owned and run out of Waltham, Massachusetts by a company called Nepco.[199]

Even the increasing amount of legitimate shopping by internet, whatever its advantages, is a more impersonal (and often frustrating) activity than going to the supermarket, and demands even greater uniformity of the customer base. In such a system human beings as individuals are a commercial nuisance.

In almost every area the concept of independence is being lost. Since aggregation of knowledge is one of the key building blocks of power it might be supposed that universities could provide a counterweight to the influence of corporations and government. But even in universities,

---

[199] See article in The Guardian 'Closure leaves thousands out of pocket' by Miles Brignall, 21st January 2006.

supposedly bastions of free thinking, more and more of their activities are being reviewed on the basis of not whether they are excellent in themselves, but the degree to which they provide economic growth. These trends are not new – they were recognised in the 1986 BBC series 'A very peculiar practice', based on the experiences of the Welsh screen writer Andrew Davies at the University of Warwick. The degree to which commercial funding is now an integral part of much university research is only one facet of the way in which corporations and the corporate organisational model have 'infiltrated' so many parts of life, but it has significant implications.

The influence of corporations begs the question of what universities are for, it also tends to distort what subjects are studied, and what areas within particular subjects are studied (there will be an inevitable bias in financially stretched universities to focus on those areas where there is additional funding coming from outside sources). The increased reliance on endowments, doubtless with some strings attached, will further determine which subjects are studied. In the UK, this is further amplified by the degree to which government funding of universities is dependent to a considerable extent on research excellence.

There is also a growing question mark about the independence of the research work done at universities. This can be of particularly great concern where such independent expertise is required for regulatory purposes in such areas as health.[200].

---

[200] In 'Captive State' for example, George Monbiot wrote "The person responsible for reviewing the data on rBST for the FDA was a researcher called Suzanne Sechen. Before joining the Food and Drug Administration, she was a graduate student at Cornell University supervised by a consultant for Monsanto called Dr. Dale Bauman....In 1987 she left Cornell to work full time for the FDA, where she reviewed her own Monsanto-funded data on rBST, as well as that of her ex-supervisor, Dr. Bauman, p.239

There are millions of people who are self employed in the UK, but the nature of their self employment has changed over the years. There are, I suspect fewer people who are, and always have been, self-employed, and increasingly more people who have worked for a larger organisation, and then have decided, either by choice or necessity to 'go it alone'. It may well be that the British equivalent of the German 'Mittelstand' is eroding rapidly. In the past many middle sized businesses were both rooted to a particular locality and interdependent with other businesses of a comparable size, so that they created a business and social fabric of a locality. This created a business community, with its own interests, and sense of identity. The new pattern, I believe, is more of a hub and spoke arrangement with smaller businesses servicing much larger businesses, like cleaner fish providing hygiene services for sharks, being grateful that they are not being gobbled up. The arrangements are very one sided – such as those with supermarkets and suppliers commented on earlier, and such businesses are increasingly separated from a business community. To what extent can a small 'independent' supplier speak out and voice opinions which may be offensive to his large client? Self censorship and self-preservation are the far more likely result.

This should not surprise us. The company is a feudal decision making structure, and it will result in feudal forms of behaviour. The behaviour of a small businessman towards a large corporation is no different in essence than the behaviour of a small tenant farmer to a large landowner. In that unfortunate but telling American phrase 'When you've got them by the balls their hearts and minds will surely follow'.

So not only is the corporation changing our society and damaging the democratic process from the outside by exerting pressure on elected representatives, and dangling the carrots and brandishing the sticks it deems appropriate, but it is also undermining the economic independence of a part of society which played a pivotal role in the expansion of democracy.

The rise in scale of corporations has led them to globalisation, as they seek increasingly larger markets for their products or services. It is arguable that the World Trade Organisation is at least as important a body as the United Nations, and certainly its transformation from the General Agreement on Tariffs and Trade illustrates the way in which has become increasingly important, a fact not lost on many non governmental organisations and protest movements.

So companies have had a tremendous impact on our lives – their priorities frame our action, our thinking and our opportunities. They guide our objectives and stifle our objections. Our lives revolve around them and not vice-versa. They are callous, cold and calculating as well as commercial. So have they transformed our society? What kind of society do we live in now under their influence?

Chapter VI

The way we live now

What have we done?

Capitalism was seen as the victor at the fall of communism, but it is doubtful whether this can necessarily be said to be good for democracy. Whatever the theoretical underpinnings of the Marxist view of the world, in the Soviet Union capital and the state were merged into one. Decisions were taken by the few and the system praised democracy in principle while denying it in practice. Economic and political power were combined together in one entity and the opportunity of the ordinary citizen to change policy, or even to have a different view, was sharply curtailed to the point of vanishing.

In the era of the giant corporation it is difficult to see a great deal of difference between the position of an employee in a large multi-national, and that in a communist state. The rewards go to the few; loyalty, not dissent, is required, the internal arrangements of the company are decided by the board who are not answerable to the employees, and the only remedy is to leave the company, if the employee wants to escape this de-humanising and stifling embrace.

However, it is not always possible to escape easily. There may be few other comparable jobs around in the area. In the consumerist society which companies have done so much to encourage there may be crippling debt to act as a chain to the workplace. The type of work may be the sort usually carried out in large corporations, with the result that an escape from one dispiriting environment only leads to entering another.

This is not to say that people who run companies are intrinsically mean or nasty. Companies are however a framework for unfairness, and their sole goal of profit, irrespective of any other motivation, is one which all but the most callous executives would be ashamed to own up to as individuals. Yet it is the mechanism of the large corporation that is being lauded by governments, as they try to reduce still further the impediments to the globalisation of corporate activity.

We cherish the virtues of a democratic society lightly at our peril. Perhaps because the current generation has grown up at a time which has been more democratic than any other in history, we have come, like Francis Fukuyama, to assume the normality, indeed the inevitability of the triumph of democracy. We fail to see that behind the façade of elections and elected government power is drifting away. Government is about nothing if it is not about power. The focused energy and resources of the corporates are everywhere wearing down the ill-organised and diffuse influence of the public on governments. The power of decision making by corporates is in the ascendant, that by governments is on the wane.

The solution to this concern, the erection of bulwarks against the unconscionable aggregation of power is by no means an easy one, but it must be sought in returning to first principles and in reviewing the way in which the values which society treasures (whatever they may be and however they may change) are provided with a mechanism so that they are reflected in the life of society as a whole.

If we accept that democracy is the best way in which societies can make decisions, and that a democracy functions best when the disparity of wealth and power between participants in society is as small as possible, then it follows that it is not in our democratic interest to have very large corporations. As an ultimate goal therefore the reduction of the size of corporations, who are participants in our society is one which is highly desirable.[201]

---

[201] E.F. Schumacher in his seminal book 'Small is Beautiful, a study of economics as if people mattered', Abacus 1974, pointed out the dehumanising influence of scale, and the unsustainability of modern growth expectations.

What is the definition of 'market' and the invisible hand of Adam Smith? A market might be thought of as a collective noun, and implying some large number – but it is as defensible to describe four dominant players as a market, as it is to describe four birds or sheep as a flock, or four cows as a herd. In English the differentiation should be made between the words 'less' and 'fewer'. The former to be used when looking at a substance or countless objects and the latter when looking at a countable number of objects – hence less butter or sugar, but fewer peas or potatoes. Similarly, we could say that there is less of a market, but fewer companies. The problem today is that there are now so few companies in certain areas that it is impossible to maintain that distinction, or realistically believe that there is any real sense of market in the way in which Smith conceived it. This is not a new phenomenon, but we are in denial if we pretend that we are, in any real sense, talking about a market when looking at the operations of companies in a range of different activities, where there are a small number of dominant players. We continue to use a vocabulary that described a different reality.

Heilbroner speculates that the reason the discipline of economics had not really developed before Adam Smith's time was that there was no market system as such,[202] just a series of markets, and it is arguable that in many areas there is equally no market system today.

The current situation is coming increasingly to resemble that of feudal times. Then the mass of the people did not count; it was merely the landed classes that were of importance and who had some say in decision making. Now we have corporate overlords rather than physical ones. It is the major players who decide on policy, and the role of government is becoming more and more comparable to the role of middle management, an implementer of policies decided elsewhere.

Elections in both the United Kingdom and the United States have been increasingly about the economy, and which party

---

[202] 'The Worldly Philosophers' pages 27-29

will deliver the greatest economic benefits, rather than being fought on fundamentally different views of society. It is perfectly true that different parties have different nostrums as to how to achieve this, and different views as to where the benefits will lie, but the goal espoused by the major political parties is that of good stewardship of the economy in order to achieve ever higher standards of living. It is equally true that policies relating to health, education etc. figure prominently in election campaigns, but the leitmotiv behind them is that the economy will keep growing while these other policies are delivered. A government can make many mistakes in office as long as the economy is run successfully, but if the economy is weak it will have to do spectacularly well in other areas in order to avoid falling. The major actors in this economic drama are, of course, not individual voters, but companies, large and small; they are the natural constituents of a government focused on economic performance. The companies are both the instruments and bellwether of the economy and governments ignore them at their peril.

The political and social landscape of today is therefore becoming more and more a system of what one might describe as 'corporate feudalism', or corporatism for short, and the system of government a corpocracy. However this nascent system is, if anything, more pernicious than its mediaeval predecessor. It knows little of 'noblesse oblige', and as an artificial legal construct it is even more remote. Although the aristocracy of the Middle Ages was often bloodthirsty and cruel, it nevertheless subscribed to certain ideals, of Christianity and of courtly love. Even though these were customs more honoured in the breach than in the observance, they nevertheless formed the backdrop against which their actions were judged, and indeed how they saw themselves. They were also mortal; evil men as well as good were killed in battle, and this vulnerability doubtless increased their sensibility to the teachings of the Church.

The modern corporate, like the church, is perpetual. It does not die, unless its very essence, money, is not there to sustain it. Money is its lifeblood; it can survive without employees, albeit in a dormant form, but it cannot survive without money. This is the defining feature of what gives it life. Like the mediaeval church it also has a mission in life; unlike the church, this mission is not to save souls, or to better mankind's condition, but to make a profit. As long as something is legal, then it is irrelevant how a company goes about its business of maximising profit. Indeed, even if an act is illegal, then if the cost of breaking the law is less than the profit gained by so doing then the corporate may well seek to break the law, as we have seen.

The modern corporate feudal baron therefore is subject to fewer qualms even than his mediaeval precursors, and in addition swears no oath of allegiance to his lord. On the contrary this corporate baron is constantly seeking ways to escape governmental jurisdiction, whether legal or fiscal, eager to gain and retain the maximum amount of money for the minimum amount of regulation, irrespective of the consequences.

This growth in corpocracy, the rule by corporates, is as insidious as it is wide spread. It is acknowledged that corporates are out of control, that they twist and distort the way in which human beings interact with one another. However there seems to be no clear indication that the democratic mechanisms of society are capable of stemming this trend, much less reversing it.

In fact what we are seeing is the gradual transformation of the political sphere by the business sphere. Through the construction of this type of corporate vehicle we have not only created a management structure which owes nothing to ideas of democracy but we have institutionalised amorality. The sole obligation of the company is to render the maximum amount of profit to its shareholders. No company has any business to be involved in any kind of charitable activity, or expenditure of any kind on anything which will not maximise the profitability of the company long term.

It can therefore be no surprise that since this is the unique mission of the enterprise type for which so many people work, and since their future prospects and livelihoods depend so heavily on achieving this corporate goal the cultural norms and niceties which govern behaviour in society at large are curtailed or jettisoned in its pursuit. It is for the shareholders once they have received their dividend to decide to which charity, if any, to donate the excess profits of the enterprise. It is not for the board of directors to make such decisions on their behalf. Indeed unless they are able to show that such donations improve the company's standing in the community to such an extent that the company will make more money in the foreseeable future then they are doing nothing more than taking the shareholders' money and giving it away – veritable Robin Hoods perhaps, but thieves nonetheless. As Milton Friedman put it:

"A corporation is the property of its stockholders. Its interests are the interests of its stockholders. Now, beyond that should it spend the stockholders' money for purposes which it regards as socially responsible but which it cannot connect to its bottom line? The answer I would say is no."

Friedman is absolutely right. We have straight-jacketed the corporate structure so that socially responsible actions are corporately irresponsible. Charitable giving by companies can only really be justified as good public relations, with the expectation that the company's reputation will be so enhanced that it will make more money than it would otherwise have done.

It is therefore palpably hypocritical for companies to pretend to a corporate mission – they have only one – which is to maximise shareholder value. It is for this reason that so many corporate mission statements ring so hollow, since after every aspiration should be included in brackets the caveat '(as long as it makes money)'. It may well be open to individual entrepreneurs to state that it is a poor business that only exists to make money (although presumably entrepreneurial bankers such as the Rothschilds might venture to disagree), but within the corporate structure all other values are set at naught. It is the ability to make money which is the sole purpose for encapsulating any enterprise in a corporate cloak.

There is, of course another reason why such corporate mission statements ring false – they are a misdescription from the start – since the corporate structure is an inanimate artifice to produce profits any additional motives to justify existence can only come from the human beings which give it life. Any corporate mission statement which appears is generally nothing more than the product of the wish of the Chairman or Managing Director or the board of directors to voice their own opinions of what the company is about, but if his or their opinions change or they themselves are replaced so too can the mission statement.

The directors, it is clear, cannot have a mission statement that is different from the mission with which they have been entrusted by the shareholders.

They can, at best, elaborate the way in which they intend to make money for the company, but apart from stating aspirations of the most bland and obvious sort, such as they wish to be the best, it is difficult to understand how such a statement could contain anything that was not already understood and needed no saying in the first place. Thus it is that even with such small commonplaces as corporate mission statements the disparity between what is said and what is meant, by what are announced as the guiding principles and the code by which a company actually works is often great enough to create an instant sense of cynicism. It is one thing for companies to be run on a hypocritical basis, but it is another when this is flaunted in writing, and employees expected to acknowledge what is at best an irrelevance and at worst a downright lie.

However the mission statement does highlight the pernicious tendency of the corporate system to seek out a value system where it has none. The purpose of a mission statement after all is really to get the employees to work more effectively than they would otherwise do, for no material reward, and perhaps for the customers and potential customers to regard the company in a better light than they otherwise would, and thereby use its services when they might be tempted to go elsewhere. All this to achieve a higher profit than would otherwise be the case.

However since a company has no values of its own these values have to be imported on a job lot basis from the outside, depending on the preferences of the senior management and no doubt after contemplation of their likely effect on their target audience.

The role of a modern day company can be compared with that of the Roman Catholic Church in Mediaeval Europe, although it works the other way round; the Church erected an institution around a set of beliefs, the modern day company imports beliefs into an already existing institution. It does so, however, not in any way to propagate a coherent set of beliefs designed to benefit mankind, but for narrow commercial advantage, for what company would propose a mission statement which would have an adverse impact on its profitability? It is a supposedly meritocratic structure, male dominated, where those who have risen to higher ranks expect loyalty and obedience from those below to achieve the goal of the organisation. Democracy, except at the very highest levels (whether boardroom or conclave of Cardinals), is an alien concept.

In the commercial world therefore we inhabit a space which is an intentional moral vacuum, and like a vacuum it sucks into itself the values that are imposed on it by the legal framework in which it operates together with those considered to be most expedient by senior management. By definition the values that the senior management hold will derive from value systems outside the corporate structure, but they will be imported through the lens of commercial acceptability and be subordinate to the requirements of profitability.

The values of those who have worked long enough and successfully enough in the corporate environment will naturally have been shaped by it, and it is probable that the degree to which their initial outlook when entering the corporate world was aligned with the existing corporate goals will have assisted their rise to senior management.

It is therefore necessarily the case that the corporate world tends to distort and subordinate the values which are drawn into its sphere, and tends to encourage people who subscribe to the amoral goal of corporate success. It is true, of course, that it acts within a legal sphere, where regulation and legislation may require the company to maintain certain standards, e.g. in respect of reporting requirements, but if a company is obliged to obey the letter of the law it knows little or nothing of the spirit of the law. Indeed, where this is possible it may seek out a different jurisdiction where the laws are less onerous in order to increase its potential of making money. In the Financial Times' review of 'Hardball' mentioned elsewhere it is pointed out that according to the authors of the book the only social responsibility of business is to be successful 'within the rules of the game', and this is not an unfair comment given the legal framework within which a company operates.

As a result the corporate culture has two significant impacts – not only does it reduce the standards of behaviour in society at large, since corporations are large and important players, but it also corrodes the values of those working in a corporate environment.

Incorporating Citizens

These problems stem from the very nature of the corporate vehicle itself. On the whole the way in which the corporate model can be adapted to fit the notions of modern democracy have been rather limited. As discussed earlier, corporates are societies in their own right. In human terms (as opposed to economic), the only way in which we can understand them as societies is if we look at them as a group of people working together for a common purpose. In order to be effective in their purpose they have to raise money. At this point if the group of people incorporate and raise equity they grant control over their own affairs to a third party – the shareholder. If they borrow money from a bank, although the bank has an important say in how they conduct their affairs ultimately it is up to them to ensure how they are going to repay the bank its money. The relationship is a contractual one, not that of master and servant. The question remains, by what special alchemy does the raising of share capital necessarily deprive a group of people working together control over their own affairs?

If we were to take the corporate analogy further, if we were to look at government, acting on behalf of a society working together, in what circumstance might it issue shares in e.g. Great Britain PLC, as opposed to merely government securities in the form of gilts or other instruments in order to secure its financial future at the expense of its liberty? Up until now no government, as far as I am aware, has reckoned that this is a price worth paying, nor, it has to be said, is there an investment market out there to take the risks. But we have the example of Huaxi in China to prove that this is by no means as fanciful as it might seem.

Huaxi in China is known as 'China's richest village'; the village (which has become a township of 60,000, partly by taking over other villages nearby) has become a quasi corporation. Huaxi Village in Jiangyin County, Jiangsu Province, has fixed assets of 3 billion yuan (US$362 million). Home to 58 village-owned businesses, Huaxi was expected to generate 10 billion yuan (US$1.2 billion) in sales revenue for the year 2003. The members of the village all have large houses, and are very wealthy by Chinese standards, with annual salaries of some $6,000, although they receive only about 20% of this in cash, the rest being withheld to invest in village enterprises.

The reverse side of the 'miracle' is that the villagers are only wealthy as long as they stay in the village – as soon as they leave, their shares in the village, their house and car are forfeit. Also their lives are geared to the requirements of enterprise – the bars and restaurants shut at 10 pm to ensure fitness for work in the morning, and the villagers are not allowed to talk to outsiders. There is no night life and individual enterprise is not allowed. Non villagers also work in the village, but for a fraction of the salaries.

This is not to suggest that the Huaxi model is necessarily replicable or even sustainable. However it is not unique. The so-called 'mini-constitution' of Hong Kong concedes[203] a long term goal of universal suffrage. However the actual voting method provided by Annexe II is that 30 of the 60 seats in its legislative council will be chosen not by universal suffrage, but by 'functional constituencies'.[204] This of course includes important business interests, and the concept is very close to the way in which the UK parliament functioned prior to the Great Reform Act, and reflects concepts of neo-corporatism which were popular in fascist Italy.

Lest it should be thought that such ideas are geographically and historically distant however, the idea has taken root closer to home. Unlike their modern day counterparts the ancient guilds of merchants of the City of London, although based on mutual self interest, were self-governing and were far more imbued with non-commercial values. They were connected

---

[203] Article 68, Clauses 2 and 3 provide that: "2) The method for forming the Legislative Council shall be specified in the light of the actual situation in the Hong Kong Special Administrative Region and in accordance with the principle of gradual and orderly progress. The ultimate aim is the election of all the members of the Legislative Council by universal suffrage. 3) The specific method for forming the Legislative Council and its procedures for voting on bills and motions are prescribed in Annex II: "Method for the Formation of the Legislative Council of the Hong Kong Special Administrative Region
and Its Voting Procedures".
http://www.oefre.unibe.ch/law/icl/hk00000_.html
[204] Hong Kong constitution, Annexe II, Section 1, http://www.oefre.unibe.ch/law/icl/hk02000_.html

with local churches, and were aware of their social and charitable obligations. It is therefore a remarkable irony that in the dying throes of historical anomaly, and to preserve the utterly artificial entity that is the City of London (i.e. the historic business district, rather than London as a whole)[205] corporations have now been given the right to vote for members of the Common Council (the governing body of the City of London) – a right that is both repugnant to a democracy and potentially pernicious in its effect. Under the new provisions for elections in the City of London:

"any eligible incorporated or unincorporated body can now appoint one or more individuals to vote as long as it physically occupies premises within the City to carry out its activities."

This means that businesses can now appoint individuals to vote for Members of the Court of Common Council to represent them directly within the decision-making forum of the Corporation. When they do vote it will be as an individual – just like in any ordinary election[206], but they will be the mere ciphers in the corporate interest. The development of the legal corporate personality will be virtually complete.

This takes the legal nature of a corporation to new heights of absurdity. In a parody of the BBC's mission statement this is

---

[205] The Corporation of the City of London is a municipal corporation (i.e. a corporation in its non-commercial pre nineteenth century sense) responsible for the historic business quarter of London, sometimes referred to as 'The Square Mile'. Its survival is a historic hangover from the days when many people lived as well as worked in the City of London (Sir Thomas More (1478-1535) for example the Chancellor to Henry VIII was brought up in Milk Street in the City of London. People elected in the 25 wards of the City of London are elected to the Court of Common Council, which is the governing body of the Corporation of the City of London.

[206] From the booklet 'A new vote for your city' published by the Corporation of London

a situation where 'corporation shall speak profit unto corporation'.[207] It is scarcely imaginable if this principle, that companies should be given the vote, were applied across western democracies as a whole what the outcome would be. It would be the most amazingly successful parasitic implant through which the forms of democracy could be retained, but behind the democratic façade power would be exercised elsewhere. It should be borne in mind that the City of London is by no means a mere minor anachronism. Although only about 7,000 people live there over 300,000 people work in the City of London in some of the most highly paid jobs available on the planet. The rateable values per square foot of the properties of the City of London (i.e. their property value calculated for the purpose of local tax) are some of the highest in the UK. The distribution of all this wealth is not subject to effective democratic control, but by business interests. It is as if the mayor of New York were to be deprived of the property taxes for the Wall Street district of Manhattan, and their control given to the business interests located there instead. The City of London is busy opening representative offices in Beijing and Shanghai, having already established an office in Brussels. The move of many banks to Canary Wharf, outside the City of London, may highlight in the future the difference between the municipal functions of the City of London and its role as a businessmen's club for the financial services industry paid for out of local property taxes. At the moment, however, the City of London is effectively strengthening its non-democratic position.

These modern day constitutional arrangements show the great similarities between corporate society and the wider community, the great degree of overlap, and the whittling away of the fundamental tenets of the democratic principle. It presents in microcosm what the rise of corpocracy is tending to create, how society is being transformed by the requirements of the corporate good rather than vice-versa. It presents in stark relief the end point of a materialistic society.

---

[207] The BBC's crest carries as its motto "Nation shall speak peace unto nation", although it is not formally part of its coat of arms.

The leader of the Huanxi village until recently, Wu Renbao, talks of what constitutes happiness: 'car, house, money, child and respect' (which could almost be a slogan for the New Labour Party in Britain). He has now made way for one of his sons to follow in his footsteps, the latter receiving 100% of the votes. One is reminded of the Aesop fable of the dog and the wolf – the latter preferring his more uncertain life to that of the dog, who though well fed is chained up during the day, the better to carry out his guard duties at night, the motto of the tale being – 'better lean freedom than fat slavery'.
The greater the extent to which the interests of the company dominate society, the greater the extent to which the non monetary values of society are excluded. The ideal corporate state is not very different from the ideal communist state: it desires conformity, it craves monopoly and the exclusion of competition, it dislikes dissent and it is intolerant to values which are irrelevant to, or in opposition to, the profit motive. Huaxi stands as a warning of the kind of society we are in the process of creating and the kind of priorities that we are adopting.

Some of the most powerful institutions in western society are entirely based on maximising profit, and such human values that are acknowledged on a day to day basis, whether as a legal requirement, or as part of the natural interchange between employees are effective not because of the corporate structure, but despite it. Companies are amoral organisations, but that does not mean that they do not carry implicit value judgements within their structure. The very focus on profit maximisation is in itself anathema to many strands of religious thought, as repugnant to the basic tenets of the Christian faith as it is to Islam.

It is not difficult to understand how the peoples of less developed countries must feel in terms of the onslaught of the corporate model; their governments are far less capable of providing the protection against corporate rapacity that is available in the West, their institutions less developed to protect individual and community rights. As Joseph Stiglitz has pointed out in his book, 'Globalisation and its discontents'[208] very often they are subject to economic nostrums, imposed upon them by organisations such as the IMF (International Monetary Fund) against their will at times of crisis in their economies, with governments being put into the impossible position of being accountable to a population for policies to which they do not subscribe and which can cause considerable hardship. In such circumstances belief in democracy is understandably weakened and its base undermined, as populations in those countries regard their governments as increasingly irrelevant and themselves as victims of colonialism carried on in the economic sphere.

The question thus arises of for whose benefit these actions are taken. On whose behalf are organisations such as the IMF acting? Few in the developing world would say it is in their interests. On the contrary these are policies imposed upon them. It is also difficult to see the benefit to the states or the citizens of the developed world. Multinational corporations and banks however do benefit from such policies. They are in the front line of economic dislocation, and it is their profits that are most nearly affected by market instability. They are also the ones most likely to benefit from the billions of public money provided for rescue operations, particularly if state assets have to be privatised as part of the IMF 'medicine'.

Even for a country with an economy as large as the UK, the markets are master of at least part of its destiny, as the devaluation of sterling as it fell out of the European exchange rate mechanism clearly demonstrated.[209] The deregulation of the markets has by definition reduced their accountability. On

---

[208] Published by Penguin in 2002. The theme pervades much of the book, but see for example Chapter 4, The East Asia Crisis.

[209] The pound fell out of the Exchange Rate mechanism (ERM) on the 16th September 1992 a date which has come to be known variously as 'Black Wednesday' and 'White Wednesday', when international speculators sold the currency so ferociously that Norman Lamont announce an increase of interest rates first from 10-12%, and subsequently 15%p.a.in a Canute like attempt to stem the tide

the contrary governments through this mechanism have made themselves accountable to markets rather than vice-versa.

It can of course be argued that this is a good thing – that it results in greater efficiencies and therefore higher living standards for all, but it should be recognised that there is a very substantial price to be paid for such corporate freedoms – they come at the expense of individual freedoms. China has not been blind to the fact that the modern corporation has more in common with the command and control structure of a communist state than with the democratic ideal. Democratically elected governments find it far easier to promote the commercial interests of bras and Boeing than mention the dreaded 'D' word.[210]

China exemplifies how corporate capitalism can be achieved without multi party democracy. The Chinese government has realised that there is no necessary conflict between capitalism as currently constituted and authoritarianism. Political freedom is not a pre-requisite to economic efficiency. It is rather the reverse; the wealth created by economic efficiency may give rise not only to a greater demand for consumer goods, but also for social goods, such as greater political freedoms, one of the last needs in Maslow's pyramid of self actualisation.[211] It is from the greater education of a

---

[210] The final abolition of quotas under the MultiFibre Agreement in January 2005 led to a surge of exports of Chinese textiles to the European Union and the United States to the detriment of both their own garment industries and those of some developing countries. This resulted in emergency measures being introduced to stem the flood of imports. The United States' discussions with China focused on trade in garments and sales of aircraft; more 'D' cupracy than democracy.

[211] Abraham Maslow (1908-1970) established a theory of a hierarchy of needs. He argued that certain lower needs had to be satisfied (such as the need for food and shelter), before higher needs such as (in ascending order) the need for safety, the need for love/belonging, the need for self esteem and finally the need for

workforce required by a competitive economy and the contact with export markets with a different political philosophy that the danger to authoritarianism comes, not from the use of the corporate model.

The justification for all this is of course that companies are efficient, and it is implicitly assumed that the only way in which this efficiency can be achieved is through the current corporate legal framework. It also, of course, begs the question, of what all this efficiency is ultimately intended to achieve; whether there is some end in sight or whether it is supposed to lead to greater and greater consumerism where choice of consumer products will be widened and deepened to an ever larger market as living standards rise. In this scenario it is presumably an unwritten assumption that this increase in human consumption will result in an increase in human satisfaction, indeed in human happiness.

The long term viability of the human race, or indeed of the planet, is of little concern to the immortal corporation, for whom ironically short term considerations are far more important than longer term ones. It is clear to all that in the long term this growth driven approach is unsustainable, but the bold decisions for change are constantly deferred.

The consequences of corporate action are all around us, and their focus on immediate return for shareholders has caused us to squander our natural patrimony. Even in the eighteenth century Thomas Paine in his pamphlet on Agrarian Justice acknowledged the revolution in agriculture as compared with hunting and gathering – a comparison that was doubtless very real to him given his time in America. Even given the agricultural techniques of those days he supposed that agriculture could support a population of some 10 times that of hunting and gathering in an equivalent area.

---

self-actualisation – which can be viewed as the need to fulfil one's perceived potential.

What we fail to acknowledge in our own times, however, is that for our requirements of energy and minerals we are still in the hunter gatherer stage of evolution. Indeed the situation is far worse than that, since the animal and vegetable worlds can renew themselves in a timescale that is meaningful to human beings. The inert resources that we are using up have taken many millions of years to form, in the case of energy, and are the product of a one off series of events in the case of the metals which we use. In view of these timescales the arguments as to whether the world could run out of oil in 50 or 100 years time are astonishing in their myopia[212]. We are squandering our natural inheritance at an extraordinary rate, and the profligacy of our actions will result in the disinheritance of posterity. This process has been substantially accelerated by the mechanism of the corporation. The concept of handing an inheritance to a successor generation is an alien concept to a theoretically immortal entity. Growth is favoured far above stability until dominance is achieved.

---

[212] The speed with which we are using up our oil resources was explained very clearly in an article in The Guardian, April 21st 2005 by John Vidal. Although estimates vary enormously, and many are deliberately enlarged or reduced for a particular audience, he quotes one expert (Colin Campbell) as saying: "About 944bn barrels of oil has so far been extracted, some 764bn remains extractable in known fields, or reserves, and a further 142bn of reserves are classed as 'yet-to-find', meaning what oil is expected to be discovered. If this is so, then the overall oil peak arrives next year." Vidal continues: "If he is correct, then global oil production can be expected to decline steadily at about 2-3% a year, the cost of everything from travel, heating, agriculture, trade, and anything made of plastic rises. And the scramble to control oil resources intensifies. As one US analyst said this week: "Just kiss your lifestyle goodbye."

Muddying the waters

Whereas from Victorian times until quite recently the actions of companies may have polluted rivers and created slagheaps, their scale is now so vast that their activities threaten the wellbeing of the entire planet. The rapacity of the corporate sector for energy is such that in the UK nuclear energy is again being looked at as a potentially serious source of power even though the colossal government and private investment of many tens of billions of pounds in UK nuclear power has resulted in a commercially unviable industry, and industrial waste that will remain dangerous far longer than recorded human history to date.

The way in which companies make workers redundant today is analogous to the environmental pollution of the 19th and 20th centuries. An important cost factor of the production process was left for society to bear, and consequently distorted the real cost of production. In modern society the ease with which workers may be fired results in society – through unemployment benefit in those countries that can afford it or through more extreme individual privation in those countries where such a safety net is more limited or non existent – bearing costs that are created by the company. In the same way much of the after-cost of physically demanding labour is met through disability benefit.

Joseph Stiglitz pointed out his impression of South Korean employers who seemed far more aware of the social compact between them and their workforce and the obligation on them to continue employing them even through bad times[213]. The lifetime employment concept in post war Japanese labour practices also recognised this important obligation of the company. It is this very distinction of course which has made Japanese companies appear to be very different animals compared to their Western counterparts. They are overtly not run solely, or possibly even mainly, for the benefit of their

---

[213] 'Globalization and its discontents', Chapter 3, Freedom to choose?

shareholders, but this has far more to do with the social milieu in which they operate rather than the legal framework within which they function. In particular profit has not been the sole driver of their goals. Market share and perfection of the product and the production system have received rather higher priorities. This approach has served the Japanese well in the manufacturing sector, although significantly less so in the case of banks where, in the absence of significant potential to increase productivity, pursuit of market share took such a toll on profitability.

The British industrial revolution also had paternalists, such as Robert Owen and George Cadbury. New Lanark and Bourneville were perhaps not so terribly different from the all embracing facilities provided by a number of Japanese companies, although, of course, far less wide spread as a phenomenon.

Such approaches are however followed in spite of, not as a result of, the corporate framework, and are dependent on the management of the companies continuing to subscribe to social values which the corporate framework tends to inhibit. Corporate management similar to that of the Japanese may be regarded as less flexible, but it is wrong to assume that Anglo-Saxon style flexibility for companies is beneficial for society as a whole just because it may be beneficial to certain companies, or indeed companies generally. Such flexibility should be considered as a cost transfer mechanism – from company to society at a rate which currently favours the company.

A World Apart

The growing difference between managerial salaries and that of the workforce is merely a recognition of the balance of power within the corporate structure, and the growing influence of the corporation on society as a whole. The new managerial aristocracy, like daleks, have gained vast new powers by encasing themselves in a near impregnable structure. The company is a modern day Land of Oz, where behind an impressive façade skulk rather ineffectual wizards whose apparent omniscience and omnipotence is provided by the paraphernalia of power. When the corporate veil is stripped away what is revealed is the disappointing sight of a merely ordinary mortal operating a machine producing special effects; the magic has proved to be illusory on many previous occasions when managers of previously successful companies have been caught unawares as market or circumstances have moved against them.

Derek Higgs in his report to the Chancellor and the Secretary of State for Trade and Industry in 2003[214] started his letter to them attaching the report with Bagehot's famous quotation of 1867 about the British Monarchy "We must not let in daylight upon magic". But the magic that Higgs was concerned about was that of non-executive directors, and the way in which they could make the board more accountable to the shareholders for the successful running of the company.[215]

This approach to corporate governance does not concern itself with the wider social implications of corporate activity. The

---

[214] Review of the role and effectiveness of non-executive directors, Derek Higgs, 2003.
http://www.dti.gov.uk/cld/non_exec_review/pdfs/higgsreport.pdf
[215] The goal that Higgs was trying to achieve is set out in his proposed amendment to the Corporate Code, as typified by this extract: **"The role of the board.** The board is collectively responsible for promoting the success of the company by directing and supervising the company's affairs. The board's role is to provide entrepreneurial leadership of the company within a framework of prudent and effective controls which enable risk to be assessed and managed. The board should set the company's strategic aims, ensure that the necessary financial and human resources are in place for the company to meet its objectives, and review management performance. The board should set the company's values and standards and ensure that its obligations to its shareholders and others are understood and met." (Suggested Code principle A.1 and provision A.1.1).

inherent structural flaws of the current corporate form underline the way in which attempts at effective corporate governance without a radical change in the way companies are structured is doomed to failure. The management are not answerable to shareholders for being socially responsible – they are answerable to them for profit.

The lack of accountability of management is but a symptom of a wider malaise within the body corporate of its decision making mechanism. The attempt to remedy this problem through the use of e.g. non-executive directors is doomed to failure. While they may start as independent, to what extent can they remain so? Is it realistic to expect them to turn to the shareholders when there are serious differences of opinion? Of course this may happen from time to time, and will depend to some extent on the strength of character of the directors involved, but this is anecdotal exceptionalism, not systemic robustness.

It is difficult to understand the underlying philosophical rationale of a system based on a part time director, with less understanding of the business than a full time director, acting as an effective deterrent against anything but the most blatant misconduct. On the contrary, such non-executive directors are being asked in some ways to be spies for the shareholders – on the basis that the shareholders need someone to keep an eye on the executive directors on their behalf. Yet such directors are equally supposed to participate in board meetings and the strategic decision making of the company.[216]

It must be the case that the meetings that the directors have with one another, and the need to work together satisfactorily will tend to militate against them doing their job wholly satisfactorily. Indeed even when an outside person is appointed to safeguard the interests of the shareholders in the

---

[216] See for example the Higgs Report, Paragraph 6.6: "The role of the non-executive director is therefore both to support executives in their leadership of the business and to monitor and supervise their conduct."

shape of the auditor the requirements of forming a good working relationship and the temptations available through earning fees for other types of work, or even the pressure to retain their role as auditors, create the permanent potential for the erosion of probity.

In addition the selection mechanism of non-executive directors will mean that they are likely to be known to executive directors, and that the incumbent directors will not want non-executives who are wholly unsympathetic to the way in which the company carries on its business, and the mindset of the existing management. Naturally these attitudes may change over time, and greater familiarity, as the adage has it, does not necessarily breed greater respect.

Nevertheless the system relies a great deal on mutual regulation by people who are likely to know well, and may be friends of, the people they are overseeing. In addition they themselves will often be senior executives in their own companies, and their behaviour will necessarily be shaped to a degree by their own views as to the way they expect non-executive directors to behave in their own companies. As a system of probity it is largely self-referential, except to the extent legal rules have to be observed.

Indeed the pool from which non-executive directors will be drawn will be largely and not unreasonably senior executives of other companies. Their own careers will have been shaped by the single minded pursuit of profit, and they will, by definition, have been successful in achieving the corporate goals set for them.

Both executive and non-executive directors will want to ensure that they are adequately rewarded for their efforts. It requires a curious view of human nature to believe that those executives who have been successful in reaching a senior position, (which will necessarily have required a successful application of attributes of self-advancement), will be slow in ensuring their own personal gain at the same time as the profits of the company.

Achieving appointment as an executive director at a company will have no doubt depended to some extent on a person identifying with corporate priorities. Indeed, as pointed out above, companies are constantly on the look-out to externalise costs to increase the bottom line, irrespective (absent legal restraint) of where those costs will lie. It is unsurprising that on a personal level directors should seek to do the same thing for themselves, in relation to the company, as they do on behalf of the company in respect of society at large. It is rational for them to seek to ensure their remuneration package is as divorced from the performance of the company as possible on the downside, whilst maximising it on the upside. They are merely applying the corporate approach to their own personal circumstances, and externalising the cost of their failure to the shareholders. It is entirely logical that they should seek to do this, and to run companies in a way that will achieve the best results for their remuneration package. Non-executive directors will frequently be or have been executive directors at other corporations and are therefore likely to be of a similar mindset.

Of course there will always be exceptions, but the actions of non-executive directors and their remuneration are likely to depend far more on their relative bargaining position than some innate and lofty feeling of shareholder service. After all, it is difficult to see why such executives should act differently as non-executive directors in the board rooms of other companies.

A Most Ingenious Paradox

In the UK system, one could perhaps draw an analogy between non-executive directors and the present day House of Lords. The non-hereditary peers are appointed for their expertise, and scrutinise the work of the House of Commons. However the system is inherently unstable, given the fact that appointments by the government of the day are bound to be biased. The very factor which provides the peers with their independence, the fact that they are virtually unsackable once appointed, is also the factor which lays the system open to so much criticism. Although the peers may be answerable to the people in some vague way this is not true in any meaningful sense, and can result in tremendous tension between the House of Commons and the House of Lords, whenever there is a difference of view, and the inevitable complaint of the lack of democratic legitimacy of the House of Lords is raised.

The current attempts to reform the House of Lords are therefore exceptionally futile. Since the current House of Lords has no raison d'être, it is impossible to decide who should be represented there. It has, of course, acquired an important role in reviewing legislation, as a sort of glorified constitutional consultancy, but that does not constitute legitimacy. It is the appendix of British democracy – an appendage with no apparent function, which may occasionally become inflamed causing considerable discomfort to the body politic; in extremis, and without proper attention it could prove fatal. It has increasingly been seen as a leading exemplar of power without responsibility, or at least accountability. No-one yet however has had the courage to perform a clean appendectomy.

If the original rationale for the House of Lords were to be replicated today then the chief executives of the largest companies, together with the partners of the most important legal and accounting firms would be members as of right. In a commercial age these are people whose opinions the government cannot afford to ignore, and yet there is no mechanism for them to provide their expertise in an open and transparent forum, where their advice and opinions have to be balanced alongside those of their peers and with the competing interests of the non commercial part of society.

It is true that there are a number of people who have been appointed to the House of Lords with expertise in various fields, but the method of appointment is neither clear nor transparent, is not limited to appointing those with expertise in a certain field, is subject to political bias, and results in those appointed being able to remain long after their expertise may have become outdated.

It would therefore be more logical by far that a coherent framework be drawn up of the most important institutions in the country and their chief executives or equivalent appointed ex-officio. This could include not only chief executives of companies, but heads of trade unions, those in charge of the major hospitals etc. They would clearly have limited time to spend in the House of Lords given their other commitments, but whether the attendance record would be better or worse than the current House of Lords would perhaps be a moot point. Those appointed would no doubt make themselves available when their particular area of expertise was being debated and they would also have the resources available within their organisation to investigate the implications of the legislation sent to them by the House of Commons, increasing the potential for improved scrutiny of Parliamentary Bills. They would have the additional advantage of not being beholden to the government of the day, and therefore fully capable of advancing their own opinions.

In addition, when the Chief Executives were replaced by their successors they would cease to be entitled to sit in the Upper Chamber. Since the great nobles of yesteryear held their land until death, and it then passed, usually under entail, to the nearest male heir it made perfect sense for membership of the Upper House to reflect this. There would be no such imperatives with the corporate executive. Whereas the nobility represented the land which gave them their power, the executive represents the company which gives them theirs. For the chief executives occupying seats in the House of Lords it would in practice be the company, not the individual, which was being represented. In this way the Upper House would have representation from the most powerful people in the commercial community.

There is also the perception that the House of Commons is increasingly represented by people who are professional politicians – i.e. those who have done little or nothing in the world outside politics and who therefore represent nothing but the interests of themselves and their parties. The reconstitution of the Upper House in this way would also have the advantage of bringing back into parliament expertise which may be less available than once it was in the House of Commons.

This is not to say that such an approach should be advocated, merely that it would approximate much more closely to some of the less democratic antecedents of the parliamentary system, where the forum of debate and decision was much more closely aligned to where actual power lay. Such a system would not, of course, be democratic. It would in fact be a massive departure from the democratic process as such representatives would be appointed and not elected. It would however reflect the realities of power more accurately than the current system.

The example serves to highlight the fact that the maintenance of the political system as a purely democratic preserve may result in its being sidelined in terms of the real influence that it can bring to bear in society at large. It exposes the inconsistency between a political system which is democratic and espouses one set of values and a commercial system which is purportedly meritocratic and is driven by different priorities.

Such a system would not be terribly different from what has existed elsewhere in similar circumstances. Until the passage of the 17th Amendment in 1913 senators in the US Senate were not elected, but appointed by the legislatures of their respective states. In the era of the Robber Barons, the influence of money on such legislatures often resulted in wealthy men being appointed senators. In the Senate they could block legislation that they thought was contrary to their commercial interests. In his book 'Wealth and Democracy' Kevin Phillips lists 22 Senators who were multi millionaires in 1902-3, (even in the currency of that period with its vastly greater purchasing power).[217].

The connexion between wealth and the growth of democracy traced in this book should give us pause for thought. We claim a notional disconnection between power and wealth, but this flies in the face of the way power has moved between different parts of society. To pretend that wealth has no claims on power merely results in wealth using more circuitous routes to exercise its influence. Companies, which are the legal personification of wealth, inevitably seek to do the same.

It must surely be axiomatic that since one of the few curbs that exist on the power of large corporations is that of the legislative framework in which they operate, they will wish to influence it. If they cannot influence it in an overt way, then it has to be in a covert way. The trend in the United States of America towards a close relationship between the political parties and big business has been highlighted by Greg Palast in his book 'The Best Democracy Money Can Buy'. It is inevitable that this should happen, and to the extent that commercial power becomes greater and concentrated in fewer hands the more pernicious this influence is likely to become. Lord Acton's dictum in respect of the corruption of power applies as much in the commercial sphere as it does in the political one[218], perhaps even more so given the moral vacuum and the less transparent atmosphere in which companies operate.

As the electoral and financial demands of democracy become greater, the room for manoeuvre for politicians often becomes smaller, fearful as they are of upsetting any potential

---

[217] Kevin Phillips, Wealth and Democracy, p.240

[218] As Jefferson implied when he wrote: "No other depositories of power [but the people themselves] have ever yet been found, which did not end in converting to their own profit the earnings of those committed to their charge." --Thomas Jefferson to Samuel Kercheval, 1816. ME 15:71

constituency either geographical or sectoral, which may influence the outcome of an election. The transformation from being the leaders of people to being mirrors of perceived popular sentiment is likely to be accelerated by increased media exposure.

The corporate world has far fewer such burdens. For the larger corporates the control of their 'electorate' in the shape of their shareholders is far less effective. In only the most egregious of cases are their activities examined in any detail. They are therefore much freer to pursue their own agendas, and this gives them even greater influence. Only with massive parliamentary majorities does bravery return to the political world, but even then such bravery is often shaped by outside influences.

In a different context this difference was encapsulated by Fisher Ames, one of the leading thinkers of Revolutionary America, if we read 'corporation' for 'monarchy' and 'democracy' for 'republic':

"A monarchy is like a merchantman which sails well, but will sometimes strike on a rock and go to the bottom; a republic is a raft which will never sink, but then your feet are always in the water."[219]

So the rough road to democracy in the United Kingdom has brought another divergence between power and government. This gap between vested political power and actual economic power has set up considerable tensions in our societies, where the corporate power has no formal place in the political structure.

During the vast majority of the evolution of the United Kingdom parliament, it was the members of the House of Commons and House of Lords who gave it its power, not the other way around. The power they were able to exert was that of wealth. At the start of the twenty first century it is

---

[219] Speech to the House of Representatives 1795

increasingly clear that much real power has shifted outside government into the hands of those undemocratic creatures, the corporations.

The American system of corporate governance is even further removed from the principles which underpin its constitutional norms. The United States system is based on the principle of the separation of powers, i.e. the separation of government into the branches of the executive (the Presidency), the legislature (Congress) and the judiciary (the Supreme Court). The system creates a mechanism of checks and balances in the democratic sphere of governance, but no such counterweights exist in the corporate sphere. The rise in the importance of the corporate vehicle requires as much time and effort to examine its ultimate effect on society as that given by the American Founding Fathers when they debated the constitutional arrangements of the young United States. Indeed if they had given as much attention to the corporate constitution as they did to the national one, we would doubtless be in a very different situation today. The constitutional issues were debated at great length by Hamilton, Madison and Jay in the 85 'Federalist Papers' as well as by many others in a host of publications and correspondence. But the lurking dangers of the corporation were nothing but a side show, even though Thomas Jefferson was alive to the potential danger of monopolies[220]. At the Constitutional Convention of 1787 James Madison twice proposed putting the federal government in charge of corporations "in cases where the public good may require them and the authority of a single state may be incompetent."

---

[220] On Dec. 20, 1787, Jefferson wrote to James Madison about his concerns regarding the Constitution. He said, bluntly, that it was deficient in several areas. "I will now tell you what I do not like," he wrote. "First, the omission of a bill of rights, providing clearly, and without the aid of sophism, for freedom of religion, freedom of the press, protection against standing armies, restriction of monopolies, the eternal and unremitting force of the habeas corpus laws and trials by jury in all matters of fact triable by the laws of the land, and not by the laws of nations."

With the example of the East India Company as their guide many delegates were unwilling to authorise corporations at a national level, wishing to reserve such powers to the individual states. Corporations ultimately failed to feature in the US Constitution. Concern centred not on the nature of corporations but on the best method of controlling them. The concept of the modern corporation was scarcely a twinkle in an entrepreneur's eye at the time.

Despite the elaborate provisions of the Sarbanes-Oxley legislation[221], and the requirement of a majority of non-executive directors, only about one-fifth of companies separate out the functions of Chief Executive and Chairman, unlike in the UK where separation of these two positions is the norm. If the UK corporate republic is an oligarchy, the US equivalent is verging on a monarchy.

The German corporate model tries to resolve this issue of management accountability by having an independent supervisory board so that the two functions are kept distinct; a sort of corporate Senate or House of Lords, but even this is only a partial answer to the problem. Although there is employee involvement in certain aspects of the company's activities, the primacy of capital is still acknowledged and the voting system for the management is based on share ownership. In addition the basic function of the company is to make profits; the legislation is about protecting workers' rights rather than the underlying democratic principles in respect of corporates as a whole.

There is therefore this central dichotomy in respect of the way in which society's affairs can be conducted. The assumed

---

[221] The Sarbanes-Oxley Act of 2002 was the legislation introduced in the United States following the Enron and similar scandals. It has imposed considerable additional compliance requirements on companies in a number of areas, including the appointment and remuneration of audit committees, and has provisions dealing with the signing off of financial reports by CEOs and CFOs and also provides for severe penalties for the alteration of documents.

underpinnings of the current form of corporate capitalism are that capital is more important than labour and is the sole qualification for the ability to decide the ultimate control of a corporation. This despite the fact that Adam Smith in the Wealth of Nations[222] clearly underlined that labour was the primary source of production.

This viewpoint derives essentially from an aristocratic or oligarchic concept of society, at least in terms of sentiment – that control of a company should not be put into the hands of the ordinary employee, but should be carried out through a form of plutocracy - where decisions are made by the wealthy, or by those who control the wealth, such as the fund managers, who act as a kind of proxy plutocrat with no real and immediate responsibility to the diffuse investor base for the decisions which they purport to take on their behalf.

Of course, theory and practice are considerably different. Actual power is very largely in the hands of the management of a company. The senior management of the company have achieved their position through a mixture of talent, particularly commercial talent, aggressiveness, self advancement during their career and a slice of good luck. The diffuse nature of shareholder control gives considerable room for manoeuvre to directors to benefit from the exercise of these skills honed through many years. It is an advantage they will doubtless be loath to give up. Democracy on the other hand allocates the primacy of decision making to the individual members of society, whatever their wealth, and allows no role to wealth for decision making.

Corporate governance as commonly understood largely confines itself to the problem of making company management more accountable to the shareholders. There has been little attempt to review the principles underlying

---

[222] see Book I, Chapter V, e.g. 'Labour was the first price, the original purchase money that was paid for all things.' and '...labour be the real measure of the exchangeable value of all commodities '

the way in which companies govern themselves, and how this affects the wider community. On the contrary there are disturbing indications that in a world driven by materialistic priorities the corporate method of decision making is making increasing inroads into the democratic decision making process.

Chapter VII

Companionism

Can democracies control companies?

As the preceding chapters show, the way in which we have arrived at the decision making processes for companies has not either been a straight forward one, or, for much of the time, a particularly principled one. On the whole the United States, like the United Kingdom, has tended to value pragmatism over principle.

In essence for companies, as for societies, the central question is who makes what decisions, on what basis, and with what degree of accountability. There are many books which review the problems of corporate power, some of which have been quoted, but what appears much more elusive is a systemic approach to reform. In this respect those who wring their hands in recognising the manifest injustices of the system have not been able to propose a comprehensive solution that will displace those who, Pilate like, wash their hands of any responsibility for the effects of the modern corporate world.

Although we use the term corporate governance to refer to the way in which companies regulate themselves, it is insufficiently recognised that companies are societies with their own form of government. The board of directors is the executive and legislative rolled into one and the shareholders are the electorate, weighted as to wealth. The workforce are the subjects of this economic state. The Memorandum and Articles of Association (in the UK, or their equivalent elsewhere) are their constitution. It is immediately clear that the system provides few of the checks and balances that we have come to expect in modern constitutional arrangements. The diffuseness of the shareholding electorate and its disintermediation by agents further dilutes control of the executive. The information flow is often attenuated in the name of commercial confidentiality. The whole system tends

237

toward the likelihood of unaccountability. There is in addition no judicial system within the corporate system. Any appeal by an employee against unfair treatment must needs be on an ad hoc basis to an executive in a higher position than that of the one complained against. If a decision is that of the board, then there is no recourse within the company. For the employees the board is no different to the court of an absolute potentate of times past.

Such a system of governance for society at large would be wholly at odds with the values which we espouse of transparency and fairness. It is difficult to imagine the population of any democracy choosing a system where the electorate votes in accordance to wealth, where there is no legal system and where the executive and the legislative is rolled into one. A company is a primitive form of government whose flaws are egregious, and wide ranging. In addition a company is not a system through which many values are weighed in deciding its future course of action. It has only one motivation and that is profit. Unlike a democratic form of government it is therefore highly focused, both in terms of the way decisions are taken and in terms of the orientation of those decisions.

As a society we would, I hope, not think too highly of individuals whose sole focus was the making of money, regardless of the consequences. Yet as a society we increasingly look to companies as entities to be admired – effective providers of the goods and services we need and overlook the darker side of their single mindedness. Social responsibility is, in practice, little more than an ineffective attempt to inject a certain amount of 'noblesse oblige' into the corporate structure. But the concept is purely notional – it hangs there, an orphaned waif, not knowing to whom to appeal.

In his book 'the Age of Consent' George Monbiot suggested that the way to reduce the power of companies was to have a world democratic system and looked at organisations such as the World Social Forum as providing the potential nucleus for a world parliament. The problem is that his idea has been tried before, and has not worked. Indeed in his own book[223] he gives an instance of this. Monbiot describes the time when the ordinary people of Rome, sorely oppressed by the Roman senatorial class, withdrew their services (referred to earlier in this book) and appointed two tribunes to represent them. He points out how eventually the power of the tribunes resulted in them identifying more with the elite than with those they represented. There are more modern instances of the problems of this kind of approach. The Chartists in Britain in the nineteenth century, for example, had their own National Convention and members even put MC (Member of the Convention) after their name, but the odds were always totally stacked against them achieving an alternative sphere of influence in their drive to reform the existing parliamentary arrangements. In fact it is difficult to think of any example of parallel institutions achieving any sort of influence except where the official ones are in a state of near collapse.

Notwithstanding the power of his arguments, unfortunately, rather like the guns of Singapore during the Second World War they are facing in the wrong direction. The problem is not that democracies are too small; it is that companies are too big. What he is suggesting has been tried before – in the New World. As has been discussed above, in its early years of independence the governmental structure of the Unites States was far larger than the corporations, indeed corporations scarcely existed at its inception. The constitutional architecture of the United States was exceptionally well thought out, and the country as Thomas Paine pointed out, was and is, even in its earliest years, continental in scale.

The United States was founded on some of the most rational and fair constitutional principles of its or indeed any day, which, by and large, have stood the test of time. There were virtually no corporations when America was founded, and there was a very substantial distrust and dislike of them. Yet, as we have seen, within a hundred years corporate influence

---

[223] The Age of Consent, George Monbiot, Harper Perennial, p.97

had come increasingly to dominate the United States. If democracy were able to contain the persistent pecuniary power of corporates it would surely have done so in the United States, when democracy was strong and corporates were very weak.

Companies are marvellously effective organisms, but they have no effective means of internal control. Like cancer they have the potential to grow rapidly and without regard for the consequences, infecting every aspect of the body politic. The democratic body will always be vulnerable to such relentless organisms, but the irony is that it has created them in the first place, and it can alter their decision making DNA. Discoveries have been made recently as to how bacteria bind together and work as a single organism[224]. In a slightly different way companies perform the same conjuring trick and we have yet to find an equivalent anti-biotic.

What is required to remedy the social malaise caused by corporations is a review of whether corporates could actually work in different ways and still be as capable of delivering society's goals.

Remote Control

There is a curious expression called 'shareholder democracy'. Like the Holy Roman Empire, which was famously described by Voltaire as neither holy, nor Roman, nor an empire, shareholder democracy often does not involve shareholders, and is certainly not a democracy. It is curious that companies should be governed on the basis of one pound one vote – it is not a formula that has found favour in other forms of human endeavour. The cry 'One pound one vote' is not one that has echoed down the centuries as the fairest way of reaching a

---

[224] See for example the article by Jerome Burne 'Meet Bug the builder in The Times, 6th November 2004, explaining the creation of 'biofilms', which are 1,000 times less likely to succumb to antibiotics than scattered and unco-ordinated bacteria.

decision. But even if one were to try to justify it in principle it is clear that in the vast majority of cases it does not work in practice. In the UK individual investors only account for 14% of the market, foreign investors for one-third and the 'other financial institutions' category (i.e. not insurance companies or pension funds), another 10.7 %. This latter category consists of hedge funds, venture capitalists etc. This is a substantial change. In 1963 individuals held 54% of shares, while the foreign ownership of shares doubled between 1994 and 2004. [225] It is something of a contrast that while democratic countries find it inappropriate to grant voting rights to non citizens they have come to accept the great direct power of foreign corporate ownership over the lives of their citizens.

The rise of the hedge funds has also highlighted the empty notion of shareholder democracy. The likes of ESL investments, a hedge fund run by Edward Lampert require shareholders with at least $10 million to invest and they must be willing to leave the money in the fund for at least five years[226]. The fund owns more than 50% of Kmart, and is the largest shareholder in Sears. Lampert was reported as earning more than $1 billion in 2004. These kinds of arbitrage and merger and acquisition activities seem worlds removed from the concept of a broadly based shareholder democracy.

Those who exercise the vote in the vast majority of large corporations are the agents of the shareholders. The fund managers, the pension funds and the insurance companies are often not the beneficial shareholders themselves. These agents seldom go to the trouble of consulting the beneficial shareholders in any meaningful way; it would be administratively burdensome, and the response likely to be meagre. The shareholders look to their shareholdings to

---

[225] Lombard column, and article by Tony Tassell and Lina Saigol, Financial Times 22nd June 2005.
[226] See for example the article in USA Today, http://www.usatoday.com/money/industries/retail/2004-11-21-lampert_x.htm

produce a financial return, and for the agents to purchase those shares which will provide the best return, and sell those which they think will under-perform. The fund managers, whether as corporates or the people actually making the investments, are mere financial delegates of the individuals who are the ultimate beneficial shareholders.

It is of course true that the ultimate beneficial owner may be many legal layers removed from the financial investment. The beneficial owner may have invested in an investment trust which invests in a variety of different shares. He or she may have invested in a fund of funds which invests in other funds which then invest in shares. He or she may have invested directly in a company, but found that the shares are actually held by a nominee company for easy electronic settlement purposes. This is the reality of share ownership today for the vast majority of investments. It is pure fantasy to suppose that individual shareholders take any meaningful interest in the way that large companies are run, where the shares are widely held. They know too well that their small shareholding will be irrelevant when the voting decisions of the big fund managers are taken into account.

As the influence of private equity investment grows, the fiction that shareholding has anything to do with democracy becomes even more difficult to maintain. Vast fortunes are being built up which are in practice answerable to no-one and about whom little is known or revealed. Nor is there any entitlement to know. The recent takeover by Koch Industries of Georgia Pacific has further highlighted the size and scale of these private companies.[227] The deal has enabled Koch Industries to overtake Cargill to become the largest private company with annual revenues of $80 billion and a workforce of 85,000. As a non-quoted company the amount of information it has to disclose is considerably less than for a

---

[227] See the Times article by Tom Bawden.
http://business.timesonline.co.uk/article/0,,9065-1872294,00.html

publicly quoted company.[228] The rise in private equity funds has stimulated the trend towards the non quotation of companies, and the elaborate framework of disclosure for quoted companies will apply to a shrinking percentage of invested wealth. The notional accountability of the large fund managers will be further marginalised.

And to whom are the large fund managers accountable, and for what? Notionally, of course, to the individual shareholders whose money they invest. In practice this accountability is a mere financial one. If they invest well they are more likely to retain the funds with which they have been entrusted. If their results are poor then the investor may well go elsewhere in search of a higher return. Whatever the valiant efforts of a CalPERS (Californian Public Employees Retirement System), or Hermes (responsible for Post Office and Telecoms pension money) with its 'Focus Funds' ('shareholder engagement investment funds') to be activist shareholders and their attempts to encourage good corporate governance, the reality is that the 'Emperor has no clothes'. They are not the beneficial owner of the shares they manage, and it is difficult to see how they could consult in any meaningful way the ultimate beneficial owners. If there is a potential conflict between a different board and a lower profit, what decision could they make? Clearly the only rational basis on which they can interfere with a company's management is on the basis of incompetence, not on any ethical or social responsibility platform. The individuals on

---

[228] Such companies are often known for their secrecy. According to Greg Palast, in "The Best Democracy Money Can Buy", pp. 106-111, Koch is the only company in the US to operate a private secure telephone network, apart from the CIA. One of the two Koch brothers, David, stood as a candidate for the Libertarian Party, campaigning against Ronald Reagan from a more right wing stance. The Kochs spent a great deal of money to establish the Cato Institute, the right wing think tank in Washington. The potential influence of private corporate wealth over the democratic process is typified by this private company.

whose behalf they act look to them to maximise their pensions, not pursue ethical agendas without consultation.

CalPERS publishes on its website an exposition of the principles[229] it uses in making decisions at shareholders meetings. Many of these reflect the normal agency concerns to ensure that e.g. the management does not pay itself too much. The fact that many of these concerns are stated as a principle is as much a testament to the fact that fund managers as a whole have been ineffective in the past, and continue to be ineffective, in ensuring that the management do not enrich themselves at the expense of the shareholders. In their statement of domestic proxy voter guidelines, they explicitly acknowledge the primacy of financial returns:

"The Board's stated fiduciary duty is to obtain the highest return for the Fund commensurate with acceptable levels of risk. This implies that non-financial considerations cannot take precedence to pure risk/return considerations in the evaluation of investment decisions. However, action taken by the Fund as a share-owner can be instrumental in encouraging action as a responsible corporate citizen by the companies in which the Fund has invested."

Further paragraphs refer to its concern that the management of the companies in which it invests "conduct themselves with propriety", and its expectation that management to 'eliminate' any improper practices that come into being (although these are not defined). They refer to companies which operate in countries where serious human rights violations occur and states that:

"For employees who are disadvantaged because of such violations, the Board expects the companies to persist in availing themselves of every reasonable and legally permissible means to ensure that all of their employees and

---

[229] http://www.calpers-governance.org/principles/domestic/voting.page01.asp

families have what they need to pursue a life of dignity and personal well-being."

As we have seen above a number of companies operating in America, and in developing countries without such human rights violations leave a great deal to be desired in respect of their treatment of employees, but this guideline does not seem to apply to them.

Having laid down the guidelines, CalPERS then lays out what it will do:

"Should satisfaction of the Board's criteria by any company not be adequate, the Board will consider what action to take, which may include, but not be limited to, correspondence with the company, meetings with company officials, sponsoring of shareholder resolutions or, as a last resort, liquidation of System holdings in the company, **if the sale is consistent with sound investment policy**".

The last part of this text, not in bold in the original, highlights the emptiness of this approach. Even if the guidelines are broken and a company ignores their advice, CalPERS will sell its shares only if they do not think that it will cost them money.

It is clear then that this is a policy where everything is subordinate to a financial return.

In their guidelines on social/political issues their list includes the following[230]:

8010 Abortion	
Warnings on contraceptives	Against
Report on human fetal tissue research	Against
Stop reimbursements for termination of human life	Against

---

[230] http://www.calpers-governance.org/principles/domestic/voting/page15.asp

8020 Animal rights	
Report on progress towards ending animal tests	For
Prohibit animal testing in laboratories	Against
Report on alternative ways to "factory farming" of animals	For
8030 Beer marketing	
Report on relationship between marketing beer to minors and driving accidents	Against
8040 Broadcasting	
Appoint an ombudsman for broadcast news	Against
8050 Burma	
Terminate investments and operations in Burma	Against
8060 Communist Countries	
Adoption of policies for dealing with Communist countries	Against
8070 Community reinvestment	
Report on lending in low-income and minority neighborhoods	For
Develop an overall fair lending policy	Against
8080 Corporate Contributions	
Publish in newspapers a detailed report of political contributions	Against
Limit corporate contributions only to those that further the interest of the corporation	Against
Forbid contributions to schools restricted by ideology	Against
Establish limitations on candidate PAC contributions	Against

8090 Drug pricing	
Report on drug pricing policy	Against
Adopt a drug price restraint policy	Against
8100 Energy	
Report on automotive fuel economy	Against
8110 Environment	
Report on safety precautions at pesticide plants	Against

These are very important moral and ethical issues. It is by no means clear either on whose behalf CalPERS are making these judgements, what consultation they have with their investors before taking such decisions, or indeed what qualifications they have to reach such decisions in a principled way

CalPERS is recognised as being at the forefront of shareholder responsibility and activism – and yet even here the overriding monetary consideration and the lack in their turn of any proper accountability is clearly evident – the system in which they operate is simply not designed to allow complex decisions on social issues to be taken.

It is sometimes lost sight of that all shares are ultimately held for individuals; however many legal layers one may go through, the final beneficial owner is a human being. Yet the attendance by individuals at shareholders' meeting, or rather the lack of it, is an ample demonstration that those ultimately entitled to the financial benefit of all this corporate action do not believe their vote provides them with a say of any significance over a company. Of course there are exceptions with newly launched companies, and where the shares of a company are tightly held, but for the titans of the twenty first century the shareholders meeting is little more than a façade, or possibly a 'farcade', a meaningless ritual to be gone through, and where the only concerns are likely to come from other corporates who are as unaccountable as themselves.

The feeling of jaded impotence of the disempowered shareholders would not be unfamiliar to those citizens who are losing confidence that they are able to make a difference through the ballot box.

The fund managers and others in the finance industry have generally neither the experience nor expertise to monitor the management of large companies; their professional specialism is to assess value, not to manage management. They know that except in a rare case they are not, in practice, accountable to the ultimate shareholders, the individuals who have the beneficial interest. Only in the most extreme cases do they find themselves compelled to act in a forceful manner. The beneficial owners of these shares, at least in the UK, often hold them through a nominee company, and are not entitled to vote at AGMs, or they hold the shares through a savings structure, such as an insurance company or a pension plan, and therefore are not entitled to vote. The fund managers are therefore agents without masters, whose supposed skill at managing money ill equips them for the role of controlling management with whom they often have far more in common than the shareholders they represent.

Finally, of course, to the extent that the board is accountable to anything, it is accountable to the money – there is no political system anywhere in the world that has accepted the principle that the power to hold people to account should be carefully and exactly calibrated according to the amount of money you have. Yet that is precisely the theoretical basis on which the management of these companies are responsible – according to a principle that is universally regarded as reprehensible in any other context, and the antithesis of many if not all of the world's religions.

In brief therefore, not only are companies notionally controlled by a system that we would regard as anathema in any other walk of life, but the system doesn't even work properly. Companies are controlled by other companies.

Some Flawed Assumptions

Is there then another way of organising companies which is capable of delivering accountability while at the same time enabling a company to be managed efficiently? This goes to the very heart of the way we, as a society, believe that decisions ought to be taken. As we have seen in previous chapters, companies are societies themselves, both in terms of their historical provenance, and in terms of the way they function. If we are to arrive at a type of osmosis, through which the values of society at large are to find their way into the corporate environment, then we have to find a way through the corporate membrane.

At the core of the problem are two key assumptions which purport to justify the way in which corporates currently operate:

First, that in order to operate efficiently corporates must be subject to shareholder discipline, with profit as the (only) measure of their success; and

Second, that shareholder voting rights are indivisible and inseparable from their financial rights.

However both these assumptions are demonstrably wrong.

There are a number of organisations which are run on commercial lines which do not have a conventional shareholder structure, from the Mondragon co-operative movement in the Basque country to the John Lewis partnership in the United Kingdom. These are not small enterprises. The brief outline of the Mondragon cooperative is succinctly put on their website:

"The Mondragon Corporacion Cooperativa (MCC) began in the town of Mondragon in 1956 when a group of five young engineers were encouraged by their socialist priest, Father Jose Maria Arizmediarrieta, to set up a cooperative to make paraffin cooking stoves. Using Arizmediarrieta's vision the five young students built a financial base for the MCC today. By 1959 they had already formed the Caja Laboral Popular (CLP), the Working People's Bank, which is not only the bank for the cooperatives but is run as a cooperative itself. MCC has grown in its forty years of operation to include 160 employee-owned cooperatives, involving 23,000 member owners, with sales grossing US$3 billion in 1991. The main focus of the Association of the Mondragon Cooperatives is the creation of owner-employee jobs to expand the opportunities for people to participate in the relationship economy. Statistics show the Mondragon cooperatives to be twice as profitable as the average corporation in Spain with employee productivity surpassing any other Spanish organisation. It is focused on social success, involvement of the people and industrial democracy. MCC has grown to be one of the twelve largest companies in Spain and is the biggest in Basque County."

The John Lewis Partnership is one of the UK's top ten retail businesses with 27 John Lewis department stores, 166 Waitrose supermarkets, and 63,000 permanent staff who are 'partners' in the business, and share its profits.

This is not to suggest that these business models are necessarily the best or only alternative to the current corporate structure, but they do show that organisations which are answerable to their employees instead of to third party shareholders can be and are successful enterprises. Such examples give the lie to the idea that if democracy of the type found in politics were applied in the business sphere then management's ability to act would be so impaired as to severely jeopardise the company's efficiency and long term survival.

However, in both the Mondragon and John Lewis cases, ownership has not been separated from voting rights. One of the criticisms sometimes levelled at such organisations is that without freely tradable shares they are unable to raise capital as effectively and as cheaply as companies with an ordinary shareholding structure. Even if this were true, the availability of low-cost capital is of far less importance in some types of businesses than others, and does not seem to have been a major impediment to the growth of either Mondragon or John Lewis.

It is clear that such enterprises have not needed the vaunted advantages of shareholder discipline.[231]

An Educational Lesson

The private education sector in Britain (and doubtless elsewhere) is a fascinating example of how a whole industry can be run without such shareholder discipline. Private schools in the United Kingdom have a mountain to climb. They are competing with the state sector which offers the same product – education in primary and secondary schools – for free. Since they obviously cannot compete on price they compete on quality, and given the rising numbers of pupils in private education in the United Kingdom, it is clear that they are doing this successfully. This is despite the fact that the relative cost of private education in the United Kingdom has increased faster than prices generally, since there are few efficiency savings that schools can make; their largest expense is salaries and the annual increase in the national average income has been substantially higher than that of prices generally for some considerable time.

Yet the UK private education industry has in the main no shareholders breathing down the necks of those managing the schools. We have not seen the amalgamation of schools into massive educational groups dominating the educational

---

[231] In Part C 'Towards a decent society' of his excellent book 'The Hungry Spirit', Arrow 1998, Charles Handy explores both the concepts of corporate as citizen and also the corporation as a town or village, yet even he, on p. 164, says of German companies 'A few near disasters have made them begin to realize that they need not only the money of outside investors but also the harsher discipline that this interest group will bring.'

landscape. The schools are generally run well and balance their books, infused by an ethos which recognises both the necessity of running a commercial venture and with integrating with their community. This is not to say that the system of school governors and Parent Teachers Associations, of Charitable Trusts etc. are replicable as a structure in a wider business context. These institutions have grown from a variety of different roots, benefiting from individual and institutional vision and generosity. An initial charitable impulse however, would not have been enough to ensure their survival. They have survived because they have provided a service that the public wanted to buy, and done so in a way in which the commercial element was subsumed in a variety of different objectives, in respect of the education provided, the balance of academic and other priorities, and the place of the school in the community.

Of course the reputation of schooling in the United Kingdom has not always been so high. When the interests of commerce were rather greater, the educational attainments of such establishments were rather less, as Charles Dickens pointed out in Nicholas Nickelby. This is the conversation when young Nicholas goes to teach at Dotheboys Hall run by Mr. Wackford Squeers:

"'This is the first class in English spelling and philosophy, Nickleby,' said Squeers, beckoning Nicholas to stand beside him. 'We'll get up a Latin one, and hand that over to you. Now, then, where's the first boy?'
'Please, sir, he's cleaning the back-parlour window,' said the temporary head of the philosophical class.
'So he is, to be sure,' rejoined Squeers. 'We go upon the practical mode of teaching, Nickleby; the regular education system. C-l-e-a- n, clean, verb active, to make bright, to scour. W-i-n, win, d-e-r, der, winder, a casement. When the boy knows this out of book, he goes and does it. It's just the same principle as the use of the globes. Where's the second boy?'
'Please, sir, he's weeding the garden,' replied a small voice.
'To be sure,' said Squeers, by no means disconcerted. 'So he is. B-o-t, bot, t-i-n, tin, bottin, n-e-y, ney, bottinney, noun

substantive, a knowledge of plants. When he has learned that bottinney means a knowledge of plants, he goes and knows 'em. That's our system, Nickleby: what do you think of it?'

'It's a very useful one, at any rate,' answered Nicholas.

'I believe you,' rejoined Squeers, not remarking the emphasis of his usher. 'Third boy, what's horse?'

'A beast, sir,' replied the boy.

'So it is,' said Squeers. 'Ain't it, Nickleby?'

'I believe there is no doubt of that, sir,' answered Nicholas.

'Of course there isn't,' said Squeers. 'A horse is a quadruped, and quadruped's Latin for beast, as everybody that's gone through the grammar knows, or else where's the use of having grammars at all?'

'Where, indeed!' said Nicholas abstractedly.

'As you're perfect in that,' resumed Squeers, turning to the boy, 'go and look after MY horse, and rub him down well, or I'll rub you down. The rest of the class go and draw water up, till somebody tells you to leave off, for it's washing-day tomorrow, and they want the coppers filled.'"

Now there was a school run on very commercial lines!

We should not take the change in regime from Dickens' Dotheboys Hall to the current private education system in the UK for granted. One of the great contradictions today is between what we teach in our schools, and the kind of behaviour that corporates require. The virtues of charity, generosity, and turning the other cheek, the principle of helping your neighbour etc. are common to all the world's great religions, and we expect schools to pass on these values. But they are an alien concept to corporations.

In the US there is a now a significant tendency towards commercialisation of public sector education. It remains to be seen whether, over a period of time, the values inculcated in such schools will reflect corporate profit priorities. There is some cause for pessimism. The companies which run such schools are in any event run for profit, and the priorities of the school and the staff will inevitable come to reflect this central goal over a period of time.

Edison schools (founded in 1992), mentioned in an earlier chapter, is the largest Education Management Organisation (EMO) in the United States, it operates in over 20 states on behalf of local government with some than 300,000 students. It is growing at a phenomenal pace. It is one of some 40 such organisations in the United States. Their intention is to own and operate schools.

Edison are now also operating in the United Kingdom, but their track record is not entirely unblemished. As pointed out by Joel Bakan in 'Corporation' their running of schools has been influenced by concerns over their profitability:

"To save money in running its Philadelphia schools, the company sold off textbooks, computers, lab supplies, and musical instruments. It also moved its executives into schoolrooms in the hope of saving $9,000 a month in rent on their corporate offices (upon learning about the move the school board quickly ordered the executives out of the schools). Edison founder and CEO Chris Whittle further proposed that the company use unpaid Edison students to do the work of paid school employees. "We could have less adult staff," he is reported to have told a group of Edison principals as he described his plan to have each of six hundred students in a school work one hour a day at administrative tasks, thus making the work of seventy-five adults redundant."[232]

Mr Wackford Squeers would have been proud.

Such incidents underline the different concerns and pre-occupations of an educational conglomerate run for profit, and the kind of institutions produced by the private sector with different motivations, in constant contact with the community they serve, and operated on a human scale.

In the United Kingdom the introduction of 'Academy' schools into the public sector is starting to replicate the American

---

[232] p.116

approach. For a contribution of a fifth of the start up costs of such schools, up to a maximum of £2 million, commercial sponsors obtain the right to control the teachers' pay and conditions and alter the school curriculum. It is still an open question whether such schools do raise standards, but this uneasy relationship with the private sector is likely to bring a considerable conflict of priorities in the running of such schools in the future and may result in the corporate ethos penetrating into the educational environment without adequate structures being put into place. The fact that Edison's Chief Executive, Chris Whittle, has been reported recently as saying "

The surreptitious privatisation of the National Health Service in the United Kingdom through the use of PFI (Private Finance Initiative) and PPP (Public Private Partnership) is another illustration of the advance of the corporate priorities of profit into institutions which embody some of the core social concerns of society. The extent to which profit is starting to replace clinical judgement as the driver of whether a patient receives treatment or not, and whether there are sufficient hospital beds or not is outside the scope of this book, but is dealt with in great detail in 'NHS plc' by Allyson Pollock.[234] It is clear from her book that the delivery of healthcare in the United Kingdom is increasingly determined by financial priorities, in accordance with the corporate view of the world, rather than the social priorities of clinical concern. However it is by no means clear that there has been any great increase in efficiency or cost effectiveness as a result of these changing priorities.

---

[233] The Independent newspaper, 18th January 2006, article by Richard Garner, Education Editor.
[234] NHS plc The Privatisation of Our Health Care, Allyson Pollock, Verso 2004.

Money without votes

There is a pervasive received wisdom that not only do companies require shareholder discipline, but that it would be difficult, if not impossible to raise money for investment if shareholders did not have the vote. However, in more traditional corporate structures there is ample evidence to show that it is possible to raise money effectively without voting rights. For example General Motors, in respect of both its acquisitions of Hughes Corporation and EDS issued 'tracker' shares ('H' shares and 'E' shares whose value and dividend flows reflected the economic success of the relevant subsidiary company), which provided no voting rights.

Bearer participation certificates and non-voting equity have long been features of the Swiss corporate scene, with global companies such as Schindler and Roche having substantial amounts of such paper outstanding. In the case of Roche the non voting equity is some four times the size of the bearer shares. In Japan the interlocking shareholding of members of the keiretsu, or business groupings, such as Mitsubishi or Sumitomo, historically rendered the idea of outside shareholder voting control a very notional concept. There are numerous quoted companies where the majority of the shares are held by one investor or a group of investors and where it is clear that the voting rights of the others, in the absence of a shareholders' agreement will be of little value. It is undoubtedly the case that non-voting equity is coming under pressure (they make the work of merger and acquisition teams in large investment banks that little bit harder, since special interests are involved). However, it is clear that there is no essential connexion between economic investment and voting control.

It is entirely logical that this should be so. As outlined in a previous chapter the assumption that economic ownership meant control grew up in the nineteenth century and before, when owners of companies had unlimited liability, and companies were comparatively small. The quid pro quo of unlimited liability was control. However with the advent of limited liability that rationale no longer existed. The position of the ordinary shareholder was then, in essence, no different from that of the bank lending money to the company, or the preference shareholder, neither of whom expected to have a say in its management. It was and is, of course, perfectly clear that shareholders should receive a higher return on their investment as a reward for the greater risk that they run – the other investors have a higher priority for the return of their money. However this is a difference of degree, not a difference of kind.

The recent Mergers and Acquisitions Directive of the European Union has brought this into perspective. This piece of legislation, which is due to be implemented by the Member States of the European Union by May 2006,[235] requires that where one company holds more than 75% of the share capital of another then the remaining shares cannot have more than one share one vote. This provision is designed to provide that takeovers cannot be frustrated by a 'golden share' with blocking powers or a minority holding of shares with multiple votes. The same Article of the Directive (Article 11) also provides that where such multiple voting rights are removed, then compensation should be paid, the terms of such compensation to be set by members States. The problem which has yet to be resolved is how such compensation can be calculated - .i.e. it seeks to put a value on the voting rights attached to shares. In a case involving Siemens decided in October 2001 the Landgericht München (the Munich district court) apparently came to the conclusion that the average market premium for voting rights was approximately 15%.

It is perhaps interesting to note that in the Annual Report of another very large German company, Allianz AG, of the same year explained in some detail about the terms and conditions of its own Bearer Participation Certificates (i.e. shares without

---

[235] Directive 2004/25/EC of The European Parliament and of The Council of 21st April 2004 on takeover bids, European Journal, L142/12, 30th April 2004.

voting rights). Their terms and conditions provide for annual distributions amounting to 240% of the dividend paid by the company in respect of their ordinary shares. Such certificates are redeemable at the option of their holders every five years (and from the end of December 2001 onwards by giving 12 months' notice). They are also redeemable at the company's option on giving six months' notice, at just under 123% of the share price.[236] Such arrangements show only too clearly that equity investment without voting rights is perfectly feasible, even though it may be difficult to calculate what economic benefit, if any, should be attached to them. It is at least clear that for all those UK investors whose voting rights are exercised by nominee companies, or through pension or insurance savings schemes, little if any value has been put by the investors on their ability to exercise those rights personally.

The reality for individual investors is sometimes quite the reverse of what is portrayed. Very often their financial interests are trampled on while their supposed voting control is of no use in protecting their real interests. An example of the powerlessness of the individual investor was the recent share buy back scheme by O_2 the mobile telecommunications company. Under the terms of a share buyback programme in March 2005 initiated by the company, O_2 offered to buy out more than 1.6 million small shareholders at a five per cent premium to the then market price. However investors who failed to respond to the offer in time had their holdings automatically repurchased. They were paid £1.30 per share. In November the share price had climbed to £1.97 as an £18 billion bid was launched by the Spanish company Telefonica.[237] The small shareholders were being disenfranchised and compulsorily ejected for doing nothing. In a curious twist, those small shareholders who had already

---

[236] Allianz Annual Report 2001, Notes to the Accounts §8, p.34.
[237] See for example the article by Joe Morgan in The Times, Money section 5th November 2005.

lost their vote, because they held their shares electronically, were not affected by the compulsory buyback.[238]

This pivotal implication of limiting liability went unnoticed. The ordinary employees of companies had difficulty enough in asserting their rights as citizens in the nineteenth and early twentieth centuries. To the extent that they thought at all about controlling the companies in which they worked, their ideas were permeated by the influence of communism and socialism, which adhered to the creed that control and economic ownership were indivisible, and that to control something the workers, and ultimately the state, had to own it.

No Laughing Matter. A New Electorate.

The formula N_2O is the chemical formula for nitrous oxide, or laughing gas. A handy mnemonic for the relationship between shares and voting rights is the chemically improbable N_3O, standing for No Necessary Nexus – there is absolutely no reason shares should carry votes or why the financial interests of the shareholders cannot be safeguarded in the same way as those of banks and preference shareholders. Neither the shareholders, nor any of their agents, such as the fund managers can in any sense be regarded as the 'members' of a large company with widely distributed shares. Their greater financial risk entitles them to a greater financial reward, but the severing of their unlimited liability, and the very construction of multiple layers of ownership, means that they must cease to be regarded in any real way as the individuals that are the human personification of the corporate animal. For this we must look elsewhere.

---

[238] Under the UK system, if the shares are held electronically, rather than through a paper share certificate, they are held on behalf of the shareholder by a broker in a nominee account; the broker and not the individual shareholder is therefore the shareholder of record. Many shareholders have therefore lost the right to vote for the administrative convenience of the fund management industry.

One of the great triumphs of modern day democracy is that it has managed to break the link between ownership and control in the political sphere – the entitlement to vote is no longer based on property. This simple premise has, however, yet to make itself felt in the commercial sphere.

The idea that the position of shareholders had fundamentally changed as a result of limited liability was an entirely alien one in the social context of the mid nineteenth century when the character of the modern day corporation was being forged. The enormous turmoil of the First World War, the titanic struggles of democracy, fascism and communism of the Second World War, and the ensuing cold war between communism and capitalism in the latter half of the twentieth century meant that allegiance to systems tended to be as highly prized as analysis of them.

Democratic accountability on a periodic basis for the good stewardship of society is as applicable to the corporate society as it is to society as a whole. There can be little doubt that the activities of companies drive many of the priorities of modern life and they are in practice, as we have seen, effectively accountable to no-one. The board of directors have a legal responsibility to shareholders, but the inflation of directors' salaries, the amoral decisions taken, and the perfunctory nature of annual general meetings all demonstrate the tenuous and ephemeral nature of this responsibility. Even in the most extreme cases of corporate malfeasance it may be the media, the employees, customers or other entities that bring the management to book, or at least start the process. As Arthur Anderson showed in the case of Enron, the accountants, who in their role of auditors are there to protect the interests of shareholders, can also be less than effective in carrying out this role.

Accountability for the merely financial return of the assets to the investors results in corporates institutionalising an attitude of a lesser responsibility to society at large than is expected of individuals. Through commonly shared values, individual citizens recognise the values of good neighbourliness, of restricting their actions to try to ensure that their neighbours will do likewise in order to reduce tension in the fabric of society as a whole. Notwithstanding self interest people act the way they do because of a complex consideration of many different values, including religious and moral teaching, views of the 'public good', their relationship with their neighbours, and potential penalties, both legal and social for transgressing social norms. Corporations, and in particular large corporations, do not enjoy (in any sense) this same frame of reference. They merely wish to maximise financial value for the shareholders and their impact on society as a whole or on certain individuals assumes a much lower degree of importance and priority. Their 'neighbours' are more likely to be other corporations or the government and the potential penalties that they suffer for corporate wrong doing are often minor compared to their resources.

The degree to which other values are taken into the equation by a company is purely the result of the values which individuals who occupy positions of importance in the company at any given time happen to hold (and which originate by definition from outside the company) coupled with the legal norms which are imposed on the company by society at large. Indeed it is arguable that individuals act differently wearing a "corporate hat" than when they act as individuals. Although their social values as individuals may inform the way in which they act on behalf of a corporation there is also a reciprocal tendency for the decision making framework and responsibilities of a corporation moulding behaviour both inside and outside the corporation.

Corporations, no less than people, are subject to Lord Acton's dictum that power tends to corrupt and that absolute power corrupts absolutely. This applies both to the power of the corporate in the world at large and to the power of the directors within a corporation to pursue their own agenda. The Enrons, Worldcoms and Tycos of this world should not be seen as exceptional cases, but as a natural consequence of the temptations inherently and intrinsically available to corporations and their management[239]

A Square Peg

In his 'Theory of Justice'[240], John Rawls spent a great deal of time in establishing the way in which individuals might come to recognise mutually beneficial patterns of behaviour resulting in an appropriate concept of justice. For example in §11 of his book he defines his two principles of justice as follows:

"First: each person is to have an equal right to the most extensive basic liberty compatible with a similar liberty for others.

Second: social and economic inequalities are to be arranged so that they are both (a) reasonably expected to be to everyone's advantage, and (b) attached to positions and offices open to all."

Such fundamental underpinnings of a civic society are of little interest to a corporate. Their liberties crowd out those of others. Commercial confidentiality often deflects requests for further information. As an entity endowed with legal

---

[239] These problems are scarcely new. As Adam Smith famously pointed out: "The directors of such companies, however, being the managers rather of other people's money than of their own, it cannot well be expected that they should watch over it with the same anxious vigilance with which the partners in a private copartnery frequently watch over their own. Like the stewards of a rich man, they are apt to consider attention to small matters as not for their master's honour, and very easily give themselves a dispensation from having it. Negligence and profusion, therefore, must always prevail, more or less, in the management of the affairs of such a company." Wealth of Nations, Book V, Chapter 1, Part 3, Article 1.

[240] 'A Theory of Justice', John Rawls, Oxford University Press 1973.

personality it can tower above all but the wealthiest of individuals in society and it is both an expression of inequality and often enough a creator of it. Indeed by seeking to out-compete its rivals its mission is greater inequality, not less. It seeks to exploit the world as it finds it to its greatest advantage.

To the extent that corporate entities become larger and larger, and in particular to the degree that they become larger in relation to the society in which they operate their ability to influence the observance of some laws and to prevent the introduction of others tends to increase. Gradually the governance of society moves in practice away from a democracy, government by the people, to a 'corpocracy' government by corporates, where the facade of democratic accountability fronts a system where decisions are made in practice by corporate boardrooms.

The perception that power lies elsewhere, away from democratically elected institutions is growing. It is not merely trade unions which feel that direct action is required to influence events. We have seen the growth in non governmental organisations (NGOs), who have their own specific social agendas which they believe are excluded from adequate consideration in the corporate and business spheres. This interaction of other bodies or 'corporations' with commercial corporations further accelerates the advance of corporatism, as deals are done between these bodies rather than through a more open democratic process.

Because of the primacy of money in the corporate decision making structure, the result is a very important inversion of investment rationale. In the political sphere we are concerned about investing money in people; in the commercial sphere management is concerned about investing people in money.

In our daily lives as citizens money is regarded as a way of improving our living standards, enhancing our lives, and increasing our freedom. It is a means of ensuring our freedom from want and liberating us from drudgery, so that we can lead lives that are more fulfilled. Money is a resource to be used to release us from necessary drudgery and to fulfil higher aspirations. Ultimately the increase of wealth is for the purpose of improving the human condition.

This rationale is turned on its head in a corporation. There the employees are the resource and the goal is to maximise the return on the money. The company does not, or should not, concern itself what the money may be ultimately used for – that is a matter for the shareholders – its purpose is merely to use the resources at its disposal to maximise the return on the invested money. It is the complete reverse of what society at large, however inadequately, is trying to achieve.

It is therefore of vital importance that the goals which are set for a company take into account the human values which they are ultimately there to achieve. As the corporate priority increasingly dominates us we move further and further towards the 'soulless society', trapped in an unending cycle of wanting to be better off, and where the rewards for our efforts in trying to achieve this are likely to be distributed increasingly unfairly.

There has been much talk over the years of 'stakeholders' i.e. different people and entities with whom a company inter-reacts, such as employees, customers, trade unions, and communities in the areas in which they operate. The problem with this concept is that it is almost impossible to decide on a clear dividing line between those who might be considered a stakeholder and those who might not, nor indeed what proportionate balance each of these voices might have and how their interests could or should be protected where there is disagreement.

The concept has impractibility and an inability to be delivered virtually written into it. It has the additional disadvantage that this is not the way society operates generally. It is not clear, for example, why customers should be considered 'stakeholders' in a company. Their connexion with the company is a purely commercial and contractual one, and if the company ceases to provide what they require they will simply go elsewhere. Because the United States purchases a large amount of its oil from the Middle East, it does not follow that the United States can be considered a 'stakeholder' in the Middle East. Important trading partner it may be, but its attempts to lay claim to a more profound status in the region have not been crowned with success.

This is not to say that the concept of stakeholding is not an extremely important one, and indeed it is clear that it can produce tangible results. But stakeholding is essentially an attempt to get companies to work together with other interested parties to come to an agreed solution, often in respect of a specific project, and taking account of the interests of the company. It is **not** an alternative method of accountability for the decision making process within a company.

If, for example, we take the Future 500 stakeholders group set up in 1995 by leaders of the Fortune 500 companies it is clear that they view stakeholding as a way of taking projects forward on the basis of discussions with interested parties, while at the same time maximising profits. Notwithstanding their concerns over the disposal of bottles and the Amazonian rainforest, they nevertheless feel it important that they have triggered "Triple Bottom Line Gains at many of the World's Largest and most influential companies". The website talks about how important it is to be open to feedback, and there is a diagram including employees and customers as well as 'interest groups' and 'community'[241] However as long as companies only have responsibility to serve their shareholders and maximise their profits then such aspirations, even if sincere, do not deal with the fundamental issue. This concept of stakeholders has nothing to do with the culture inside companies; it has a great deal to do with the way in which companies inter-act with society on terms that are designed to achieve the companies' objectives on a profitable basis.

---

[241] http://www.globalff.org/

In order for a corporation to realistically act as a single cohesive and coherent body, there needs to be a clear and easily understood dividing line between those who are members of the company and those who are not. This can certainly be said in respect of the investors, albeit even here a number of legal layers have to be stripped away, and the actual ultimate member may not be known, merely his or her proxy at one or several stages removed. The shareholders may have only held the shares for a few days or for many years, but they are an identifiable group of people. However there is also another body of people who are readily identifiable and whose lives are intimately tied up with the success or failure of a company – far more so, in fact, than the investors, and that group is the employees.

As GlaxoSmithKline said succinctly in their Social Responsibility Report 2002:

"People are the greatest single source of competitive advantage for any company. At GlaxoSmithKline, we believe that attracting, retaining and motivating the very best people is the best foundation for our future success."

It is the employees who are the real life blood of any company. It is by their combined efforts that the company performs well or badly. Of course lip service is often paid to their importance, with expressions such as 'our company's assets go up and down in the lifts', but the reality is that in most large companies, except for the top layer of managerial talent, the employees are viewed as an amorphous resource to maximise profit.

It is a remarkable but largely unremarked fact that when companies are acquired, the acquisition of the workforce is one of the most important considerations. There are a variety of ways of valuing a company from book value, and break up value to going concern, but they all ignore any explicit valuation of the workforce. Frequently a merger will be justified by the reduction in costs that will flow from reducing the workforce. In any event, although it is notionally the case that a workforce could resign en masse to resist a takeover, the reality is that they will continue in work. In practice therefore, when companies are bought and sold, people are bought and sold. Since the workforce have to be paid this could not be categorised as slavery, but for those at the bottom of the heap there is less and less to distinguish their ability to influence their destiny from that of mediaeval serfs. They come attached to the financial and property assets that are being bought and sold. As we have seen elsewhere in the book, when the directors are looking at the wellbeing of the company their framework of reference is very largely a financial one.

As we have seen the organisation of companies is highly autocratic. It is by no means clear on whose authority those who are supposed to call them to account, act themselves. Such accountability is, in many instances, rather weak and ineffective and is very constrained. Whatever the current fashion might be for the social responsibility of corporations[242], this goal can only be partially accommodated within a framework of profitability, given the way that companies are currently organised. Those boards that go beyond this remit do so despite the company structure, and run the risk of being accused of unlawful largesse with the shareholders' money.

The Transferable Vote

Since companies are societies themselves, it seems neither logical nor fair that they are run along non-democratic lines in

---

[242] See for example the article in the Financial Times by Craig Smith and Craig Cohon on 8th December 2004, suggesting that corporate responsibility should become mainstream in companies "..closing down the CSR [Corporate Social Responsibility] department would be a good first step towards true social responsibility". Given the restrictive obligations of boards of directors to their shareholders CSR at the expense of profit seems an unlikely outcome.

a society which subscribes to the democratic ideal unless there are compelling reasons that this should not be the case. There appears to be no proof or evidence to show that the curtailment of democratic rights is a pre-requisite for the efficient functioning of a company. It seems clear that democracy's domain should extend to corporate societies as well as to political ones. It is obvious that if we as a society believe in the democratic process, then we should apply this to the corporate sphere as well as the political sphere.

The conversion of a company from a feudal structure to a democratic one can be accomplished remarkably easily. In practice it can be implemented by transferring the voting rights currently held by shareholders to the employees of a company. The directors would then be responsible to their employees at the Annual General Meeting (AGM). In particular the employees, through the AGM, would have the right to appoint and dismiss directors. This would be analogous to the right to elect a government in the political sphere.

In the same way that in a representative democracy individuals have no right to formulate policy, so too the employees would not have to have a right to manage the company. They would, however, be in a position to hold the board of directors to account. The employees are likely to have a very good idea of how well the company is being run on a day to day basis, and they collectively have a greater knowledge of and stake in the company's success and the effectiveness of the managers than even the investors.

In this context, and to identify a company run along these lines, it is helpful to have a term to encapsulate this vital distinction. We describe a system run for the benefit of the capital invested as 'capitalism'. A system under which a company is run by its employees should be described as '**Companionism**'. This encapsulates the reality that it is the people banding together for a business goal who are the core of the company, not the capital applied to the business. The word companion, though derived from the same root as company, embodies a very different set of values. It emphasises the individual rather than the institution, it has an implication of egalitarianism, and it also has a commercial heritage. Adam Smith remarked[243]:

"In France, the duration of apprenticeships is different in different towns and in different trades. In Paris, five years is the term required in a great number; but before any person can be qualified to exercise the trade as a master, he must, in many of them, serve five years more as a journeyman. During this latter term he is called the companion of his master, and the term itself is called his companionship."

It is in this sense of being a person of informed views within a decision making structure that the term of companionism should be understood. As we move towards a knowledge based economy, where the skills of the workforce are of paramount importance 'companionism' well encapsulates the concept that it is the workforce, individually and as a body, that is responsible for the destiny of the company.

The creation of companies based on companionism would not be particularly complex. The provision that the voting rights of the shareholders at an annual or an extraordinary general meeting should be transferred to the employees of a company on the basis of one person one vote may be radical but it is not complicated.

It is, of course, another matter to discuss whether the powers currently held by the shareholders in any jurisdiction are themselves appropriate or sufficient; what is key is that, as in a representative democracy, they would have the right to dismiss the board.

There are a number of ways in which it is possible to envisage that a proper corporate democratic structure could evolve, from elections of the whole board, through a rotating retirement of certain members (as in the US senate for

---

[243] Wealth of Nations Book 1, chapter X

example) to votes of confidence of individual board members. In the same way that democratic institutions around the world work in very different ways to achieve the same goals and through the same mechanism of one person one vote, reflecting as they do the values and customs of the societies in which they operate, so too is it likely that democratic companies would adjust their internal voting systems and powers to reflect their own communities.

Some smaller companies could perhaps contemplate a rather larger measure of democracy, more along the lines of the Swiss political model. For example there is the well established international Scott Bader group in the United Kingdom. All the companies in the group form part of the 'Scott Bader Commonwealth', the shares of which are owned by a foundation created by Scott Bader, the founder, and which has a number of principles:

"The intention of the Founders was to create a radical company, its well-being entrusted to those who work in it. It must encourage a spirit of co-operation and help to eliminate social injustice and waste —making the world a better place to live. Scott Bader companies are the business units of a larger membership organisation called The Scott Bader Commonwealth. Everyone working in Scott Bader is expected to become a member of the Scott Bader Commonwealth. Members share the responsibilities and privileges of being trustees-in-common and working the Scott Bader way, and must accept the challenge of ensuring the company is sustainable for the benefit of future generations."

The Scott Bader companies and those who work within them have a set of principles which are set out in Appendix III; these go far beyond just looking at profit as the goal of the company. Ethical considerations, equality of opportunity, and the need to keep staff well informed and consulted on day to day working and wider company issues are all principles to which all employees have to sign up.

The company is small, with over 600 employees of whom some 300 are based in the UK. Its turnover in 2002 was just under £100 million, it had total assets of £64 million and had an operational profit of £1.28 million (although its profit in the previous year had been nearly £3.5 million). The company has been going since 1921 and the Scott Bader commonwealth structure was created in 1951, so it has been operating successfully in this way for more than half a century. The way in which the company operates shows how corporate architecture can influence outcome.

The company actively seeks to support the community in which it operates, and to use its surpluses for charitable purposes. In 2004 it donated 26.1 percent (£217,048) of its pre-tax profits to charitable causes and in 2005 won an award[244] for its work in the rural community.

The Company supports the local rural community via the use of its land and facilities. It regularly hires out its large 'Commonwealth' Centre that accommodates a maximum of 200 people; its facilities include a bar, dance floor, stage, food preparation area, chairs, tables and toilet facilities. The local community uses it for functions such as weddings and parties at a rate between £100 - £200 dependant on the day, charity and fundraising events are charged between £60 - £80.

Each year every employee is given £150 to spend on a charity of their choice. Much of this is spent in the village to support local activities. Many individuals are active members of their local community and this money supports that work.

The company has a swimming pool, built primarily for employees that village families use during the evenings and weekends and local schools and other organisations use during the day.

---

[244] The EMRAF [East Midlands Rural Affairs Forum] Rural Charter Award

These and many other examples of the way in which the company seeks to help its community can be found in its citation for its rural community award in 2005.[245]

The principles underpinning the company and the absence of a structure requiring the company to maximise profit for its shareholders has created a completely different relationship between the company, its employees and its surrounding community. Indeed it is precisely because the company essentially consists of its employees that it has become a very different kind of institution than one answerable to money alone. The fact that it is not constantly striving for maximum growth also enables it to operate at a more human scale and provides a far more sustainable model of commercial activity than the global corporations so prevalent in our society.

The Scott Bader Commonwealth is unusual, but it is by no means unique. The John Lewis Partnership and the Mondragon Co-operative, as mentioned earlier, share some similarities of approach in terms of their decision making process, and they too have been very successful.

In the United States there is the Springfield Re-Manufacturing[246] company in Missouri (which also has an operation in Canada). In 1989 Jack Stack and his colleagues bought out a unit of International Harvester, with an astonishing debt to equity ration of 89 to 1. In five years the company was transformed into a profitable $43 million enterprise with a debt-to-equity ratio of 1.8 to 1. Meanwhile, the appraised value of SRC stock had soared to $13.06 per share from 10 cents per share at the company's founding--an increase of almost 13,000%.[247] The company is in the rather unglamorous business of reconditioning engines. It is not particularly large, with some 330 employees. How did it achieve its success? The key was 'open book management –

---

[245]http://www.bitc.org.uk/resources/case_studies/sbcawards05.html

[246] http://www.srcreman.com/

[247] See article in Inc., magazine 'America's 25 most fascinating entrepreneurs, by Bo Burlingham, April 2004, http://www.inc.com/magazine/20040401/25stack.html

the company shared its financial and other operating information with the employees, and the company became employee owned. As a result of treating employees as partners, rather than merely 'human resources', there was an increase of knowledge about the company's problems, and a greater motivation and ability to find solutions, with corresponding financial benefits to match.. However it is not just that the employees are informed and incentivised. They are also the owners of the company. Their approach to the business reflects their priorities rather than just maximising short term investor return. Jack Stack wrote a book about his approach called 'The Great Game of Business'.

Of course a similar result can be reached when companies are run by 'benign dictators', as in the case of SAS (the world's largest privately held software company). James Goodnight, one of the founders has decided not to list the company. It means that he is not subject to shareholder pressure for short term returns. The company provides facilities that are more often associated with a previous era. An article in Inc. magazine points out that:[248]

"There's a 77,000-square-foot health and fitness centre, playing fields for soccer and softball, an on-site medical clinic, a dining hall with live piano music, two daycare centres, an eldercare referral service, unlimited sick days, and a masseuse who makes the rounds several times a week. Goodnight's explanation for this largesse is fairly simple: "If we keep our employees happy, they do a good job of keeping our customers happy." If SAS has a relatively low profile for a company of its size, that's because its software is employed mostly in corporate environments, in serious jobs."

It is rather ironic that, as the article mentions, among work on anti-money-laundering programs, customer-relationship marketing, pharmaceutical research, companies use its applications to gather and mine huge amounts of data for Sarbanes-Oxley compliance.

---

[248] http://www.inc.com/magazine/20040401/25goodnight.html

However, as in the political sphere enlightened dictatorship is a difficult act to follow. The companies above are notable not only because their daily activities are infused with a humanity lacking in more traditional companies, but also because they are quite rare. They are different not only because they treat their employees with a great deal more of respect, but because in cases such as Scott Bader, Springfield Remanufacturing, John Lewis and Mondragon, the corporate architecture is different. The success of these companies gives the lie to the idea that the workforce is not to be trusted, or that companies can only be run efficiently if they are answerable only to invested money.

It is true that an increasing number of companies in the United States are looking at the concept of open-book management, and providing more information about what drives a company's profitability. But this alone is not enough. Such a move can enhance productivity, but on its own it will not, in the long term, enable a company to take on board values other than profitability, which is essential if the way in which companies work is to change. The concept of Companionism encapsulates the key principle that a company consists of a company of people, not a company of money, and without the ultimate decision making vested in the people of a company, as it is in the political sphere, the fundamental flaws of the corporate structure will remain.

It should perhaps be emphasised that such an approach is very far from the socialism/communism propounded by Marx and Engels. Companionism does not involve redistribution of wealth, nor does it suggest whether assets should be publicly or privately owned. It does however provide the democratic mechanism of civic society in the corporate context. It is through this mechanism that corporate decision making can be judged by individuals rather than by money. The way in which the employees of a firm exercise their votes in respect of the board of directors will depend both on the values that they hold, both individually and collectively, and their perception of the actions of the directors. The decision making of the directors would be moulded by the requirements to keep the confidence of the workforce as well as that of the investors. The directors would operate within a system which would favour a community of interest between them and their workforce, in contrast to the current system which often pits them against their workforce in the (often short term) interests of the shareholders. Companionism is above all the application of the representative democratic principles already accepted in the civic sphere in the commercial sphere.

Some consequences

There are, of course a number of very important ramifications which would result from this very simple change. One of the objections that can be raised against the democratisation of companies is that it would stifle initiative – that entrepreneurs would cease to be interested in starting companies if they thought that they would be unable to have control of their start up venture. One of the advantages of companies as they are currently constituted is that they are almost infinitely scalable, from start up to multinational, without much change in the management structure.

However this advantage hides to some extent the fact that given the different impact on society of a company with five employees and 50,000 there <u>ought</u> to be a substantial difference in the structure of such companies to reflect this difference. In the same way that families are not democratic, but are the building blocks for a democratic society, and they provide a desirable environment for raising new members of society, so too it is reasonable to have a structure which distinguishes between the decision making processes of small and large companies.

It is both feasible and desirable that there should be a distinction between voting rights in smaller and large corporations. The smaller a corporation is the more the employees and the management meet together on a daily basis, and the more likely it is that the views of the employees are known to the management. It is also the case that a smaller company has less of an impact on the society in which it operates, and therefore the formalisation of a democratic structure is less essential, as the way it is run is more likely to be susceptible to the values of the community around it. However, as companies grow larger they change internally and externally. Internally they become much more formalised in their decision making structure – inevitably given the larger number of people involved, and externally they have more of an impact on society at large, and instead of the company being dependent on a community, a community can become dependent on a company. This metamorphosis from micro-enterprise to multinational requires a different framework to accommodate the changes in the personality and practices of a company.

Although such distinctions are always arbitrary, if we use the headcount criterion used by the European Commission[249], we can define a micro company as a company with fewer than 10 employees, a small company as one which has fewer than 50 employees, and a medium size company as one which has fewer than 250 employees. Although the European Commission uses other criteria as well, it is the number of employees which is of paramount importance in respect of the democratic arrangements within a company.

In order to provide a simple transition mechanism as a company grows larger it is proposed that all the voting rights for a small company would remain with the shareholders until it reached the size of a medium sized company – i.e. 50 employees, and at that point the shareholders would retain 80% of the voting rights and the employees would receive 20%. For each additional 50 employees a further 20% of the votes would go to the employees, until the workforce reached

---

[249] COMMISSION RECOMMENDATION of 6th May 2003 concerning the definition of micro, small and medium-sized enterprises (notified under document number C(2003) 1422, 2003/361/EC, Official Journal of the European Communities,20th May 2003, L124/36.

250 employees at which point the company would become a 'large' company, and all the voting rights would belong to the employees.

In this way as a start up company grew, the changing impact of a larger organisation would be reflected in the way in which it was run. It should perhaps be re-emphasised that this would not affect the financial rights attaching to the shares – the shareholders would still be entitled to their dividends, but of course the directors would need to explain to the workforce their reasoning for the dividend policy, and the importance of ensuring the investors receive an adequate return on capital to enable the company to continue to access the capital markets.

There might well be attempts to manipulate such a system, to try and ensure that voting control is not transferred to the employees by, for example, setting up a multiplicity of companies, or having a large number of temporary employees or attempting to limit the rights of part-time employees etc. It would not be difficult to have legal provisions constraining these practices, but there would also be business and managerial considerations as to whether such an approach was in the best commercial interests of the company. There would perhaps also be an inbuilt bias against expanding companies beyond a certain size as a result of a potential loss in voting rights; to the extent that there tends to be a closer understanding between directors and employees in smaller companies, and the power of the company is likely to be less daunting, this might be no bad thing.

A transfer of voting rights to the workforce should also result in the board having to justify their own remuneration to the workforce. It is one thing to justify large pay packets to remuneration committees composed of people, many of whom doubtless aspire to similar levels of remuneration. It is perhaps more difficult to explain to the workforce of the same company why the difference between the highest and lowest paid within the company continues to diverge. Since the workforce is also involved in the creation of wealth within a company they should have a good understanding of the relative contribution made by management and employees.

The way in which corporations function in different countries would also change. At the moment companies can be seen as the advance guard of a westernising influence. This can be considered as good or bad, depending on one's point of view and on both the country and the company, but the workforce still have little influence on the way in which the company is run. There may be numerous rules and regulations affecting a number of the company's activities, but inside the company the employees have little scope to get the company's policies and work practices to accord to local sensibilities. The democratisation of the company structure would have the effect of making the management of overseas subsidiaries responsible to the workforce of those subsidiaries. This would undoubtedly increase the awareness of companies operating outside their own countries of the different sensitivities. It would provide a degree of reality to the nostrum 'Think globally, act locally'.

There are some who may argue that the route of democratisation has already been taken in other countries. There are for example works councils (comités d'entreprise) in France, (Betriebsrat) in Germany and also the over-arching system of 'Mitbestimmung' or co-determination in Germany. Both of these have grown out of different roots and are more a way of balancing certain interests in an institutional way, and in respect of certain aspects of a company's relationship with its workforce rather than a fundamental acceptance that ultimate decision making power in a company should belong to the employees rather than the shareholders.

The French Works Council, for example, was instituted at the end of the Second World War, and was a consultative body in respect of company welfare and cultural purposes. However, its consultative role could be said to overlap with that of the trade unions involved in collective bargaining. Notwithstanding the ambiguity of this role, the required provision of a similar body is being rolled out across Europe.

A 2002 EC Directive requires all enterprises with over 50 employees to establish a framework "setting out minimum requirements for the right to information and consultation of employees in undertakings or establishments within the Community."[250] The requirement for the employer to inform the employees is subject to exceptions, e.g. in respect to commercially sensitive information, so it remains to be seen to what extent such a framework will have any real impact on transforming the way in which companies manage their affairs. In any event, this is merely a mechanism to protect the employees' interests to some extent; it does not go to the root problem of today's companies which is that of the accountability of the senior management and of the company itself.

In Germany, companies with over 500 people have two boards, a management board or 'Vorstand', and a supervisory board or 'Aufsichsrat', a non-executive supervisory board which elects the management board, the Chairman of the Aufsichsrat representing the shareholders. In all companies with more than 2,000 employees, 50% of the supervisory board are elected by the workforce. In practice the influence of the trade unions is pervasive in this structure. If the British government was willing to try new constitutional arrangements in Germany after the Second World War which it was unable or unwilling to institute at home, this was also true for the British trade union movement. Victor Feather, who was subsequently to become General Secretary of the TUC and other British trade unionists were instrumental in persuading the Germans to organise their unions on an industry wide basis, resulting in just 17 large unions, with only one union per industry, thereby avoiding demarcation disputes.

---

[250] DIRECTIVE 2002/14/EC OF THE EUROPEAN PARLIAMENT AND OF THE COUNCIL of 11 March 2002 establishing a general framework for informing and consulting employees in the European Community, Official Journal of the European Communities, 23rd March 2002, L80/29

This powerful union presence meant that that the unions were the mouthpiece of the workforce. It was they who negotiated with management on behalf of the workforce. They were not affiliated to any particular party (unlike the trade unions in the United Kingdom, who founded the Labour party and many of them still consider it to be the political wing of unionism) and spoke for an entire industry's workforce which enhanced their standing.

These arrangements have therefore become institutionalised in practice, with the employees, through their trade union (rather than directly), in some ways acting as a corporate body. This interposition of the trade union to some extent dis-intermediates the democratic role of the workforce.

This approach echoes the theories of corporatism and neo-corporatism which were pioneered by the likes of Adam Müller[251] in the early 19th Century, which harked back to feudal times, and did much to inform fascist thought in Italy in the 1930s; the stability of class interests discussed by the main protagonists being thought preferable to democracy in the raw. This type of corporatism embodies not only commercial companies, but also non incorporated bodies, such as trade unions, and looks to a forum of interest groups to work together on behalf of society as a whole. Its view of society is more geared to the rights of interest groups than to those of the individual. Indeed before the Great Reform Act it could be said that the British Parliament was constituted on a similar basis – to reflect groups of interests rather than individual electors. Like modern day commercial corporatism it is inherently undemocratic; it exists within democratic societies, but is based on a very different view of the way in which decisions ought to be taken.

This aspect of corporatism was taken up by the Canadian thinker John Ralston Saul in his Massey lectures.[252] He felt

---

[251] (1779-1829)

[252] The 1995 Massey lectures, "The Unconscious Civilisation". In the lectures Ralston Saul examined the way in which corporations

that corporatism in the modern age has led to the undermining and denial of the individual as citizen in a democracy, leading to an 'adoration' of self interest and a denial of the public good.

Would it work?

The transfer of voting rights from the shareholders to the workforce of a corporation is therefore quite different from these corporatist models, and is a reflection of a different concept of governance. What we are looking at is the fundamental point that corporations should be corporations of people; currently commercial corporations are corporations of money.

One of the arguments that can be advanced against the use of democracy in corporate affairs is that it would not be practical or even practicable to conduct the affairs of a company on this basis. This has been dealt with above, but it is worth noting that exactly these kinds of sentiments were expressed and these sorts of arguments used prior to the passage of the Great Reform Act of 1832 in the United Kingdom. It was feared that chaos would result if the franchise were widened to include even the 'middle class'. In fact the Act was a very much watered down version of what was originally intended. However when it transpired that the increase in the franchise did not result in a breakdown in the system, then gradually the system was further reformed to make it even more democratic.

These same visceral fears are undoubtedly at the root of our acceptance of the current corporate structure; innate conservatism and fear of the unknown militate against us

---

have developed and the way in which our modern corporatist society seems unaware of its predicament, quoting John of Salisbury's question in 1159 "Who is more contemptible than he who scorns knowledge of himself?" as applicable to modern civilisation as a whole.

wishing to change too radically a framework which appears to have had such tangible benefits in terms of improvement in living standards. The United Kingdom had been tremendously successful in both expanding its influence internationally and in improving its domestic economy. Yet it is difficult to imagine what sort of country it might have become if it had not embraced change, but continued to defend the old system. One of the drivers of the 1832 Act was a great apprehension of unrest and possible revolution if change did not take place and the example of the French Revolution was by no means absent as a guide to the potential consequences. Change was in the air and it was seen that a little change was preferable to a possible revolution.

In the United States on the other hand, their unusual geographical and historical situation was such that the Founding Fathers were able to discuss from first principles the sort of society and constitution that they would like to see. Seldom has there been such a philosophical and enlightened approach to the creation of a constitution and a sense of nationhood.[253] There can be no doubt about the care and

---

[253] Sadly, of course, even excellent constitutional arrangements are not always enough. The recent death at the age of 92 of Rosa Parks on 24th October 2005, Alabama reminded the world that discrimination (cloaked in legality) in the United States was a recent phenomenon. Rosa Parks, a black lady who refused to give up her seat on a bus for a white man on the 1st December 1955, in Montgomery sparked a movement of non violent protest. The Supreme Court ultimately ruled that the segregation of blacks and whites on buses was illegal, but it was sadly a reflection of attitudes that had its roots in the earliest days of American society. The tragedy of the appalling treatment of the North American Indian tribes is graphically described by Peter Farb in his book 'Man's Rise to Civilization as shown by the Indians of North America from Primeval Times to the Coming of the Industrial State' 1969 Secker & Warburg. In the chapter entitled 'End of the Trail', Farb highlighted the treatment of the peaceable Cherokee (one of whose intellectuals, Sequoya, is commemorated in the name of the Pacific coast redwood), who were sent on a thousand mile march to the

thought with which the United States constitution was crafted out of a multitude of divergent views, nor in respect of the sheer talent of the leaders of the debate.

But the remarkable edifice of the American constitution has no counterpart in the corporate sphere. The framework of corporate law is embedded in business initiative and conservative pragmatism rather than founded on principle. There seem to be no cogent reasons why the principles that underlay the crafting of the American constitution should not apply to corporate societies as they do to society as a whole. It is difficult to see how our concerns about the impractibility of democracy in the commercial sphere are, in essence, any different from the concerns that assailed the Founding Fathers of the American constitution who were fully aware that democracy in its purest form was impractical. As Jefferson wrote from Monticello to his friend John Taylor:

> "Such a government [i.e., a pure republic, which Jefferson equates to direct democracy] is evidently restrained to very narrow limits of space and population. I doubt if it would be practicable beyond the extent of a New England township."[254].

This was perhaps an echo of Jean Jacques Rousseau, who in the Social Contract defined democracy so narrowly that every citizen was a member of the government. [255]

In exactly the same way corporate governance cannot be carried out, except in the very smallest companies, on the basis of a pure democracy, but that is no bar to the

---

west from their homeland in Georgia, Tennessee and North Carolina, called 'the trail of tears'. Clearly the protection of the constitutional edifice did not extend to native Americans.

[254] Letter of Thomas Jefferson to John Taylor, 18th May 1816.

[255] The Social Contract, Jean Jacques Rousseau 1762. See Book 3, chapter 4, which concludes in respect of the purest democracy: "If there were a nation of gods, it would be governed democratically. So perfect a government is unsuited to men'.

introduction of representative democracy in the corporate sphere just as it has happened in the political sphere.

Often the current situation is defended in terms of market efficiency and so on, but the markets we have today are very far from those envisaged by Adam Smith. Indeed at the time of Adam Smith the Bubble Act was still in force, and society greatly alive to the evils of incorporation, albeit more from the point of view of fleecing an unwary public than from the implications of the effect of corporations on society.

The corporate economy has undoubtedly delivered large material benefits to society, and although these have by no means been shared equally, standards of living have undoubtedly risen for society as a whole. However this is not to say that this could not have been achieved without corporations. Even in the world of the eighteenth century, it was possible for Adam Smith to write:[256]

'...and yet it may be true, perhaps, that the accommodation of an European prince does not so much always exceed that of an industrious and frugal peasant, as the accommodation of the latter exceeds that of many an African king, the absolute master of the lives and liberties of ten thousand naked savages.'

The carrying on of business does not depend on the existence of feudally run corporations. In what way then, can the concept of democracy be integrated into the corporate model? Firstly we must recognise that there is an issue of scale. In democratic countries generally the larger the size of the democracy the less representative it becomes. The federalism of the United States mitigates this effect, and the confederalism of Switzerland enables a far higher degree of democracy than would be possible if Switzerland were centralised. This paradigm is also true for companies. The more removed the board of directors is from their workforce, the less their actions are likely to be open to control. We must

---

[256] Wealth of Nations, Book I, Chapter I

acknowledge that we have to deal with a number of very large organisations in the world today who must also be made democratically accountable. To the extent that they have numbers of subsidiaries it will be easier for the democratic process to work effectively.

It should be emphasised that this in no way takes away from management their rights and responsibilities in respect of being able to manage, in the same way that representative democracy does not take away the right of a government to govern. What it changes fundamentally however, is to whom the management is responsible; under companionism they would be responsible to the people, not the money. The standard by which they are judged and the people who make that judgement will change. The benchmark for their success will therefore also change.

Under such a system management will have to take account of the norms operating in society as a whole, rather than just the requirement to make money with scant regard for the priorities of society as a whole. Their workforce will only be a partial reflection of the priorities of society as a whole but this is not, in essence, very different from the democratic process at large where large numbers of people disagree with the government of the day, but accept its legitimacy, because it has been elected by a majority of their fellow citizens.

The democratisation of companies will not make companies enlightened overnight, but it will make company decision making susceptible to preoccupations and priorities, that are not purely driven by the profit and loss account.

No doubt it will not be seen by all board directors in this light, but it will also release management from their commercial straightjacket. It is remarkable how many entrepreneurs and successful businessmen, from Andrew Carnegie to Bill Gates feel the need to give something back to society out of the fortunes they have made. The charitable donations made and the socially responsible attitude of the management of a number of companies illustrate the basic human instinct of concern for others, which the corporate structure does so much to suppress and destroy. Currently it is not possible to give effective vent to these feelings within a corporate context without depriving the shareholders of something which is currently theirs.

The fact that the management serves the money, and is therefore often regarded as 'on the other side' by the workforce provides a permanent potential for friction in the conduct of industrial relations. What workforce would strike against a management for which it is ultimately responsible? Clearly there will sometimes be crises, but these will be resolvable in the knowledge that if the workforce is dissatisfied with the job that the management are doing then they can replace them, and it is their own jobs that will suffer if they get the decision wrong.

In the struggle between people and property, Europe has come a long way from the concept of people as property, in days of the feudal villein and serfs. We have now arrived at a stage where we entrust the appointment of our political decision makers to the people through a democratic process, but we have yet to muster the courage to cross the bridge and use the same process for our commercial decision makers.[257] There is no rational justification for this, and the arguments against strike at the very roots of democracy itself.

Companionism will not solve all the current major ills of the world at a stroke. What it does provide however is a mechanism through which the values of society can be expressed democratically in a commercial as well as a political forum. A company is as properly part of democracy's

---

[257] The defence of liberty is as important in the commercial sphere as in the political sphere, and current position of employees reflects the comments of the Irish judge John Curran, who said in 1790: "the condition upon which God hath given liberty to man is eternal vigilance; which condition if he break, servitude is at once the consequence of his crime, and the punishment of his guilt".

domain as is a country. As democratic systems vary from one country to another, so we should expect variations of companionism. It is likely that, as with political democracy, companionism will be more effective in some countries than in others. But once the concept is in place, it will provide a pathway for dissent against overt greed and the over concentration of power.

Companionism will provide members of a company's workforce with the same rights that in many Western countries they now take for granted in the political sphere. It has the potential to re-ignite a belief that the individual matters, and start a re-engagement with politics by many who currently feel disenchanted. Companionism will enable the voice of the workforce to be heard in respect of the major decisions to be taken by a company, and in respect of who should be taking those decisions. It will end the pretence that there is something reasonable or acceptable in running business purely for profit, and on a completely different basis from the rest of society. It will give the whole workforce the freedom to decide their priorities, for good or ill, and it will give campaigners of all persuasions the opportunity to win their hearts and minds, knowing that it could make a difference.

As a society we have to decide whether we truly believe in the democratic ideal. If we do, then we have as much reason to trust people to vote for those who run their company as to vote for those who run their country. If we do not take the less travelled road of democracy to Companionism, then the bleakness of our future is not hard to imagine – the trends of a soulless selfish society, whose demands are insatiable, and whose motivation is greed are with us already, and grow stronger with each passing year. They are the inevitable consequence of having powerful corporate organisms who serve not mankind but money. Only by making them democratic can we start to recapture their humanity and ours.

Appendix I

Typical Controls in Corporate Charters Prior to the Civil War[258]

Activities	Each corporation was limited to performing a specific function, such as operating a school or a bridge.
Lifespan	Typically, charters of incorporation were issued for terms ranging from 20 to 50 years, after which they would have to be renewed. Banks were subject to especially tight restriction, with some states limiting terms to 3 to 10 years.
Property ownership	Most states limited corporations to owning only property that was directly needed for the authorized activity.
Size	Charters directly limited on the amount of capital that an individual corporation could control. Some charter provisions also had an indirect effect on size, including restrictions on property ownership, the requirement for unanimous shareholder consent in major decisions, geographic restrictions, and limits on permitted activities.
Geographic	Most corporations were not allowed to operate beyond the borders of the state in which they were incorporated. Sometimes a corporation was even restricted to a single county.
Inter-company ownership	As a rule, corporations were not allowed to own stock in other corporations.
Performance criteria	In addition to stating what sort of activities were allowed, charters also

---

[258] Taken from Table 5.1 in Gangs of America by Ted Nace, pp. 68-69

frequently specified project completion dates and output requirements. Sometimes the two were combined; e.g. an iron company being required to reach a certain tonnage of production within three years.

Profits

Charters sometimes limited the profit a corporation could earn. In addition, many charters required that profits from a company be used to buy back stock, so that eventually all stockholders would be eliminated and the company would in effect become a public entity under the supervision of the state legislature. Under the Turnpike Corporation Act of 1805, Massachusetts authorized the legislature to dissolve turnpike corporations once their receipts equaled the cost of construction plus 12 percent.

Public privilege

Charters for turnpikes typically exempted farmers, worshippers, and poor people from paying tolls.

Shareholder restrictions and protections for minority owners

In some cases incorporators had to be citizens of the state. Some charters prevented a single powerful individual from controlling the corporation; some required a minimum number of shareholders. Some charters required that the corporation use a voting formula that increased the leverage of small investors. Most required unanimous consent for key decisions, such as issuing new stock or selling the company.

Special restrictions on banking

Bank charters were limited to three to ten years. Banks had to get special approval to merge. In some states banks were required to direct their loans to local industries. Banks were also required to lend money to the state government if requested. Maximum interest rates were designated. Both Illinois and Indiana actually banned private banking corporations in their state constitutions. Wisconsin and four other states amended their constitutions to require that all bank charters be approved by popular vote.

Shareholder liability

Limited liability - the principle that shareholders can't be held responsible for judgments against a corporation or for unpaid corporate debts - wasn't a widespread feature of the corporation until after the Civil War. Some charters required full shareholder liability. Others capped liability at twice the value of a person's stockholdings In addition to other restrictions, corporations were subject to the general ban on activities not expressly permitted in their charter.

Ultra vires

This doctrine of limited authorization, known as *ultra vires*, translates as "beyond the powers." Courts would not enforce any contract outside the scope of a corporation's charter.

Appendix II

Table 1: Differences in structure of US and European Sports Leagues[259]

	US Sports	*Football in Europe*
League system	-closed, no promotion or relegation-teams compete in single league competition	open, annual promotion and relegation - teams may compete simultaneously in many competitions
League functions	-collective sale of TV rights -centralised marketing	-collective sale of TV rights
Competition between clubs Competition between leagues	-limited substitution by consumers -numerous cases of entry by rival leagues	-significant potential for substitution -all leagues contained within the established hierarchy
Player market	-rookie draft -salary caps (NFL, NBA) -collective bargaining	-active transfer market

[259] From: **Equality of opportunity and equality of outcome: open leagues, closed leagues and Competitive Balance by** Luigi Buzzacchi (Politecnico di Torino), Stefan Szymanski (Imperial College London), Tommaso M. Valletti (Imperial College London and CEPR), Table 1.

Revenue sharing	-equal division of national broadcast income -gate sharing (NFL 40%, Baseball average 15%, NBA 0%) -sharing of television income	-little or no sharing of league gate revenues -some sharing of gate from cup competitions
Competition policy	-antitrust exemption for baseball -Sports Broadcasting Act exempts national TV deals from antitrust	-centralised sale of TV rights under attack -selected interventions (ticket allocation FIFA)

Appendix III

"The Spirit of Scott Bader[260]

This leaflet states the Principles and outlines the Commitments which guide the way Scott Bader works as an organisation, at all its locations around the world. These Principles and Commitments are developed from the Constitution and Charter which were written by the Founders of the company. The intention of the Founders was to create a radical company, its well-being entrusted to those who work in it. It must encourage a spirit of co-operation and help to eliminate social injustice and waste — making the world a better place to live. Scott Bader companies are the business units of a larger membership organisation called The Scott Bader Commonwealth. Everyone working in Scott Bader is expected to become a member of the Scott Bader Commonwealth. Members share the responsibilities and privileges of being trustees-in-common and working the Scott Bader way, and must accept the challenge of ensuring the company is sustainable for the benefit of future generations.

---

[260] From the Scott Bader website,
http://www.scottbader.com/pub.nsf/AttachmentsByTitle/UK_PR_S
piritBooklet/$FILE/Spirit.pdf

Principles

Scott Bader companies, wherever their location, work to a common set of principles - these are:

- ♦ Care
- ♦ Equality [of opportunity]
- ♦ Ethics
- ♦ Involvement
- ♦ No discrimination
- ♦ Respect [human dignity]
- ♦ Service

Commitments

All those working within Scott Bader commit to the following:

1. The Scott Bader way of working — the Scott Bader Spirit

To be sustainable we must maintain a reputation for honesty, integrity, service and quality in all our dealings.

Each Scott Bader company must work in a spirit of co-operation and partnership — with colleagues, our local communities and all those with whom we do business. We must ensure we provide equality of opportunity by informing and training one another to help meet our full potential as individuals and so drive the business forward.

2. Taking Responsibility

As individuals we accept personal responsibility for our actions, recognising all staff must be trustworthy, avoid conflicts of interest and constantly seek to improve their skills and knowledge As an organisation each company must behave in a caring and ethical way and work to grow mutually beneficial long term relationships insisting on honesty and integrity in all its affairs. Managers have a special responsibility to enable these individual and corporate behaviours and also to ensure open and accurate reporting at all times.

3. Working for a Better Society

We must care about all those who rely on us and respect the dignity of all people. Discrimination on grounds of race, age, religion or gender is not tolerated. Distribution of a proportion of profits must be made to benefit those less fortunate than ourselves. As a sustainable, caring company our success can influence others to follow our example. We must help those who wish to follow. Also, while the company will not make payment to any political organisation — it will, where possible, support staff who wish to be engaged in community activities.

Self Governance

The Scott Bader spirit encourages personal responsibility and self governance where all staff are kept well informed and consulted on matters affecting their day-to-day working and wider company issues, and in turn staff commit to working in the best interests of the organisation. There must be involvement in decision making which includes some form of elected representation. Ultimately accountability lies with the General Meeting of Members of the Commonwealth."

Printed in the United Kingdom
by Lightning Source UK Ltd.
124659UK00001B/13-30/A

9 781846 856808